GOODNIGHT, SEATTLE

The Unauthorised Guide To The World Of Frasier

David Bailey and Warren Martyn

Also available:

I CAN'T BELIEVE IT'S AN UNOFFICIAL *SIMPSONS* GUIDE
THE AVENGERS DOSSIER
THE NEW TREK PROGRAMME GUIDE
X-TREME POSSIBILITIES
   – A Paranoid Rummage Through *The X-Files*
THE BABYLON FILE
   – The Definitive Unauthorised Guide to *Babylon 5*

First published in 1998 by
Virgin Books
an imprint of Virgin Publishing Ltd,
Thames Wharf Studios,
Rainville Road, London W6 9HT

Reprinted 1998

Copyright © David Bailey and Warren Martyn 1998

The right of David Bailey and Warren Martyn
to be identified as the Authors of this Work has been
asserted by them in accordance with the Copyright,
Designs and Patents Act 1988.

ISBN 0 7535 0286 0

Typeset by Galleon Typesetting, Ipswich
Printed and bound in Great Britain by
Mackays of Chatham PLC

CONTENTS

Acknowledgments

David's Dedication:

To my family – Mum, Dad, Ian, Virginia, John, Faye, Jonathan and Emma – for a great deal of much-needed love and support.

Thanks:

This is a list of those who kept me going through a pretty tricky 1997.

Rebecca, Peter, Kerri and James, first of all.

At Titan: Marcus, for giving useful advice in every arena; Katherine, for still loving *Frasier* when I'd almost had enough; John, Leigh and Térése, for letting me have time; Ness, for being Ness; Chris and Darryl, for that family feeling and the 'just one'; and everyone else, for making it a good place to work.

John Binns, for faith and wheelie-bins.

Neil Corry, for being there, then there, then round the corner.

The Sandgrounders (Louise, Gillian, Lisa, Mel, Claire and Nick, and the honoraries, Adrian and Ian), for being proud.

Jim Sangster, for having an idea in the first place.

Gary Gillatt, for being jealous.

Robert and Davy, for a breath of fresh air.

The Seventh Door gang, for the training groung (sic).

Phil, improbably, for helping with an angle.

And a last-minute entry for Fido, from Spike.

Warren's Dedication:

For Allan Smith, who was there when we got hooked on that Friday night comedy 'thing'!

And on the 'Thanks to' front, well, firstly to Gary and Grayson who made me watch my first *Frasier* – 'Travels with Martin'. Also, this book would not have been remotely possible without the help of Sarah Booth, Kathy Sullivan and, most importantly of all, Stephen James Walker, without whom . . .

Introduction

Why an unofficial episode guide to *Frasier*? That's easy – why not? It is a television show that has been near the top of Channel 4's ratings since the day it started (much to C4's surprise) and has proven so popular recently that the station opted to run the fourth and fifth seasons one after the other without the customary few months' break.

But to the uninitiated, what exactly is *Frasier*? And who is Frasier Crane? And Niles? And Daphne? And . . . oh, you get the idea.

Frasier Crane started life in the third series of the hugely successful American sitcom, *Cheers*. Set in and around a bar in Boston, called Cheers oddly enough, the series focused on the lives and loves of its staff and customers. Frasier was a psychiatrist, brought in as a short-lived love interest for Diane Chambers (played by Shelley Long), a regular for those first three years. She dumped Frasier at the altar but the producers clearly saw the potential of the character and, by the time *Cheers* ended after eleven seasons, Frasier was among the most popular characters. During his time in the bar we discovered a lot about him – he was married once before his first appearance in the bar (to a children's entertainer, Nanette Gooseman – aka Nanny Gee – played by Emma Thompson) and then during the last few seasons he was married to the formidable ice maiden Dr Lilith Sternin (played by Bebe Neuwirth). He also implied that he was an only child and both his parents were dead. In fact, before her passing, Hester Crane (played by Nancy Marchand), another psychiatrist, turned up in Boston to ask Diane not to marry her beloved son.

When *Cheers* came to its natural conclusion, the producers opted to spin Frasier off into his own series, and that is where we begin.

Frasier has upped roots and left Boston, his home of fifteen years. His marriage to Lilith has ended acrimoniously after she had an affair, and so he leaves her and his son Frederick and heads home to Seattle. Here, he takes up a three-hour radio psychiatry programme with KACL 780 AM every afternoon between 2 p.m. and 5 p.m.

There he meets Roz Doyle, his new producer, reacquaints himself with his psychiatrist brother Niles and his socialite wife Maris, and finds himself living with his ex-cop father, Martin, crippled by a gunman's bullet. To help out, he enlists Manchester-born Daphne Moon as Martin's live-in health-care worker.

What follows is, to date, five years of top, sophisticated wit and satire – and even the occasional farce – as Frasier comes to cope with those around him and, more importantly, they try to cope with him.

The Characters

Frasier Crane
played by Kelsey Grammer

Snobbish, arrogant, conceited and pretentious (underlined!) are just some of the words used to describe him by his friends. We shudder to think what his enemies call him (although Derek Mann of the local Seattle paper has had a few choice words on the subject). Ultimately, though, Frasier is a modern hero – determined to help his friends when they're in need and sort their lives and loves out for them. Of course the methods he uses might not always be quite what you would expect, but there is no getting away from the fact that his heart is in the right place.

Niles Crane
played by David Hyde Pierce

Younger brother of Frasier and another psychiatrist, he is fastidious, prissy and effete, and desperately jealous of his brother's fame – a jealousy he buries under an ill-concealed loathing of the 'popularising' of psychiatry. He feels that the idea of Frasier wasting his talents by doing a radio phone-in is almost a betrayal of the years of schooling they put themselves through. Niles is married to the bizarre creature known only as Maris – never seen but often mentioned. Although Niles is very much in love with his wife, he is lustfully attracted to Daphne Moon, a state she is blissfully unaware of and everyone else is resigned to.

Martin Crane
played by John Mahoney

As far removed from his two sons as it is possible to be – they clearly inherited Hester's genes. He is a down-to-earth Seattle cop, retired through injury after getting shot by a thug robbing a convenience store. As a result, he has come to live in Frasier's swanky new apartment and feels like a fish out of water. While his two sons argue over the merits of the Metropolitan opera or the quality of the local restaurants (judged by their spirit menus more often than not), Martin would rather head to one of his favourite bars, Duke's or McGinty's, for a beer or three with his ex-force buddies, or play a devastating round of poker, or watch an Angie Dickinson movie, or . . .

Daphne Moon
played by Jane Leeves

Sent by an agency to fill a vacancy as Martin's health-care worker, Daphne quickly becomes the archetypal female around the house, taking on the housework chores as well as administering to Martin's every medical need. However, no wilting flower is our Daph, offering her own unique brand of sage advice and bizarre psychic premonitions learnt through years of interacting with her rather large and frankly odd English family, led by the formidable Grammie Moon, she of the odd recipes and peculiar hip problems.

Roz Doyle
played by Peri Gilpin

Roz is Frasier's producer. Initially resistant to the job, she was placed there after his original producer Dave resigned, before the first show even went out! As time passes, Roz and the extended Crane family become the best of friends, learning to deal with Roz's never-ending search for the right man (or at least, a good lay) and her inevitable inability to get either. Roz's main confidante is her mother, the Attorney General of Wisconsin, another character we hear an awful lot about and witness people talking to on the telephone, but have yet to actually meet. Roz is undoubtedly the sanest of the bunch, but, then again, how sane can anyone be to work with Frasier every day and then socialise with him at weekends?

Eddie
played by Moose

If there's one thing about his father moving into his apartment that Frasier was resistant to (well, apart from the barcalounger), it was the additional arrival of his Jack Russell terrier, Eddie. Prone to long bouts of staring impassively at his master's eldest son, eating everything going and – since having 'the snip' – playing with his favourite Barbie doll, Eddie is beloved of everyone. Except Frasier.

And then there are . . .

Those who flit in and out of episodes on a regular basis. At KACL, we meet Bob 'Bulldog' Briscoe, the loud-mouthed womanising sports jock (played by Dan Butler); Gil Chesterton, the gay restaurant critic (played by Edward Hibbert) whose pomposity almost reaches Niles's levels; Noel Shempsky (Patrick Kerr), the Roz-obsessed, *Star Trek* fan who can faint at will; Kate Costas, the fiery station manager (played by Mercedes Ruehl) who sets out to take Frasier down a peg or ten and ends up becoming romantically involved with him; Sherry Dempsey (Marsha Mason), the less than genteel lady who captures Martin's heart and is the first woman he is able to say 'I love you' to, and mean it sincerely, since his beloved Hester passed on. There are many others (Father Mike, Bonnie Weems, Elizabeth – but we'll meet those as we go through the episodes). At Café Nervosa, Niles and Frasier's favourite coffee bar and respite from the traumas of cranky fathers, insane health-care workers and smelly wet dogs, there seem to be innumerable waiters and waitresses who know the Crane boys' every foible – but rarely their taste in coffee. And finally there are those who come to visit Frasier from his *Cheers* days – bar owner Sam, former fiancée Diane and, of course, the frighteningly formidable Lilith (and, lest we forget, Frederick).

So, those are our characters – and their players. Now here are the plays . . .

For the purposes of this book, we have followed the UK Channel 4 transmission order rather than the original US transmission order. (S4C (Wales) transmission times are different from Channel 4's.)

Channel 4 began showing *Frasier* on Wednesday nights, but, midway through the initial run, moved it to Friday as one of the prime ingredients of what is now seen as their highly successful comedy night. The first episode to be shown on a Friday was 'The Show Where Lilith Comes Back'. This was the first time that the running order differed from the US, where that episode came after 'Can't Tell A Crook By His Cover'. This explains the fact that Maris is with her sister in Chicago in the Lilith episode, although for UK viewers she didn't actually go until 'Can't Buy Me Love'.

Sorry, that was an observation for mega-trivia fans only!

The only other time Channel 4 deviates from the US running order is in Season Two, where 'Burying A Grudge' moves before the two 'Adventures In Paradise' episodes instead of following them, and Season Four, where they split a one-hour special ('Three Dates and a Break-Up') into two episodes, shown one per week – with rather unfortunate consequences for a majority of the jokes.

Right, that's it. No more sad trivial nit-picking. Oh, except . . .

We have broken each episode down into a variety of different sections, each highlighting a regular *Frasier* occurrence.

Episode: Episode number and title. Bit obvious, really.

Writer: The person who is credited with writing it.

Director: The person who is credited with directing it (this is the easy section, by the way).

First UK Transmission: Because we're going by the Channel 4 first transmissions and not any US ones, American readers may note a few differences.

Skyline: You know how the Seattle skyline draws itself at the start? Well, this tells you what is seen after it has been drawn. Sometimes a helicopter, sometimes balloons or fireworks . . . and sometimes nothing at all.

Synopsis: What happened in the story, but without giving away too much of the ending in case you've not seen it. We're nice like that.

Guest Cast: The characters and actors who appear in just this particular episode.

Where Everybody Knows Their Name: Appearances or mentions of recurring characters. Lilith, for instance. Or Hester Crane. Or Sherry Dempsey. Or any of the staff of Café Nervosa who crop up on a regular basis (we like the waitress, played by Luck Hari, best). Basically anyone who is in more than one episode. Plus namechecks for regular KACL workers and, of course, our old friends from Boston . . .

Who's On The Line?: *Frasier* is well known for its heard-but-never-seen troubled callers to the show. Famous names such as David Duchovny, Mel Brooks, Cyd Charisse . . . they've all done it. We also note characters we hear of having rung in as well but not actually heard ourselves. And occasionally, we'll even tell you of callers to Bulldog's show as well!

Subtitles: Most episodes are punctuated by a series of witty captions between scenes. The amount varies, the quality rarely does.

Culture Vultures: We all know Frasier and Niles are snobs, and here are some (but not all) of our favourite 'casual' references to fine wines, good food, operas and books.

Strange Bedfellows: Roz's sex life is fascinating (mainly because she actually has one), so we thought it a good idea to highlight just who she's bedded over the series.

Full-on Moon: As well as noting her psychic abilities, Daphne's extended family and friends both back in Manchester and in America make for delightful moments for our favourite dippy damsel.

Out Of Sight: Ahhh . . . Maris. The most-talked-about but never-ever-seen character (although we sort of get a glimpse in the fifth season). But just how much do we know about Niles's rich, neurotic, diminutive wife? Well, quite a lot really, most of it rather alarming . . .

The Buddy Show: Martin frequently regales us with stories of fellow cops or army colleagues, as well as his drinking buddies down at Duke's or latterly McGinty's. They're all namechecked here.

Eddie Takes The Biscuit: More often than not, the little terrier steals the scenes he's in and, whenever he does something particularly cute, we've noted it here. Of course, cuteness is in the eye of the beholder (or some such) so we may have missed your favourite . . .

Frasier Has Left The Building: What is going on while the end credits are playing. We were going to cite the ever-changing closing-theme lyrics here as well, but, apart from the sheer tedium of doing so, we think that without Kelsey Grammer's marvellous voice, they lose their impact when written down.

On The Couch: Capsule reviews of the episode, where we think they did well, where we think they slipped up, plus other odds and ends that didn't obviously fit into any of the above categories.

Season One

1.01

'The Good Son'

Written by David Angell, Peter Casey and David Lee
Directed by James Burrows
First UK Transmission: 20.04.94

Skyline: The light atop the Space Needle glows.

Synopsis: Frasier Crane, everyone's favourite inept psychiatrist from *Cheers*, has made a break on his own. Back in his home town of Seattle, he's got a job as a radio psychiatrist and has settled into his own, finely furnished, gorgeously appointed apartment. But then his delicately rebuilt life comes under threat.

Niles, his effete brother, meets with Frasier to discuss their father, Martin. Forced to quit his job as a policeman when he is shot in the hip during a raid, Martin is very obviously having serious problems adjusting to his new life. His injury has quite seriously incapacitated him, and, when he's found lying prone on his bathroom floor ('You can still see the tile marks on my face'), the Crane boys decide that he can no longer be left on his own. A nursing home seems too harsh an option, and Niles is unable to let him live with him and his wife, Maris, as she and his father do not get on. Which leaves only one option . . .

Guest Cast: Delivery Man (Cleto Agusto), Waitress (Gina Ravarra).

Where Everybody Knows Their Name: A tacit mention of Lilith Sternin, Frasier's ex-wife, is made during his passionate speech about starting a new life. 'Six months ago, I was living in Boston. My wife had left me, which was very painful. Then she came back to me, which was excruciating.' Not the last mention of Lilith, and by no means the final time she will make a big impact on Frasier's life in Seattle. We also hear that Frederick is not enjoying sport at all (like father, like son indeed).

And Hester Crane, Frasier's deceased mother, receives the first of innumerable mentions when Niles reminds him that she always said 'a handshake is as good as a hug'.

At KACL, we hear our first mention of Chopper Dave's Rush-Hour Round-Up while Niles mentions Yoshi, Maris's gardener, who destroys her flowers after an argument with Niles. We'll hear more of Yoshi as the series continues but, as with his mistress, we'll not actually meet him . . .

And Moose the dog gets an on-screen credit for playing Eddie, a fairly haphazard credit as the series goes on that is forgotten by the middle of the second season.

Who's On The Line?: Russell (Griffin Dunne), who feels his life is going nowhere and Claire (Linda Hamilton), who isn't coping very well with a break-up and may not have heard of Lupe Velez. We also learn of Jerry – who has an identity crisis not helped when Frasier calls him Jeff and Bob – who is obsessive about someone. And, of course, Martin Crane . . .

Subtitles: The Job; The Brother; The Father; Eddie; The Home Care Specialist; Lupe Velez.

Culture Vultures: Frasier's very first off-air and in-character words are a dead giveaway of the high-culture whirl the viewer is about to enter into. He asks Roz what she thought of his show, but she seems unwilling to answer. Frustrated that she is avoiding telling him that it was bad, Frasier pleads, 'I am not a piece of Lalique: I can handle criticism.' Frasier describes his arty-farty taste in furniture as 'eclectic', which doesn't wash with Martin, but he at least gets his own back when Frasier complains that Martin's beloved barcalounger won't fit into the style of the apartment. 'It's eclectic!' he triumphantly smirks. The first of the series' real anti-snob jokes, and undoubtedly one of the very best.

Full-on Moon: And a big hello to Daphne, who starts out here a little more kooky than we shall ever see her again. Without warning, she wheels on Martin and states, 'You were a policeman.' Explaining she is a little psychic, she goes on to take a stab at Frasier. 'You're a florist.' It seems that her powers come and go: 'It's strongest during my time of the month. Oh, I guess I let a little secret out there, didn't I?'

She redeems herself, though, by accurately reading that Eddie is a dog.

Out Of Sight: At the impeccably named Café Nervosa, Niles and Frasier discuss the elder brother's feelings on Maris. 'I like her from a distance – the way you like the sun. Maris is like the sun. Except without the warmth.' And so begins one of the most entertaining strands of the series, as we hear again and again about the little darling.

The Buddy Show: We learn that Martin was shot in the hip two years ago by a kid robbing a convenience store.

Eddie Takes The Biscuit: There is very little build-up to the first appearance of one of the show's most popular characters, but every split second of it is genius.

'Oh no, Dad,' begs Frasier. 'No, no, no. Not Eddie.' But Martin is immovable because 'he's my best friend . . .'. Frasier shivers at the thought of this new intruder in his home. 'He gives me the creeps. All he does is stare at me . . . I'm putting my foot down. Eddie is not moving in here.' Cut to a black screen, with one simple word written on it: 'Eddie'. In the background, sinister music plays, obviously from a television set. We fade back to Frasier's apartment, where father and son are watching the box. Sitting next to a deeply disgruntled Frasier is Eddie – a long-haired Jack Russell terrier. He is staring at Frasier. Fade back to black.

Although the staring gag doesn't last long – it gets replaced by far funnier and more varied antics – it is milked for all it is worth. Frasier's deep hatred of the animal is obvious whenever they're together, but Eddie's strange fascination is soon replaced by a more simple disrespect of the owner of his home – echoing the way Martin initially behaves towards his son's hospitality.

Frasier Has Left The Building: This is what the entire episode has been simply and elegantly building up to. Just after a week since the story began and the 'happy family' is together. Martin is in his barcalounger, while Daphne, Frasier and Eddie sit on the couch. Eddie, of course, stares.

On The Couch: A wonderful episode. Though not as manic or charged as the series will later become in its finer moments, this is the pilot episode and it has a job to do. A job that it does with remarkable effect.

Any pilot episode is charged with putting together the component parts of a future series, and putting those elements clearly on show. *Frasier* would, of course, become known for the comic effect of its subtitles, which make their first appearance here. But here, they don't serve as the witty, clever asides they will become (with the exception of the aforementioned 'Eddie' caption): here, they are used to introduce each touchstone of the series. Once these are all in place – each one taking its pot shot at Frasier's carefully crafted lifestyle – Frasier is reminded that life has a way of working out, whatever gets thrown into the mix. This is pointed out to him by Roz, when she tells him the bizarre story of Lupe Velez, a failed actress who wanted to be remembered for committing suicide in a glorious way, but while setting up her final exit tripped and cracked her head on the toilet seat and was found dead thus. Needless to say, she never received the posthumous fame she sought although she does have a star on Hollywood Boulevard.

The series makes its first exploration of Frasier's desire to reconcile himself with his father: the two men are disparate in every way. Martin, understandably annoyed with having to move in with his son, makes it clear that there is a great deal of ground to cover here, especially when Frasier explains, 'I want you here. It'll give us a chance to get reacquainted,' to which Martin retorts, 'That implies we were acquainted at some point.'

As in this exchange, almost every line in this episode is a signpost for the subjects, both dramatic and comic, at which the series will be looking. Rarely does a pilot show do so much, so well, to set up the future of a series.

1.02
'Space Quest'

Written by Sy Dukane and Denise Moss
Directed by James Burrows
First UK Transmission: 27.04.94

Skyline: The elevator goes up the Space Needle.

Synopsis: It is the morning after. Frasier pads, half-asleep, through his apartment, while Daphne and Martin bustle about. When he finds his breakfast changed, his coffee spoilt and his newspaper read, Frasier decides to make it clear how he feels about the invasion of his personal space.

As the long day goes on, Frasier begins to find it increasingly difficult to get some peace and quiet. All he wants to do is read his book. But first his studio is invaded by Bulldog Briscoe, then – when he thinks he might actually have the place to himself – Martin and Daphne arrive back at the apartment. Finally, he fails to find sanctuary even at Café Nervosa: Niles arrives to break the silence and spoil the end of his book.

That evening, in the apartment, Frasier makes a last-ditch effort to get on with his father, but when even that fails he begins to think that maybe it is time for Martin to go.

Where Everybody Knows Their Name: A momentous time for the series as Bob 'Bulldog' Briscoe (Dan Butler) makes his first ever appearance. Frasier's studio is not normally where *The Gonzo Sports Show* comes from (that's an honour reserved for Studio C) but, owing to a power cut, he has to use Frasier's. Presumably he prefers it, since, from here on, *The Gonzo Sports Show* always replaces Frasier's.

Niles and Frasier mention Hester Crane, deciding they take after her far more than their father (well, she was an opera-loving psychiatrist, remember . . .). A mention is also given to Lilith and Frederick as Frasier recalls the time he almost killed himself when he realised Lilith was leaving him for Dr Pascal and his biosphere (in the *Cheers* episode 'The Girl in the Bubble' Part Two).

Dean Erickson's waiter at Café Nervosa, Eric, is seen very clearly throughout the scenes set there, but receives no credit because he doesn't speak. The café would appear to be directly opposite the building where KACL is situated.

Who's On The Line?: Leonard (Christopher Reeve) has a problem with wide-open spaces but Frasier is less than helpful to him and a kid who fantasises about killing his parents.

Subtitles: Dear God, It Wasn't A Dream; The Best Laid Plans . . .; A Coupla White Guys Sittin' 'Round Talkin'; One Man's Storage Room Is Another Man's Sanctuary.

Culture Vultures: Frasier's beloved coffee – a 'finely ground Kenya blend from Starbucks' – is bastardised by Daphne, who throws in a broken eggshell and some allspice. Niles's embarrassing display of familiarity in Café Nervosa is wonderful: ordering his Latte in Italian, and thanking Eric the waiter with a pat '*mille grazie*'. Frasier's look of amused bemusement is brilliant.

Strange Bedfellows: As Frasier is trying to leave the studio, Roz is on the phone talking about her latest conquest. It seems she has dumped Gary because he's boring in bed. She reckons that he's thinking of someone else while they have sex. Well, that's what she's doing anyway. Graphic, and gossipy, comments continue, until she hangs up with a cheery goodbye – to her mother. In many ways, Roz's mother, like Maris Crane, will be a frequently referred-to but never seen character.

Full-on Moon: Frasier's new-found hell comes in the form of Daphne, bustling about his apartment as he blearily tries to wake up. 'They don't serve much tripe in Seattle, do they?' she comments. Frasier just stares back at her, from under stormy brows, and says, 'And you are . . . ?'

A little later, Frasier meets Daphne in the lounge, his dressing gown hanging open. Glancing down, Daphne – without shame, and with very little cruelty – comments, 'Oh, six more weeks of winter, I see.'

Daphne has now moved into her room, which isn't the room opposite Martin's at all (as mentioned in the previous episode), but is another old study of Frasier's situated down a small corridor behind the kitchen – where it will remain for the rest of the series' run.

Eddie Takes The Biscuit: More staring, as Eddie unnerves Frasier while he tries to read his newspaper. When Martin suggests, 'Just ignore him,' Frasier says that's just what he's trying to do. To which Martin replies, 'I'm talking to the dog.'

Frasier Has Left The Building: We are in the storeroom where the study furniture has ended up. Alone at last, Frasier settles down in his armchair to read his book.

On The Couch: Very obviously the second part to 'The Good Son', *Frasier*'s 'Space Quest' is an examination of just what it's like to have to share something you've kept to yourself for so long. As ever, it's the little things that Frasier finds annoying. His morning paper is no longer crisp or sealed in its rubber band. His breakfast routine is shattered by the threat of high-cholesterol food. He is even unable to read a book in peace without asinine comments from his father (who is, to his credit, trying to show concern for his son's interests). Early in the episode, greeted with all this invasion, he mutters to himself (à la Wicked Witch of the West) 'I'll get him for this . . . and his little dog too.'

Frasier's final test for the idea of his father sharing a flat with him is to sit the two of them at the dining table to have a conversation for a few minutes. To the ticking of an egg-timer, they try to disclose secrets to each other. While Frasier willingly admits to once considering suicide, Martin can only offer the fact that he recently discovered that he can turn his eyelid inside out. This marvellous scene pinpoints the moment when Frasier changes his mind about the situation he has ended up in.

While ploughing the same turf as the first episode, 'Space Quest' digs the furrows deeper to reveal even richer comedy. Although there is little in the way of story for the actors to get their teeth into, they more than make up for it in the way they begin to flesh out their characters and the relationships between them.

1.03

'Dinner at Eight'

Written by Anne Flett and Chuck Ranberg
Directed by James Burrows
First UK Transmission: 04.05.94

Skyline: Lights go on in various buildings.

Synopsis: Frasier and Niles decide it's about time they paid their father back for all his kindness and good parenting over the years. And what better way, they decide, than a slap-up meal at one of the best restaurants in town. Disasters beset their plans, though, when firstly Maris drops out and then their reservation is lost.

Martin suggests they go instead to one of his favourite restaurants – the Timber Mill. Niles and Frasier are initially reluctant, but Martin persuades them by pointing out that he was ready to go to their favourite restaurant. So the Crane brothers head over to the Timber Mill and a night of pure terror.

Arriving there, Frasier and Niles are disgusted by the place. Firstly, their ties are hacked off to conform with the dress code. Then the horror of the menu is unleashed upon them, as they are invited to 'Claim their Steak' when a trolley full of raw meat is hauled over to their table. Coping the only way they know how, Frasier and Niles bitch and snipe about the place all evening, until their cattiness finally drives their father away.

Guest Cast: Waitress (Laurie Walton), Hostess (Eve Brent).

Where Everybody Knows Their Name: Frasier and Niles consider Hester Crane to have been their inspiration, whereas Martin recalls that no matter how classy Hester was compared to him, she never, ever made him or anyone else feel small in comparison, a trait his sons could do with learning.

Among the seemingly endless list of staff at Maris's Gothic mansion is a housekeeper called Mary.

Who's On The Line?: Pam (Patti LuPone), a woman plagued by terrible in-laws, plus Monday's line-up includes a couple of jilted lovers, a man afraid of his own car, a manic depressive and three people who feel their lives are going nowhere. Typical post-weekend fodder really. Oh, and the number to call is 555-KACL.

Subtitles: Shh, They're Here; How Many Sharks Died . . .?; Honey, Don't; Dinner At Eight; Tim-berrr!

Culture Vultures: Frasier and Niles are on top posh form in this episode. Their barely disguised disgust and mockery of the Timber Mill is them at their best. At least the hostess gets her revenge when she hacks off their ties.

A bit of designer-label-dropping here, too. Niles's ill-fated tie is a Hugo Boss, and Frasier initially intends to take Martin to Armani in search of a suit (but Martin spots his favoured sharkskin outfit before they can reach the Emporio).

When reminded that he once considered Tchaikovsky's *1812* overture 'a great piece of classical music', a stunned Niles asks, 'Was I ever that young?'

Strange Bedfellows: Roz's latest date is a disaster (no change there, then). After making her pick him up, fill the car with petrol herself, and cook dinner for him, he baulks when she asks him to pass the honey. It seems he has a 'deadly fear of touching anything sticky'.

Full-on Moon: Initially flustered that Daphne is messing with his smalls, Frasier is soon calmed when she explains that she is only 'fluffing' them. When Frasier feels how soft they are, he is amazed. Daphne also reveals she plays a mean game of poker with her girlfriends – she's actually got quite a few non-court sporting talents, as revealed over subsequent shows, including pool and darts.

Meeting Niles here for the first time she reveals her psychic powers. Frasier just shrugs it off saying, 'We've decided to find it charming.'

Out Of Sight: This episode marks Maris's first 'episode'. As she and Niles were getting dressed to go out for dinner, she slumped upon the bed and sighed. It was then, Niles explains, that he knew 'dinner was not to be'. She also owns a home tanning bed.

The Buddy Show: A cavalcade of misery for Martin, it would appear, as he receives news of his ex-colleagues at Phil's retirement party. But he seems perfectly unfazed by the fact that Mo Hanson was killed in a boating accident, Hank Krinski had three heart bypasses and died, and Jimmy Berman wasted away with a 'weird disease' that turned his skin yellow.

After the disastrous meal at the Timber Mill, Martin heads to Duke's, name-checking his favourite bar for the first time.

Eddie Takes The Biscuit: On being told that Martin will bring him back a bone from the Timber Mill, Eddie remains still, his chin firmly on the sofa cushion. 'He's ecstatic!' explains Martin.

Frasier Has Left The Building: To make recompense for their ill treatment of their father's love of the Timber Mill,

Frasier and Niles decided to remain behind and finish their meal. Over the closing credits, we see the brothers chew their way through their dinners in an empty restaurant, their only company a man sweeping the floor, plus the equally bored waitress and hostess.

On The Couch: If you look at the first three episodes as a kind of introductory trilogy, then from here on *Frasier* has established its concepts, characters and setups adequately. We really get to see how well, or badly, the two Crane brothers interact with their father, and we also see the very proud, strong man that Martin Crane is, rather than the stereotypical miserable old git, as Daphne would say, of the first two shows. The meal at the Timber Mill is essential viewing to understand how the three family members tick, and it reinforces so many of the threads that will run on in this series – particularly the snobbery and Martin's kicking against it.

Daphne and Roz have little to do (although we see the beginning of Niles's fascination with his father's health-care worker) but that is not really a problem, since they become more developed as the season progresses.

What we have here is a quality episode that firmly establishes the male leads and prepares us for the start of the formulaic shows (that's an observation and certainly not a criticism) that immediately follow.

By the way, there used to be a pub in London's Soho in the early eighties that did the same thing with customers' ties as the Timber Mill does here. It also decorated the walls with the spoils of war – and very colourful it was, too.

1.04

'I Hate Frasier Crane'

Written by Christopher Lloyd
Directed by David Lee
First UK Transmission: 11.05.94

Skyline: Nothing happens.

Synopsis: Frasier is bruised, and Niles amused, when Derek Mann, newspaper critic, states simply in his column, 'I hate Frasier Crane.' Frasier retaliates on his radio show, criticising Mann for his weak idea of a witty riposte, and before long the situation has spiralled out of control.

Mann prints a detailed, point-by-point list of exactly why he hates Frasier. Frasier then takes Mann's criticism to pieces on air, prompting Mann to phone in. The time for talking, it seems, is over – Mann wants to meet Frasier for a high-noon showdown. Frasier initially dismisses the idea as stupid but, with a bit of persuasion from his father, he finally decides to face up to Mann like a real man.

Guest Cast: Harry (John Brandon).

Where Everybody Knows Their Name: Eric the waiter (Dean Erickson) finally gets a credit, and there's another for Moose as Eddie.

Who's On The Line?: Lorraine (Judith Ivey), who has a problem facing up to her present situation. Her problem is evidenced by her constant switching to other incoming calls while Frasier is trying to talk to her. In the end, his angry prognosis is given, only for him to discover that she has been on another call. And Derek Mann (Joe Mantegna) phones in to challenge Frasier to a fight.

Subtitles: I Hate Frasier Crane; Oh, Yeah . . .?; Yeah!

Culture Vultures: Frasier, ever the fan of sophisticated wit, namechecks Voltaire and H. L. Makin on air while he is attacking Mann for the first time.

Strange Bedfellows: Roz relates, in what appears to be disgust, how the garbage man was watching her as she was naked in the bathroom. It is only when he smiles, revealing a missing tooth, however, that 'the romance went right out of it'. It's worth noting here that we see the start of an ongoing battle between Niles and Roz (which may or may not be genuine or Niles just winding her up) where, each time they meet, Niles can never remember who she is. Although this is their first on-screen meeting, it is clear they have encountered each other before.

Full-on Moon: Daphne's psychic powers are back, as she begins to 'get something' from the photos of an unsolved murder case, that of the Weeping Lotus, that Martin is studying. Her wires get crossed, however, and unless Frasier was responsible for killing a prostitute when he was twelve, the case is closed again. Martin is probably saying this to shut Daphne up, because it's a twenty-year-old case and Frasier is now forty-one.

Daph's down 'n' dirty fighting methods are brought to light, too. When she is advising Frasier on how to approach the fight with Mann, she recommends a good knee to the groin. That always worked for her, she explains: just ask the victim back in Manchester.

Out Of Sight: Maris declines to accompany Niles this episode, because she's just had a row with an operator on directory enquiries. She was after the number of an analyst, since she had been through all the others in Seattle.

The Buddy Show: Harry, the policeman who broke up the fight between Frasier and Mann before it could begin, was doing a favour for Martin. They agree to meet up later at Duke's although the clarinet reference (see **On The Couch**) is lost on Harry, who wasn't at the precinct when Martin was.

Eddie Takes The Biscuit: More staring, but this time Frasier enquires of the dog the reason why. 'Does my head look like a big piece of kibble?'

Frasier Has Left The Building: Without the real thing around, Eddie resorts to staring at a photo of Frasier.

On The Couch: 'The best response is no response at all.' So says Frasier, before starting a war of words with Derek Mann which eventually progresses to a playground-style fist fight between the two. This suggestion of childishness is used to great effect, highlighting Frasier's inability to ignore criticism (an inability Niles finds very entertaining).

A fun episode, once again bringing out the difference between Martin and sons in their approach to life. Once, as a boy, Frasier was challenged to a fight after school by Billy Kriezel, which he declined – because he had a clarinet lesson to attend. As Billy's dad was a cop at Martin's precinct, Martin had to suffer the indignity of his son's wussy excuse. Confronting Frasier with this, he goads him on to fighting Mann – while simultaneously, behind the scenes, making sure that the fight is broken up before any harm can come to Frasier: a very genuine portrayal of Martin's love and concern for Frasier.

1.05

'Here's Looking at You'

Written by Brad Hall
Directed by Andy Ackerman
First UK Transmission: 10.05.94

Skyline: The elevator goes up the Space Needle.

Synopsis: Frasier, concerned that his dad is just sitting round the house all day, decides to buy him a telescope to keep him occupied. Martin is very pleased with the present – he says that he can watch a pair of nesting falcons – but Daphne and Frasier soon persuade him that there is much more fun to be had in being a voyeur.

Before long, Martin has found Irene, a woman in the apartment block opposite with her own telescope, and they strike up a long-distance friendship through messages on large notepads. Frasier begins to tease Martin about his new 'girlfriend', and gives Irene his telephone number so that the two of them can finally speak. Although Frasier and Daphne have high hopes for the relationship, it seems that Martin is less than comfortable with the idea.

Guest Cast: Aunt Patrice (Kathleen Noone).

Where Everybody Knows Their Name: Frederick phones his father for comfort after he dreams about a senator hiding in his wardrobe. Lilith gets a mention too, as it is explained that she smashed Freddie's toy gun (a present from Martin) with a croquet mallet. We discover that Hester died six years ago (not long after her appearance in *Cheers*, then) and her middle name was Rose.

Who's On The Line?: Doug (Jeff Daniels) is worried that his mother does nothing but 'literally' hang around the house. Once Frasier has corrected his grammar (she could not, of course, 'literally' hang around), this sets him wondering about his own father.

Subtitles: A Room With A View; Getting To Know You; Forcas Fracas; Gu-Gulp!

Culture Vultures: An amusing anecdote from Niles's latest wine club meet. The members switch the labels on two bottles of wine, and the duped president proclaims the inferior wine to be better than the other. But, as Niles explains, 'rough-house [turned] to tears', and the president resigned. This is no bad thing, however, as Niles has taken his place. Even Frasier can't take this degree of high-societal mischief seriously, his only comment on the events being, 'What scamps you are.'

Out Of Sight: Maris's Aunt Patrice has never been fortunate enough to see her niece standing up when she visits – the little thing is always being floored by one ailment or another. 'To this day,' she comments, 'I've no idea how tall she is.'

Frasier Has Left The Building: While Frasier and Daphne sleep in the lounge, waiting for Martin's return from his date with Irene, Eddie peers through the lens of the telescope.

On The Couch: A very sweet, very funny episode, with John Mahoney turning in a great performance as Martin at his most delicate. Frasier keeps pushing and pushing for his father to take an interest in Irene, but Martin's protests that he simply doesn't like her won't wash. Martin eventually has to lie, and say that Irene has the same middle name as Hester. Of course, Daphne comes to the rescue, working out that Martin is simply ashamed of his cane, and doesn't want Irene to see him as 'disabled'. Once this hurdle is overcome, the two of them go on a date (although we never find out how it went).

The real star turn of the episode, though, is Kathleen Noone as Patrice. We hear much from Frasier and Niles about how unbearable she is, but when we first see her she seems to be only a friendly, chirpy woman. Frasier and Niles leave her and Martin alone, to get to know each other, but on their return we see the full horror of what this woman is like. A rictus grin on her face, she is burbling to Martin in some incomprehensible manner. Sentences of this strange, choked tongue spew forth, and Martin turns to Frasier and says he thinks she is having a stroke. Niles explains that she is simply talking in G-speak, where you insert a 'g' sound in every syllable. Martin's name would therefore be 'Magartigin Cragane'. Terrified by this woman, Martin is thankful when Frasier invents an excuse to get rid of her. When she has left, Martin simply asks, 'What the hell was that?' Noone's cleverly restrained, then frighteningly manic, performance is a delight.

1.06

'The Crucible'

Written by Sy Dukane and Denise Moss
Directed by James Burrows
First UK Transmission: 25.05.94

Skyline: Nothing happens.

Synopsis: Frasier announces on the radio that he's just bought a painting by renowned local artist Martha Paxton. When she phones to speak to him after the show, he invites her round to a cocktail party as his guest of honour. The only problem is, he hadn't planned a party at all.

When she accepts, he gathers a throng in his apartment to view the painting and meet the painter. But Martha, when she arrives, doesn't recognise the painting and claims she didn't paint it. After Frasier has recovered from his embarrassment, he decides to take the painting back to the gallery from which he bought it – without success, though, as they refuse to give him a refund. When a call to the police is met with derision, Frasier decides that all that is left is revenge. But can even Frasier stoop so low as to throw a brick through the gallery window?

Guest Cast: Martha Paxton (Rachel Rosenthal), Phillip Hayson (John Rubinstein), Diane (Eugenie Bonderant), Ronald (Gregory Eugene Travis).

Where Everybody Knows Their Name: Moose receives another credit as Eddie.

Who's On The Line?: Gary (Robert Klein) wants some marital advice. She wants to holiday in Italy, he wants to spend the money on a sump pump. Frasier, apart from being aghast that anyone would not want to go to Italy, doesn't even know what a sump pump is.

Subtitles: What A Swell Party; #$&%*!!!; After He Left . . .; Peachfuzz.

Culture Vultures: There's snobbery aplenty in this episode. As everyone at the party waits for the arrival of Paxton, Frasier frets about having everything right: he worries that the Pinot Noir is 'far too stagy', and that no one except the dog is eating the canapés.

There is a quite brilliant scene in the gallery, when Frasier is trying to get his money back on the painting. He is almost side-tracked from his aim by his rampant tastebuds, when the gallery owner offers him a glass of fine wine from the Loire Valley. Although he seems more than impressed by the wine, a disgruntled Frasier later comments, 'Loire Valley, my ass!'

Full-on Moon: Daphne has a psychic moment as she traces Maris's lost earring – to Eddie's stomach!

Out Of Sight: Maris finally ventures forth, to attend Frasier's party but of course we don't see her. When Frasier asks Niles where she is, he explains that she 'exhausts easily under the pressure to be interesting', and she is currently lying on the bed under the guests' coats.

The Buddy Show: To give Frasier a 'bite of a reality sandwich', Martin gets his son to phone the police station and ask for the Fine Arts Forgery Department. He is greeted by laughter from Doris, the phone operator.

Frasier Has Left The Building: Frasier finally finds a home for the painting that has caused him so much trouble and embarrassment. He hangs it above the toilet.

On The Couch: We all love to see Frasier wriggle his way out of an awful, usually self-imposed, situation, and this episode is a great one for that. His excitement at his party is wonderful, and he continually spouts classic lines, like when he hears the doorbell: 'That must be la Paxton – and fashionably late, of course!' His attempts to interpret the terrible news Paxton gives him are hilarious: of course she didn't paint the picture, she 'gave birth' to it!

Frasier's coping with his father at a party also gives us a few wonderful moments. He drags him away from poor Bethany Van Pelt, to whom he is showing pictures of Helen, the murdered prostitute in the Weeping Lotus case (see 1.04, 'I Hate Frasier Crane'). Martin explains that she had said, 'Aren't these Swedish meatballs the messiest things you've ever seen?' But the maltreated Martin gets his revenge after Paxton announces that the painting is not one of hers: 'And you thought I was going to embarrass you.'

Frasier tells Paxton that his apartment is in Elliot Bay Towers, on the Counterbalance. As can be seen in various episodes, the number of his apartment is 1901. We see more of the Niles/Roz war and this is the first time Roz makes her way to Frasier's place, finally meeting Martin and Daphne as well.

1.07

'Call Me Irresponsible'

Written by Anne Flett and Chuck Ranberg
Directed by James Burrows
First UK Transmission: 01.06.94

Skyline: Lights go on in various buildings.

Synopsis: Another day at KACL, and another caller with relationship problems. Marco feels unable to commit to his girlfriend Catherine; he says that he is just staying with her until something better comes along. An appalled Frasier advises him either to make the decision to commit, or to dump his girlfriend Catherine, which he duly does.

Catherine, however, is not very happy about this and comes to the studios to complain to Frasier in person. Over a bag of M&Ms, ire turns to desire and Catherine and Frasier start dating. A horrified Niles reminds his brother of the ethical problem of getting involved with his patients (and their girlfriends), but Frasier carries on regardless – the only hiccup occurring when Marco phones in again thinking that he's done the wrong thing.

Marco suspects that Catherine is dating someone else and is worried because he is beginning to think that he wants her back. Frasier, much to the disapproval of Niles and Roz, advises him to forget her and move on. But will Frasier's desire win the battle against his ethics?

Guest Cast: Catherine (Amanda Donohoe).

Where Everybody Knows Their Name: Another mention of Lilith. While getting to know Frasier, Catherine comments that his wife 'must be really lucky'. Wryly, Frasier observes that this is probably true – now. And Martin is keeping up the Christmas card tradition he started with Hester.

Who's On The Line?: Marco (Bruno Kirby), who starts the ball rolling, and Hank (Eddie Van Halen), who complains about his neighbours. We never get to hear his gripe in full, though, because he can't hear Frasier over the sound of his own radio. There is also Todd, whom Roz 'accidentally' cuts off.

Subtitles: 'Twas Two Months Before Christmas . . .; M And Ms And Sympathy; Kiss Me, Kate; He's Baaack; How Am I Driving?; The Obligatory Sex Scene.

Culture Vultures: Entertaining Catherine at his apartment, Frasier cracks an awful pun. On choosing a wine, he decides to plump for the La Fête, quipping, 'La Fête don't fail me now!' Unfunny as it may be, it at least shows Frasier's excitement and desire to impress Catherine.

Strange Bedfellows: Much to her disgruntlement, Frasier drags Roz into the conversation with Marco with a merry, 'Hey, Roz, you've been round the block a few times . . .' Marco's classic male indecisiveness and 'grass is always greener' attitude puts Roz in mind of just about every man she has ever met: 'I've seen the future, and its name is Marco.'

Full-on Moon: In an aside sequence that has nothing to do with the main plot (but is, however, one of the funniest parts of the episode), we see Daphne and Martin decorating a Christmas tree (in October) in order to photograph the 'family' in front of it for their Christmas cards. Frasier, meanwhile, is napping – a habit that reminds her of the demise of Grandfather Moon.

He spent so much of his time asleep that Grammie Moon would comment that 'he might as well be a dead man'. One day, he *was* a dead man, but '[Grammie] kept insisting, "He's napping! He's napping!"' There's a curious ease and lack of sympathy with which Daphne relates this tale; perhaps the implication is that, as she is a grass-roots Northern type, something as 'real' as a death wouldn't affect her that much. Whatever, the matter-of-fact way in which she tells this story only furthers her wonderful earthy image: a marvellous break from the stereotypical norm of the English in the USA's media – that of a prissy, airy-fairy character.

This is the first reference to Grammie Moon, by the way, but, along with Billy, Daph's ballroom-dancing brother of dubious sexual orientation, she will become the most famous of Daph's extraordinarily large family.

Eddie Takes The Biscuit: Moose lives up to his name, as Eddie dresses up in a pair of foam antlers for the Christmas photo shoot.

Frasier Has Left The Building: An amusing sequence of – presumably rejected – shots for the Crane Christmas card.

On The Couch: Not one of the first season's stronger episodes, perhaps let down by the somewhat slapstick dénouement to the main plot. Hampered by the ailing stomach that always accompanies Frasier's breaches of his own ethics, his attempts to finally have sex with Catherine are constantly interrupted by his 'I'm about to be sick' noise – a strange, strangled gurgling that is frankly too silly to be funny. Amanda Donohoe puts in a good turn as Catherine but, true to form, she is relishing her special-guest status a little too much. This episode smacks of a possibly nervous production team getting a 'name' in to assure ratings for the show, something that *Frasier* – even then – didn't need.

1.08

'Beloved Infidel'

Written by Leslie Eberhard
Directed by Andy Ackerman
First UK Transmission: 08.06.94

Skyline: The light atop the Space Needle glows.

Synopsis: Having dinner at a restaurant, Frasier and Niles spy their father spending the evening with Marion Lawlor, an old family friend. Years ago, a rift formed between the Lawlors and the Cranes; this new meeting prompts Niles to investigate why the fall-out happened.

They are horrified when Niles, digging through his boyhood journals, turns up some clues that make the brothers think that, years ago, Martin and Marion had an affair. Frasier is more surprised to discover that, while his father admits to the infidelity, he was only trying to protect his son from the truth – that it was Hester, Frasier's mother, who had an affair, with Marion's husband Stan.

Guest Cast: Marion Lawlor (Pat Crowley), Waitress (Julie Gill).

Where Everybody Knows Their Name: Another namecheck for Lilith, as we learn that she cheated on Frasier while they were married. Much to Frasier's shame, Lilith once had an affair with a Frenchman, Dr Pascal, who 'lived in a self-contained, underground eco-pod' (another reference to the two-part *Cheers* story 'The Girl in the Bubble'). There's no accounting for taste, obviously. Frasier wonders if he'll ever tell Frederick about this affair, which led to their divorce.

Hester Crane is of course mentioned throughout this episode, while Moose gets another credit as Eddie.

Who's On The Line?: Poor French Danielle (JoBeth Williams) is having a problem with her 'meutheot'. Frasier, though, can't understand what she's saying, so palms her off with the advice that she should confront her 'meutheot' ... or something.

Subtitles: Not Now ... Now!; The Lady Vanishes; Dr Shecky Crane; Things Best Left Unsaid; Like Father, Like Son.

Culture Vultures: In the restaurant, straight after telling Niles that he should act like a real man, Frasier orders a 'Fuzzy Navel, blended nice and frothy'. Grammer's timing in this scene is perfect. Niles rationalises that it cannot be a 'good' restaurant because Martin eats there – presumably thinking back to Martin's choice of eateries such as the Timber Mill.

Strange Bedfellows: In this episode, Roz is dating someone whom she describes as 'a very successful media consultant', who arrives to pick her up in his cab. And we have more of the Niles/Roz war of words.

Full-on Moon: More of Daphne's crazy family history is brought to light. She explains that all the Moons have worked on the docks, 'except for [her brother] Billy, who couldn't stand the smell of fish and went to teach ballroom dancing'. Billy was always 'mum's favourite', and the script's hints of Billy's sexual orientation go gloriously unexplored by the normally astute Daphne. Or maybe she was being discreet. Jane Leeves gives a great little performance here, never once milking those hints, leaving their comedy purely in the mind of the viewer.

The Buddy Show: The Crane boys are surprised to find Martin with Marion in the restaurant, since they thought he was drinking at Duke's.

Eddie Takes The Biscuit: The duplicitous dog makes Frasier think he is obeying his orders about the couch – but he ceases to rub the fur of his back all over it for only a scant second before Dr Crane walks through the door.

Frasier Has Left The Building: . . .and since that is the case, Eddie is back on the couch, back-rubbing to his heart's content.

On The Couch: A great episode, and one that shows us both how delicate Martin thinks Frasier is, and how much he loves him and his cherished memory of Hester. Although the plot may be a tad predictable – Marion's revelation about the truth of the affair is hardly a surprise – it is the performances that make this episode stand out. The morally affronted (and, as usual, hypocritical) Frasier, the nosy (but considerate) Daphne, the surprisingly sensitive Martin, and Niles's dogged pursuit of the facts – all the actors involved do their usual best.

1.09
'Selling Out'

Written by Lloyd Garver
Directed by Andy Ackerman
First UK Transmission: 15.06.94

Skyline: The elevator goes up the Space Needle.

Synopsis: Frasier comes across a moral dilemma when he is asked to start endorsing products on his show. Can he justify misusing his position as a respected fountain of wisdom to make people buy products? He can, it seems, but only on two stipulations. One: that he has tried, tested and approved of the product or service. And two: that he gets that lovely fat pay cheque in return.

Bebe Glazer, Bulldog's agent, soon gets wind of Frasier's new-found love of advertising, and tries to persuade him to let her represent him and get him more work. But just how far is Frasier prepared to go to make sure he can pay for Frederick's college bill?

Guest Cast: Walnut (John Drayman), Almond (Michael David Edwards), and Dr Joyce Brothers. A credit is given for Director (Paul Perri), but the character doesn't appear.

Where Everybody Knows Their Name: Bulldog (Dan Butler) steps in at the last minute to advertise a Chinese restaurant on Frasier's behalf. His cod-Chinese accent and appallingly racist jokes prompt Roz to comment that 'this time, we're really going to get sued'. We also see the start of Bulldog's trademark knocking on Frasier's skull and his bark at women (hence the sobriquet 'Bulldog').

The marvellous Harriet Sansom Harris makes her debut as Bebe, with a performance that treads a fine line between frighteningly inspired craziness and over-the-top campiness. Harris, thankfully, never goes too far, making her turn the highlight of this episode.

Dr Joyce Brothers is Frederick's favourite psychologist and we are told that Frasier's son is now five. Oh, and Moose gets another credit as Eddie.

Who's On The Line?: Roger (Carl Renier) calls in to explain his problem with his wife: she wants to call their new boat *Lulu-Belle*, while he favours *Intrepid*. Frasier listens, staring into the middle distance, as Roger asks what the good doctor thinks the boat should be called. In a great piece of scripting, Frasier explains to Roger about a fantastic invention called a tunnelling electron microscope. This microscope is the most powerful magnifying device in the world. 'Roger,' continues Frasier, 'if I were using that microscope right now, I still wouldn't be able to locate my interest in your problem.'

Subtitles: Would You Buy An Eggroll From This Man?; That Better Be Your Foot; 780AM On Your Radio Dial; The Big Kahuna; Knees Together, Lips Apart; Frasier Crane To Block.

Full-on Moon: Sadly, the script makes Daphne out to be a bit of a dunderhead in this episode, as opposed to the astute wise woman we all know she is. But a great moment of glory comes as she reveals her intimate knowledge of television contracts. It transpires that, when she was younger, she appeared in a British television show called *Mind Your Knickers*, about the exploits of a group of young, 'ethnically diverse' schoolgirls. She played Emma, 'the short, spunky one. Of course, by the end of the series, I was sixteen, five foot ten, and they had my boozies bound up tighter than a mummy.' Daph has also bathed in champagne 'once or twice'. Lucky girl . . .

Out Of Sight: Niles speaks of the night he and Maris rented *Basic Instinct*. 'I don't mind telling you, we pushed our beds together that night,' he says, adding, after a typically well-judged pause, 'And that was no mean feat. Her room, as you know, is across the hall.' And we learn that Niles's car has the personalised number plate 5HR1NK.

Eddie Takes The Biscuit: God alone knows where Moose gets his knack for comic timing from. Frasier prangs his BMW against the wall in the car park, and angrily demands to know what happened to the tennis ball he hangs there to make sure he doesn't reverse too far. Eddie appears, dropping the ball at his feet.

Martin explains he only wants to play, suggesting Frasier throw the ball for the dog. So Frasier does. Right off the balcony, and across the Seattle skyline.

Frasier Has Left The Building: In one of his product tests earlier in the episode, Frasier, Daphne and Martin take a dip in a Jacuzzi showroom. Frasier panics when he thinks he sees the head of the Seattle Psychiatric Association, and plunges beneath the bubbling surface to avoid being recognised. Over the closing titles, we see Daphne and Martin relaxing in the Jacuzzi. Eventually, Frasier runs out of breath and crashes into the air again, ruining their peace.

On The Couch: However good the rest of this episode is – and it's filled with the series' typical sharp wit – 'Selling Out' is notable for Harriet Sansom Harris's debut as Bebe Glazer. The scenes between her and Kelsey Grammer sparkle with a wonderful energy. The series' star once again gets to show his ineffable talent for physical comedy, and Harriet more than manages to keep up. A case in point is the scene where she is persuading him to appear in a television advert for nuts, a product he really does not like. Harriet shoving the can of nuts across the coffee table to a stony-faced-but-cracking Kelsey Grammer is irresistibly funny, and her insinuating and calculated tones create the perfect soundtrack to this faultless scene.

1.10
'Oops'

Written by Denise Moss and Sy Dukane
Directed by James Burrows
First UK Transmission: 22.06.94

Skyline: Lights go on in various buildings.

Synopsis: Frasier, disapprovingly, gets involved in the whirling world of office gossip. It seems that KACL has budget problems and word is that someone is going to get sacked. The conclusion is soon drawn that Bulldog's for it, and everyone tries to keep it under their hat. Frasier manages to do so, until Father Mike asks him if he thinks the redundancy could be heading for his own priestly self. Frasier tells him not to worry, and that Bulldog's going to be the one. The only problem is that Bulldog is just around the corner, and has heard every word.

Unprepared to be fired, Bulldog heads straight for the office of Ned Miller, the manager of KACL, and tenders his resignation. Unequivocally. And violently. But, as Frasier soon discovers, the word on the grapevine has changed, and Bulldog wasn't the one who was going to get the chop. But can Frasier persuade Miller to give Bulldog his job back? And just who was going to be culled?

Guest Cast: Ned Miller (John Glover), Teddy (Wayne Wilderson).

Where Everybody Knows Their Name: 'Oops' marks the first major role in an episode for Bulldog (Dan Butler), as the events rotate around him and we even see him out of the studio, where he encounters both Daphne and Martin for the first time. Other KACL staff get an airing here as well: the irrepressibly shouty Chopper Dave (Richard Poe) making his first screen appearance (his penchant for shouting is explained by his frequent need to talk over the blades of his 'copter); an engineer called Terry; Father Mike Mancuso from Religion on the Line (George Deloy); and Ned Miller in his first and last appearance. Other staff members are mentioned as part of the chain of gossip: Arlenc (Miller's secretary, who gets sacked as well), Ray the greengrocer, and Bonnie 'The Auto Lady' Weems.

Who's On The Line?: Don (Jay Leno) has a weight problem. He explains that, although he eats a healthy diet and regularly works out, he just can't seem to lose even a pound. As he is talking, the voice of a drive-in takeaway waitress can be heard in the background, although no one is credited for this.

Subtitles: Heard It Through the Grapevine; Did I Do That?; One Dog Night; It's Miller Time.

Culture Vultures: Frasier's prissiness about his apartment is heightened when Bulldog pays a visit. He carefully moves his *objets d'art* out of the reach of his visitor and, when he is persuaded to let Bulldog stay the night, he snarls, 'What's the point of having a priceless suede couch, unless you have a bunch of people crashing on it?'

Strange Bedfellows: Just before leaving to launch his attack on Ned Miller, Bulldog grasps Roz and gives her a passionate kiss, saying, 'Wait for me.' Disgusted, she runs into Frasier's studio and asks, 'What was that?'

Full-on Moon: Another psychic episode for Daphne, as she detects an aura of guilt around Frasier, before he admits he was responsible for Bulldog leaving KACL. She soon realises she's on a high when she also detects that Miller cheats on his wife.

Out Of Sight: A bizarre number of images are conjured by Niles's stories of Maris's drama-group rehearsals for *Cats*: a bunch of middle-aged women in leotards crawling around his house, one of them even scent-marking the furniture. The nightmare ends, though, when she calls her husband, distraught. She has been ejected from the cast – she couldn't remember the words to 'Memory'.

Niles's weak excuse for visiting Daphne this week is to see whether she can nurse a critically ill plant back to life; it's one of Maris's favourites. Asked exactly what she did to it to let it get in that state, Niles replies, 'Nothing. Just loved it.'

Eddie Takes The Biscuit: Bulldog seems to hold a magnetism for animals, as well as women. Before he even has a chance to knock on Frasier's apartment door, Eddie is scratching at it trying to get to him.

Frasier Has Left The Building: Following through on a bet he made earlier in the episode, Bulldog presents his show upside down, hanging from his feet above the mike. Frasier and Roz look on, captivated.

On The Couch: An excellent examination of the lifeblood of the workplace – office gossip. Peri Gilpin shines in the scenes when Roz is chastising Frasier for letting Bulldog know that he was, apparently, for the chop. She is filled with a marvellous manic energy, as she screams some frighteningly astute lines on the acceptable side of rumour-mongering: 'The whole point of gossip is to talk behind the person's back, not in front of them! I didn't realise you were unclear on the concept!' Gilpin invests Roz with an appropriate zeal for gossip, lending the character the kind of juiciness and greed you would expect of someone so corporeal.

1.11

'Death Becomes Him'

Written by Leslie Eberhard
Directed by Andy Ackerman
First UK Transmission: 29.06.94

Skyline: Nothing happens.

Synopsis: Daphne is telling Niles about the sort of men she likes – 'more on the manly side,' she explains. Niles immediately hides the napkin he has been shaping into a swan and tries to be more macho.

Frasier has received a call from Dr Jennings, who says that Martin has not been for his physical. They challenge their father on this, and Martin explains he doesn't like Dr Jennings, mainly because he keeps his tongue depressors in a colon-shaped container. Frasier and Niles discuss who should be responsible for taking Martin to his appointments and right now it has to be Frasier, as Niles has to oversee his Fear of Abandonment workshop – and he's been a 'no-show, twice!'

On Niles's suggestion, they go to see a Dr Newman, who fails to arrive because he has had a heart attack and died.

Frasier discusses this with Roz the next day, but she doesn't worry about death very much – 'Maybe it's because you're forty-one,' she tells Frasier, 'and I'm . . . not.'

Frasier becomes obsessed with his own mortality, and wants to set his affairs in order. He gathers Niles, Martin and Daphne and explains why he is doing this. He suggests they all put stickers on whatever possessions of his they want after he dies. His family find this a bit weird, but Daphne can see the point of it. 'I'm a health-care worker,' she reminds them. 'I've had my fair share of patients die on me.' 'That's comforting,' murmurs a clearly discomforted Martin.

Late that night, Martin finds Frasier still awake, thinking about why Dr Newman died so young, and Martin says there could be any number of reasons, so Frasier resolves to go to Dr Newman's shiva and find out exactly why he died . . .

Guest Cast: Aunt Bobbie (June Claman), Gail (Maddie Gorman), Jill Newman (Stephanie Dunnam), Allan Freedman (Murray Rubinstein), Woman at Shiva (Shawn Huff), Patient (Marion Duggan), Receptionist (Amy Lloyd).

Where Everybody Knows Their Name: 'You're not Jewish, are you?' asks everyone at the shiva of Frasier, and he therefore feels obliged to point out that Lilith is and, therefore, so is Frederick.

Subtitles: Well, I'm Lousy At Tennis; A Family Meeting; Kugel, Fras And Allen.

Culture Vultures: Dr Gary Newman 'sounds perfect' as a doctor for Martin in Frasier's eyes because he has a Liechtenstein hanging in his office, and a weekend home on Lake Chalon. When he was young, Frasier used to recite Puccini's operas to take his mind off getting shots – 'Right then,' says Martin darkly, 'I knew you'd never be a cop.'

Strange Bedfellows: Roz has been dating an older guy and wonders what she would do if he died on her. Literally.

Full-on Moon: Daphne's mother was very keen for her daughter to go out with one Reginald Glower, the butcher's son, but Daphne never took to him because he was a 'pasty little thing'.

The Buddy Show: Martin reveals how he was on a drugs bust with seven or eight other cops. They burst in and the first guy through the door was shot dead. For a while Martin became worried about this but eventually realised that life had to go on. 'Next time I came across one of those doors, I went straight through it. The fact that I got shot in the hip was pure coincidence.' So that's how he got his injury.

Frasier Has Left The Building: Roz, doing some tidying up, chucks a towel over Frasier's African mask.

On The Couch: Without a doubt, the best parts of this episode are at the shiva, as Frasier bumbles his way through the Jewish ceremony and manages to offend almost everybody there. As a result, the call of 'You're not Jewish, are you?' becomes the catchphrase of the show. When Frasier tries to talk to Dr Newman's widow and find out what might have caused his death, she is delighted to find a psychiatrist to talk to. She asks him what he would say to one of his listeners unable to accept that her husband had died too early. He is honest, and explains there is nothing he can say that enables it to make some sense, but adds,

'You can't spend your life being obsessed with death.' If the idea of taking his own advice takes root, it is swamped by Jill Newman's delightfully resigned delivery of 'You're not Jewish, are you?' Beautifully timed.

The rest of the episode is a rather drawn-out prologue to this scene and there are some nice touches: Niles trying to be butch, Niles attaching stickers to things of Frasier's to be claimed after his death, and Roz telling Frasier that the reason all their conversations turn to her sex life is because she has one and he doesn't. But overall it's unevenly paced. Not bad, but not superb either.

1.12
'Miracle On 3rd Or 4th Street'

Written by Christopher Lloyd
Directed by James Burrows
First UK Transmission: 06.07.94

Skyline: The elevator goes up the Space Needle.

Synopsis: It is Christmas and Frasier has bought Roz a water-squirting microphone. For her part, Roz gives Frasier a very classy briefcase (which he is still using four seasons later). And, despite Bulldog's requests, Frasier refuses to take the extended Christmas Day slot, because Frederick is coming for Frasier's first Christmas in Seattle. At the Christmas party, things get slightly out of hand when, as the 'new boy', Frasier assumes the responsibility of taking the seductive, and lush, Bonnie Weems home.

Back at the apartment, Niles is trying to persuade Daphne to join them for the family Christmas at their mountain retreat. 'It's an actual log cabin with actual deer grazing through the snow in our front yard. Of course, Maris fires off her shotgun from time to time to scare them from our garbage, but still, it's enchanting.' Unswayed by this image,

Daphne elects to head to San Francisco to stay with Uncle Jackie.

Meanwhile, Frasier and Martin are arguing over how to decorate the rather extravagant Christmas tree which dominates the rear of the apartment – both are in a bad mood because Frederick won't now be joining them because he and Lilith are going to Austria.

As a result of his row with his father, Frasier agrees to do the Christmas shift (and thus receives the full wrath of a Roz Doyle denied her Christmas Day with her mother) but regrets it when the callers are such a depressing lot. He eventually sends Roz home and, hours later, escapes the studios to find a meal. As he's dressed rather casually for Frasier and hasn't shaved, he is made to feel at home when he comes across Lou's Place, the only eatery open on Christmas Day, which is packed with the local down-and-outs. When he realises he's left his wallet back at work, he explains he cannot pay, and the other customers, thinking this is his first Christmas on the streets, want to help him out . . .

Guest Cast: Lou (Christine Estabrook), Bill (Hawthorne James), Tim (John J. Finn).

Where Everybody Knows Their Name: Lilith gets a mention, because, rather than sending Frederick to Seattle for Christmas as planned, she's taking him to Austria, to the locations where they filmed *The Sound of Music*, Freddie's favourite film. He's also going to be dining with Julie Andrews, then taking a horse-driven sleigh towards the alps and getting a hot-air balloon ride over the mountains. Oh, and he's gong to EuroDisney on the way back. Any wonder Frasier realises he cannot compete. Bulldog (Dan Butler) is of course preparing for Christmas, and, at the party, Chopper Dave (Richard Poe), Elizabeth (Bette Rae) and the legendary Bonnie Weems (Katherine Danielle) make an appearance, while Father Michael gets a brief mention.

Who's On The Line?: Ned, who got mugged on his way home from the soup kitchen; Don (Eric Stoltz), who left his favourite trainers on top of his car and when they fell off they were picked up by a homeless guy, so he feels he has contributed something to the Christmas spirit; and Barry (Ben Stiller), who cannot stop crying. To add to Frasier and Roz's misery, we also hear from Tom (Mel Brooks), whose puppy died at Christmas when he was little, Gladys (Rosemary Clooney), who keeps falling in the shower but has so many pins in her hips, they can't fit any more, and Jeff (Dominick Dunne), who is watching *The Sound of Music* to cheer himself up (and so finishes off poor Frasier).

Subtitles: The Office Christmas Party; Miracle On 3rd Or 4th Street.

Full-on Moon: Daphne makes her first mention of her Uncle Jackie, who lives in San Francisco. He's a transvestite who is 'getting a bit long in the tooth too, if you ask me. Thanksgiving – he ate too much turkey and I had to cut him out of his pantyhose.'

Out Of Sight: When trying to justify having dressed Daphne in some very . . . well, skimpy dresses, reputedly because he's thinking of buying one for Maris, Niles protests to Frasier that 'Maris and Daphne are roughly the same size.' Frasier nods, 'Give or take a foot.'

Eddie Takes The Biscuit: While Martin and Frasier have their row, Eddie (very sensibly we feel) hides.

Frasier Has Left The Building: Eddie tears the Christmas presents to pieces.

On The Couch: A great show, where the best moments involve Niles trying to help Daphne in and out of her dresses (pity the poor coffee cup when Niles hears that Daphne isn't wearing any knickers) and also a fabulous moment where Eddie gets his own back on the ever-prissy Niles by drinking from his coffee cup.

The Christmas cheer clearly doesn't extend to the lonely souls who populate Frasier's phone-in, but the sequences in Lou's Place as Frasier tries to convince the homeless people that he's not one of them are excellent. Their generosity and friendliness after listening to the moans of lots of well-fed, housed people really touches Frasier and after his abortive attempts to get into his BMW outside, it's great that he just gives up and walks home.

A 'feel-good' show (nice to know that Don's trainers got a good home) that never sinks into the schmaltz that often ruins other comedy shows that try to blur the line between those that have and those that have not. Or indeed, the saccharine movie from which the title of this episode is nicked.

1.13

'Guess Who's Coming To Breakfast'

Written by Molly Newman
Directed by Andy Ackerman
First UK Transmission: 13.07.94

Skyline: Nothing happens.

Synopsis: When Niles hurts his head while trying to impress Daphne in the kitchen, Frasier is less than charitable about his motives, claiming, 'You're shameless.' Niles is not in the mood for Frasier's lack of sympathy. 'I have a very sore head and crackerjack lawyer, so don't crowd me.'

Frasier wants Niles to take Martin out on Friday night as he has a date. 'Hoping to "get lucky"?' Niles jokes. 'Oh, Niles, no one refers to having sex as "getting lucky" any more.' 'I do,' moans Niles. Martin agrees to go to Niles and Maris's on Friday night to watch an Angie Dickinson movie, if Frasier agrees to be out on Thursday night when he has a date with Elaine Morris from downstairs.

On the Friday morning, Daphne and Frasier are discussing breakfast and the bizarre play they saw the previous evening when Martin comes in, followed by Elaine, who clearly stayed the night. Frasier deals rather badly with this, embarrassing both himself and Elaine with his unintentional double entendres.

On his show that afternoon, Frasier uses his awkwardness in dealing with Martin and Elaine's relationship to explain to a caller how to deal with sex in her family. Martin is livid and Elaine won't speak to him.

On Monday, an apologetic Frasier, over the strains of 'Moon River', tries to talk Elaine into having dinner with Martin that evening in their apartment at 8 p.m.

Trouble is, when an already hesitant Elaine arrives, she discovers half the residents of Elliot Bay Towers outside Frasier's door, all anxious to find out how the evening goes . . .

Guest Cast: Elaine (Linda Stephens), Tony the doorman (Robert Colbert), Marjorie (Patricia Fraser).

Where Everybody Knows Their Name: The first appearance for the *Star Trek*-loving nerdish Noel 'the Mole' Shempsky (Patrick Kerr), who has an ill-concealed crush on Roz (he gives her a home-made spice rack, with a place for cumin), suffers from night blindness and keeps a photo of Captain Kirk on his desk and gives Vulcan salutes, saying 'Live long and prosper' at odd moments.

Who's On The Line?: Janine, who thinks her husband is an obsessive hand-washer (which, as he's a county coroner, is probably just as well), plus Ethan (Elijah Wood), who is bullied at school (quite rightly as it turns out), Al (Henry Mancini), who hates the sound of his own voice, and Marianne (Piper Laurie), who is appalled to discover that her twenty-two-year-old daughter Judy is having sex, and thus starts Frasier off on the rocky road to disaster by talking to her about his sixty-three-year-old father and Elaine. 'Kids,' mutters an unconvinced Marianne. 'You can't live with them, you can't shove them back in the womb.'

Subtitles: Boy N The Hood; Foot In Mouth Disease; This Is Where We Get Off.

Culture Vultures: Trying to smarten up his father's image, Frasier suggests that Martin play canasta with Elaine, while Niles says that PBS is showing a documentary on thirties swing bands they might like to watch. Frasier shops at Bon Marche, so he is delighted to learn Elaine works there.

Strange Bedfellows: Frasier finds it hysterical that Roz has agreed to go on a date with Noel. So do we.

Full-on Moon: Daphne's Friday morning breakfast consists of eggs, sausages and Grammie Moon's fantastic sticky buns. Grammie reportedly made them every Sunday but added a pint of rum to the recipe. Daphne used to go to Grammie Moon's after church and find her face down in the birdbath, wearing her wedding dress, which is hardly surprising. Daphne also uses her psychic powers later to send 'Come to dinner, come to dinner' messages to Elaine in apartment 1410. Trouble is Elaine lives in 1412, so Daphne ponders whether to set an extra place for the occupant of 1410.

Eddie Takes The Biscuit: When Frasier returns from the studio, like Daphne, Eddie flees the room, knowing Martin is livid with his son. He is also instrumental in persuading Frasier to sort out the mess he has created by, as usual, just staring at Frasier.

Frasier Has Left The Building: Noel leaves another gift for Roz in her control room.

On The Couch: The first of *Frasier*'s really farce-based episodes, and a brilliant one at that. Frasier's dialogue to Elaine the morning after she has stayed is nothing short of brilliant (one of our all-time favourite *Frasier* moments), and the final sequences outside his apartment and in the elevator are exquisite (Elaine telling Frasier to stand in the corner is inspired). On top of this, the period where Frasier and Roz are so bored by their callers that they begin messing around in the studio with chopsticks and a backscratcher are hilarious, and we adore the fact that Martin is always 'seeing things no one else does' and the closing dialogue between Frasier and Daphne – if Niles were there, he'd be apoplectic!

Great stuff.

1.14
'The Show Where Lilith Comes Back'

Written by Ken Levine and David Isaacs
Directed by James Burrows
First UK Transmission: 29.07.94

Skyline: Lights go on in various buildings.

Synopsis: 'Congratulations, Frasier. You've done it again.' Thus begins Lilith's return to Frasier's life by phoning in to his show to correct a piece of advice he has given to a caller. Quick as a flash, Frasier tells his audience that there is a celebrity on the phone. 'What do you mean by celebrity?' comes the icy voice down the line. 'Ohhh . . . they know you,' Frasier says darkly.

Lilith and Frasier agree to meet for dinner that night at Frasier's place. Niles is horrified – after what she did at his and Maris's wedding, he doubts he can ever forgive her. Martin puts on a brave face, and Daphne is intrigued to meet her. Within seconds of Lilith's arrival, they all remember what it was about her that terrified them so. Lilith is particularly pleased to see Martin again. 'Knowing, as I do, the nature of your relationship with Frasier, when I heard that he'd taken you in, I immediately flipped to the Weather Channel to see if hell had, indeed, frozen over.'

After the others have gone (Daphne flees due to her headache, Martin retires defeated and Niles escapes after Lilith apologises for her wedding behaviour), Lilith and Frasier finally talk. It transpires that, after his last visit home, Lilith found the letter he left, suggesting they get back together, and so she has flown over, eager to see whether a reconciliation would work because she's lonely. The trouble is that the letter is not a recent one at all, but one Frasier wrote just as they were getting divorced and so isn't applicable any longer. Lilith composes herself the best she can – 'Here I am, humiliated, emotionally drained, and I've used up all my frequent-flier miles.' She begs Frasier to let her slip away with dignity, which he does, but her handbag gets caught in the door and thus her exit becomes decidedly undignified.

The following day Frasier and Niles discuss the possibility of a reconciliation and Frasier heads to Lilith's hotel for dinner and a discussion. Things, however, do not go as planned. 'There's a bed and an honour bar. What more do we need?' They end up together for the night, but the following morning, amid conflicting emotions and the wrong breakfast, Frasier and Lilith must decide what to do next . . .

Guest Cast: Waiter (Roger Keller).

Where Everybody Knows Their Name: This is the first ever mention of Gil Chesterton, during a discussion about his show, *Restaurant Beat*. Frederick Crane is talked about, obviously, as he's off to Chess Camp (although he can't go out much since he's allergic to seven varieties of ivy). And Lilith (Bebe Neuwirth) makes a magnificent return.

Who's On The Line?: Hank (Timothy Leary), who wants to diet, and receives advice from Frasier which provokes Lilith into calling. 'I happened to hear your voice on the radio,' she later explains. 'I kept hoping you'd introduce Pearl Jam's latest hit but much to my chagrin, you were dealing out worthless advice pills from your psychiatric Pez dispenser.'

Subtitles: The Return Of The Magnificent Sternin; Look What I Found With The Dust Bunnies; Fried Eggs And Other Small Tragedies.

Full-on Moon: Daphne suffers a psychic headache the whole time Lilith is in Seattle, and, when she shakes Lilith's hand, she loses all feeling in her arm.

Out Of Sight: Maris wrote her own marriage vows, which Lilith sniggered through at the wedding. These included lines concerning Maris sailing up the transplendent river of Niles's love, and eternally sipping from the fount of Niles's perpetual adoration. Maris, who has a cold, is currently in Chicago visiting her sister. Martin sums up the two Crane daughters-in-law most adequately: 'Maris is a little strange. Lilith is weird.'

The Buddy Show: Martin is telling a story from his cop days, when he was stalking a knife-wielding villain. He was using his night stick as he walked down a dark alley and used it to disarm the villain and subdue him. Lilith asks him if he was suffering any repressed sexual urges during this. Martin gives up.

Eddie Takes The Biscuit: 'Go away,' says Lilith unemotionally to Eddie as soon as he cheerfully bounds over to say his hellos to her. Without any hesitation, he does exactly as he is told. We would, too.

Frasier Has Left The Building: Daphne's headache clears as we see Lilith's plane take off.

On The Couch: 'Roz, what exactly does "call screening" mean?' asks a terse Frasier, as Lilith's voice is broadcast. 'It means I get to put on the air the calls I want to hear!'

Yes, yes, yes, this is it. The pinnacle of the series so far – as the studio audience watching *Frasier* being taped cheer at Lilith's first words, so do we. She's back, and suddenly everything about Frasier makes sense. Of all the elements that made the character work so well in *Cheers*, Lilith was the icing on the cake and her lack of presence in this show has been noticeable. What is also so great is that you don't want her there every week (too much of anything this good quickly makes you ill), but the promise of regular reappearances can only be applauded.

This is Lilith's episode, her one-liners, her looks, her demeanour, everything about her inspires hysteria. The sheer terror on Martin's face as he talks to her is a delight, and Niles becomes even more of a bullied schoolboy than ever as she mercilessly mauls Maris's marriage vows.

But there is a rarely seen softer side to Lilith as well, as we witness when she reads Frasier's letter, hoping that they will reconcile, and during her departure from his apartment, severely humiliated. As with the best antiheroes, you never feel anything but sorrow for her. Lilith is the last person you'd actually wish ill upon, regardless of her waspish tongue, cruelly stinging our other favourite characters. When she cries into Frasier's arms because 'I'm raising a child. Alone. I'm scared,' you cannot help but be pleased that she and Frasier put (most of) their harsh words aside for a moment of genuine concern – they were married for six years after all. They may no longer be in love, but this episode proves that both characters still have the ability to care for each other, and that further develops Frasier's ongoing character. We need a few extra bricks to build upon now and again or things get stale, and this episode gives the lead character an incredibly solid bedrock.

1.15

'Can't Buy Me Love'

Written by Chuck Ranberg and Anne Flett-Giordano
Directed by James Burrows
First UK Transmission: 05.08.94

Skyline: The light atop the Space Needle glows.

Synopsis: Martin informs Frasier that a charity bachelor auction is taking place and he wants Bulldog to take part, but Frasier thinks Martin wants him – so he gets both.

Horrified by the frenzied women, Frasier and Bulldog await their turns to be 'bought' for an evening. Frasier explains that all his purchaser will get is a 'well-prepared gourmet meal and a handshake at the door'. Bulldog thinks that is 'Boring! My date gets a stretch limo, moon-roof, dinner, floor seats at the Sonics game and these incredible buns of steel!' As a result, Frasier gets sold for $500 to a model from *Seattle Style* magazine, Kristina Harper. Bulldog only raises $100 – from a shell-shocked Daphne!

Kristina arrives at Frasier's on Friday night full of apologies – she has a photo shoot, her regular babysitter is busy with the same shoot, so could Frasier look after Renata until she gets back, and they'll have dinner then?

Daphne and Bulldog, however, are having a great time. Seated in the back of their limo, stuck in traffic, a drunken Ms Moon is proving to be more than even Bulldog can cope with. 'Now, don't go getting any ideas,' warns Daphne. Then she giggles, spilling champagne over him. 'Oh, look who I'm saying this to. You don't have an idea in your head!' She then gets lippy with another driver who is honking his horn and eventually Bulldog is dragged out of the limo, presumably to face retribution from the angry driver.

Frasier meanwhile is coping with a precocious, sullen, teenaged girl, who is running up a huge phone bill, eating her way through Frasier's kitchen, and begins telling Frasier some of the nightmare stories about how her parents are divorced, how Kristina abandons her when and wherever possible, and how she's told everyone Renata's been nine years old for three years, so they won't think Kristina is too old to be a model. Appalled by Renata's harsh treatment, Frasier resolves that, when Kristina comes back, she'll get a piece of his mind. Trouble is, it never occurs to Frasier that teenaged girls don't always tell the whole truth . . .

Guest Cast: Kristina Harper (Claire Stansfield), Renata (Ashley Bank), T. J. Smith (Brett K. Miller), Stage Manager (Shawna Casey).

Where Everybody Knows Their Name: Another credit for Moose as Eddie, a brief mention of Frederick when Frasier and Martin wonder what he'll be like when he's twelve, and of course another stunning performance from Bulldog (Dan Butler).

Who's On The Line?: Frasier's show isn't seen, but a hapless sports fan called Chuck has at some point during *The Gonzo Sports Show* incurred the biting wit of Bulldog.

Subtitles: A Chump Off The Old Block; Going Once . . .; Going Twice . . .; . . . Gone; Shrink Rap; Driving Miss Daphne.

Strange Bedfellows: Roz 'buys' T. J. Smith after the auction. 'I saw what I wanted and went after it!' T. J., bless him, is terrified . . .

Out Of Sight: Maris has gone to Chicago to see her sister, but is afraid to fly since a 'harrowing' incident when she was 'bumped' from First Class. She still wakes up screaming at the memory . . .

The Buddy Show: Joe Linski is running the benefit for the Widows and Orphans Fund (presumably Widows and Orphans of police officers).

Eddie Takes The Biscuit: Eddie acquires a liking for Cheetos, as Renata feeds him copious amounts all evening.

Frasier Has Left The Building: Frasier, Daphne, Martin and Niles quaff champagne in the back of Bulldog's hired limo.

On The Couch: Another top-form show, in which the terrible stories related by Renata are truly horrific, and Kristina's reaction to them is just as awful. Predictable it may be, but getting there has never been so much fun. On top of that, Daphne gets the chance to shine during her night on the town with Bulldog (she delightfully keeps calling him Pit Bull) and gets astonishingly drunk.

This is one of the nice nice episodes – nothing too great, nothing too damning. Just good.

1.16
'Can't Tell A Crook By His Cover'

Written by David Lloyd
Directed by Andy Ackerman
First UK Transmission: 12.08.94

Skyline: The light atop the Space Needle glows.

Synopsis: Martin is getting his first tour of Frasier's work-place when Roz turns up, having been duped into giving a con artist ten bucks. Frasier thinks Roz is a fool to be taken in but Martin sympathises. He knows how good these guys can be and says Frasier is wrong to assume he can easily spot them. 'Dad, don't lecture me on the complexities of the human mind,' he says. 'Are you forgetting I graduated with honours from Harvard on psychosocial behaviourism?' But Martin certainly hasn't forgotten. 'I was at your graduation. Impressive bunch. A car backfired and half of them wet their gowns.' Martin says he's having a poker evening tonight with three police force buddies and Frasier should watch. He bets Frasier $5 that he cannot work out which one is the ex-con. Roz bets $10 that he can't either.

That evening, Frasier watches intently as Linda, Frank and Jimmy play cards, each of them giving him possible clues as to which may be the wrongdoer. Eventually he guesses that it is Frank. Wrong. Linda? Wrong again. And Frasier feels very foolish because Jimmy was the least suspicious one. Daphne feels equally foolish because, she explains later, she's going out on a date with Jimmy. Martin is appalled – Jimmy's a nice guy, but he still knows a lot of the wrong types. Frasier thinks Martin is being ridiculous. 'Don't you believe in second chances?' 'I did,' explains Martin. 'Then we had Niles.'

The next evening at Café Nervosa, Frasier and Niles are drinking 'gutless wonders' (decaf latte, skimmed milk) and Frasier tells his brother that Daphne is at the Topaz Rooms with Jimmy. Niles is all for mounting a rescue mission but Frasier is still sceptical, until Eric the waiter explains just how rough the Topaz can be.

Arriving at the Topaz, Niles asks the barman, already astonished by the sight of the two decidedly out-of-place doctors, if he has seen Daphne. Or rather 'has a young woman been in here this evening? Approximately five foot nine and three-quarters, with skin the colour of Devonshire cream and the sort of eyes that gaze directly into one's soul with neither artifice nor evasion?' Both Crane boys subsequently get into a potential bone-breaking, head-pulping session with a couple of thugs until Daphne challenges the bruisers double or quits at pool. If she wins, they go home. If she loses, they get all her money and indeed pulp Frasier and Niles . . .

Guest Cast: Jimmy (Tony Abatemarco), Linda (Katherine McGrath), Rocco (Robert Miano), Leo (Marco Rodriguez), Bartender (Ivory Ocean).

Where Everybody Knows Their Name: Once more, we see a credit for Moose as Eddie, and this episode introduces us to one of Martin's force chums, Frank (Ron Dean), who we will see again one day. This is also the second credited appearance for Eric (Dean Erickson), a waiter at Café Nervosa, who alerts the Crane brothers to just how much of a trouble spot the Topaz is.

Subtitles: Pick A Con, Any Con; Oddball In The Corner Pocket.

Full-on Moon: Daphne shocks the boys at the Topaz by proving to be nothing short of a genius at the pool table, although she talks her way around the table as if she's as dizzy as, well, a very dizzy thing. She claims she never understood pool, even when she started playing with her older brothers at the age of six. Nor did she understand it during her formative years spent mostly in the pool halls of Manchester. Nor while playing in local competitions and local tournaments, winning cup after cup 'until our poor dad had to convert the pantry into a trophy room. And I can't really claim to understand it even today. But I certainly do enjoy it.' And with that she pockets a large amount of winnings. But one of her best lines ever comes at Frasier's place, when she's introduced to Frank, Linda and Jimmy and is asked if people ever call her Daffy for short. Without so much as a blink she says offhandedly, 'Not twice.' You just know no one is ever going to call her Daffy now . . .

The Buddy Show: When they were little, Martin used to take his sons down to the police cells and lock them in, pretending to leave them there.

Eddie Takes The Biscuit: Eddie does not want to be washed and knows exactly what B-A-T-H means. 'He may smell like swamp gas,' observes Frasier, 'but his spelling's improved.'

Frasier Has Left The Building: Eddie follows a trail of treats towards the B-A-T-H but then escapes just in time.

On The Couch: A strange episode that starts off telling a highly moralistic tale of people being given second chances, which is reduced to a bizarre runaround in the last third as the boys enter the unknown territory of the Topaz bar and Daphne has to rescue them. As a result, it's all very uneven and you certainly can't blame Frasier for getting the criminal wrong: all three card players are pretty shifty. But then, so is Martin at times . . .

Exactly why it works is definitely down to the odd one-liners and exchanges, rather than the overall story. The best moment again falls to Daphne as Jimmy comes on to her, and asks her where she's from. 'Manchester,' she replies, quite charmed by him. 'That's where the Beatles were from, right?' 'No,' explains Daphne. 'You're thinking of Liverpool.' Jimmy is undeterred. 'Then who's from Manchester?' Quick as a flash and with the sourest of shrugs, Daphne replies, 'No one. That's why I live here now.' Marvellous.

1.17

'A Mid-Winter Night's Dream'

Written by Chuck Ranberg and Anne Flett-Giordano
Directed by David Lee
First UK Transmission: 19.08.94

Skyline: The elevator goes up the Space Needle.

Synopsis: As Daphne and Eric begin to date after a charming discussion over coffee beans, Niles becomes more grumpy. Frasier is actually worried about his brother's obsession with Daphne and Niles explains that his marriage with Maris is in a deep rut.

At the station, Frasier asks Roz what she does when a relationship gets into a rut. 'I get dressed and go home,' she offers unhelpfully. She does however suggest role-playing as a way to spice up the bedroom.

That night, Niles turns up at Frasier's apartment dressed as a pirate – his role-playing has not gone well, and these were the quickest clothes he could find to put on. Niles feels like crying but explains to Frasier that he actually can't. 'When Maris's Uncle Lyle died, I had to shut my hand in the car door just to make a decent showing at the funeral.' Leaving Niles to sleep on the sofa, Frasier and Martin go back to bed. Moments later, Daphne and Eric return and say a romantic goodnight. After Daphne goes to her room, Niles can be heard crying himself to sleep.

The following morning, Niles is irritable, especially with Daphne, who keeps talking about Eric. Martin suggests that Niles buy Maris flowers and fix her a nice romantic dinner for when she gets home. 'That's enough to make any woman forgive you,' he says. Niles remains unsure. 'You really think it'll work?' Martin just shrugs. 'If it didn't, you wouldn't be here.'

A few nights later, Daphne is at Maris's house, preparing to cook the required meal. She and Niles are soaked through because it is raining, and Daphne changes into a nightgown. And then confesses that she and Eric have broken up.

At the apartment, Frasier realises that with Niles desperate for Daphne and her upset about Eric, anything could happen, especially as Maris is stuck in Arizona now and can't get back till the morning . . .

Where Everybody Knows Their Name: Hester Crane is mentioned (by inference anyway) and Eric the waiter (Dean Erickson) makes his last appearance. We think he deserves an award for dealing with Niles's ever-changing coffee tastes. This episode, he requests a double cappuccino, half-caf, non-fat milk with just enough foam to be aesthetically pleasing but not so much that it leaves a moustache. And cinnamon.

Subtitles: Ahoy Matey; It Was A Dark And Stormy Night. No, Really.

Strange Bedfellows: Roz and an old boyfriend once went to a bar and pretended to be strangers and thus pick each other up all over again. It worked once but the next time it worked too well and her guy went home with another woman.

Out Of Sight: The first time Niles ever saw Maris, it was a dark and stormy night, and she was banging on the electric gates to her home with a tyre iron. She'd been to an antiques fair and bought a bell jar once owned by Sylvia Plath, when the gates failed to open. Three years later they got married and honeymooned in Zürich. She has now thrown Niles out because, in an effort to spice up their sex life, Niles left a treasure map and clues for her to find him. Hiding in a cupboard upstairs, wearing nothing but an eyepatch to cover his modesty, he was found not by Maris but by the upstairs maid. As a result, Maris has gone to Arizona, to her favourite spa, to contemplate her future. Oh, and on top of all this, we learn there are certain foods she cannot eat. Shellfish. Poultry. Red meat. Saturated fats. Nitrates. Wheat. Starch. Sulphates. MSG. Dairy. And nuts.

Eddie Takes The Biscuit: Eddie listens intently to Niles's message on the answerphone.

Frasier Has Left The Building: Daphne, Niles and Frasier gather around the piano while Martin is stuck outside in the storm.

On The Couch: 'It's a recipe for disaster! A vulnerable woman and an unstable man in a Gothic mansion on a rainy night. The only thing that's missing is someone shouting "Heathcliff!" across the moors!' One of those marvellous episodes that mix drama, pathos and comedy. This really is Niles's show: his love for Daphne is in full motion and the cracks in his marriage are beginning to really show up. It's hardly surprising that, having convinced himself that Daphne is the greatest thing since sliced bread, every move she makes is encouraging him further – into making a fool of himself ultimately. Frasier's belief that Niles would make a move on Daphne seems a little overdramatic – it's not really in his character to do more than flirt. Yet. But even so, his reaction to Daphne in the nightgown and their beautiful discussion about what love is and the subsequent realisation that he really does love Maris very much is fantastic. A really welcome feel-good episode.

1.18
'And The Whimper Is . . .'

Written by Denise Moss and Sy Dukane
Directed by James Burrows
First UK Transmission: 26.08.94

Skyline: Nothing happens.

Synopsis: It's time for the SeaBees, Seattle's annual radio awards, and Roz is determined to win one after waiting for the last decade. It's Frasier's first time and, although he pretends to be uninterested, his ego would naturally be mass-aged were the show to be nominated.

Niles is rather down – a patient has left him for another therapist. However, he rapidly forgets his troubles when Bebe Glazer arrives in Café Nervosa and hurries to his sexual-addiction group (he doesn't like to leave them alone for too long). Bebe tells Frasier he's been nominated and agrees (without actually ever being asked) to be his date for the event.

At Frasier's place, he and Roz discuss ways to influence the judges. They end up preparing to send each member of the Nominations Committee an expensive item from a Tiffany's catalogue. Martin is horrified at their bribery, but it's too late. They've made up their minds.

At the ceremony, Frasier is awed, Martin wants the bar and Daphne is wearing tight shoes, which make her feet swell. Niles of course offers to massage them. Roz arrives with Noel (her original date having had to work) and they see the other nominees. Among them is Fletcher Grey, a well-respected broadcaster who has been nominated eleven years in a row without winning, much to the annoyance of his aged mother, who comes to the ceremony each year just in case. Fletcher Grey is retiring, and Frasier begins to have doubts about his and Roz's behaviour. The award ought to go to the newsman – he and Roz will have other years. Perhaps they could refuse to accept it . . . 'Listen Frasier,' snarls Roz. 'I have waited ten years to get this award and if I have to crawl over Fletcher Grey's mother to get it, I will!' Frasier is horrified. 'Roz, I've never seen you like this before.' Roz agrees, adding, 'It isn't pretty, is it?'

Then the winners are announced . . .

Guest Cast: Fletcher Grey (John McMartin), Hannah Grey (Maxine Elliot), Keith Bishop (Wren T. Brown), Tawney van Deusen (Trish Ramish), Bob Peterson (Mark Sawyer), Committee Member (Aileen Fitzpatrick).

Where Everybody Knows Their Name: Moose receives another credit for playing Eddie. Noel Shempsky (Patrick

Kerr) returns, once again to try to monopolise Roz, and making a very welcome second appearance is the fabulous Bebe Glazer (Harriet Sansom Harris).

Who's On The Line?: Angela, who has been considering cosmetic surgery.

Subtitles: Roz And Frasier Hatch A Merry Plan; The Plot Thickens; The Thrilling Denouement.

Culture Vultures: At prep school, Frasier was nominated by the existentialist club as 'Most Likely To Be'. And Frasier gets a rare snobbish come-uppance when a large amount of his $200 champagne goes down Eddie's throat.

Strange Bedfellows: Roz has the hots for Brad McNamara, television's most handsome man. He has agreed to be her date for the ceremony, and Daphne is a wee bit jealous.

Out Of Sight: Niles begins to explain Maris's absence from the ceremony as due to something she saw in the mirror, but Frasier decides he doesn't want to know any more and we don't blame him.

The Buddy Show: Martin is delighted that the newsman Fletcher Grey remembers him from a murder case back in 1968, during which Martin found the head.

Frasier Has Left The Building: Roz and Mrs Grey knock back Pink Ladies (or rather, a very crafty Mrs Grey knocks back Roz's).

On The Couch: A superb episode that kicks off the annual occurrence of the SeaBees. Roz is at her best here, determined to take that award home, no matter what the cost, while Niles gets the best laughs as, during the course of the show, everyone from Bebe to Noel mistakes him for a waiter – and, what's worse, he actually serves them! A nice touch too, when Frasier tells Daphne that he considers her part of his family. Ahhh. Of course, he then proceeds to treat her like dirt, but that's what a family is for, isn't it?

And any episode that gives us Bebe Glazer is perfect in our book.

1.19

'Give Him The Chair!'

Written by Chuck Ranberg and Anne Flett-Giordano
Directed by James Burrows
First UK Transmission: 02.09.94

Skyline: The light atop the Space Needle glows.

Synopsis: Niles has bought Maris an emerald necklace, which he asks Daphne to try on first. 'Your practice must be doing awfully well,' she says. 'Who'd have thought the mentally disturbed had this much money?' In trying it on, she drops the necklace down her cleavage, and Niles is trying to remove it when Frasier returns home to find them. He is swiftly followed by Martin and Eddie, the former rapidly repairing another split on his favourite armchair with duct tape.

Frasier decides he's had enough and opts to go and buy his father a new recliner.

At the store they find one that vibrates gently and order it to be delivered.

Eddie is in the apartment, staring mournfully at the space where the chair used to be, fearing Martin has gone as well. Leo, the Elliot Bay Towers labourer, brings in the new chair and Daphne tries it, finding the vibration very . . . soothing. 'This is almost enough to make me give up my search for a meaningful relationship.' Martin is very upset, however – he is very sentimentally attached to his old chair and persuades Frasier to get it back. Leo reveals that he dumped it and now it has gone, so, on his radio show, Frasier requests its return.

Eventually it is located – a prop in a junior high production of *Ten Little Indians*, a play Frasier himself did once. But Mrs

Warren, the drama teacher, is not going to give up one of her main props without a fight. Or, at least, some blackmail . . .

Guest Cast: Leo (Phil Buckman), Mrs Warren (Valerie Curtin), Salesman (James Greene), Joey (Marc Robinson), Olsen (Brittany Murphy), Brown (Scotty Nguyen).

Where Everybody Knows Their Name: Moose gets his now regular namecheck as Eddie, and Hester Crane and Frederick (and probably Lilith by implication) all receive another passing reference.

Who's On The Line?: Dr Helmut Bruger (Malcolm McDowell), who is far more interested in flirting with Roz than promoting his book. Later on Frasier tries to help John and Stephanie through some emotional instability while a variety of people phone in, claiming to have seen Martin's chair. One saw it at the top of the Space Needle, another in the Governor's mansion, while yet another believed it flew over his house, and mistakenly thought it was a spaceship from a tacky planet.

Subtitles: Sitting Pretty; Good Vibrations; Best Seat In The House.

Strange Bedfellows: Roz had a hot date on Saturday night. On Sunday morning, returning home, her car broke down outside a church and now she has a date with the preacher.

Out Of Sight: Maris has recently donated her old cocktail dresses to a shelter for the homeless. Martin also jokes about getting his daughter-in-law a ratchet set but, as Frasier points out, 'as if there's anything left on her that needs tightening!'

Frasier Has Left The Building: The chair back in its place, but with a throw draped over it. Martin quickly disposes of that.

On The Couch: At first glance, it looks like this episode is going to be a bit average – Frasier moaning about the chair, then getting shot of it. Predictably enough, Martin is upset and wants it back. What makes this stand head and shoulders above so many others is possibly the best single scene of pathos ever in the show, as Martin reveals why he loves that chair. It was the chair he sat in as he watched Neil Armstrong walking on the moon. It's the chair he cheered the US hockey team from as they beat the Russians in the 1980 Olympic Games. It's the chair he was sitting in when Frasier rang to tell him he had a grandson. Most of all, it's the chair he used to fall asleep in, only to be awoken by Hester with a kiss. And sometimes, when he falls asleep in it now, he wakes up expecting her to be there still. It's only a chair to Frasier, but to Martin it's part of his life, his past, and Frasier has dumped it.

When Martin talks about Hester, you can see the full realisation of what he has done hit Frasier and Niles right in the face, and, although the rest of the episode bounds along with the usual hysteria, every time you laugh, you also remember how important it is to Martin that he get this chair back. It's a beautiful moment for the characters that make up our favourite ensemble, and one from which the episode benefits enormously.

On other topics, one cannot help but wonder if the character of Leo was perhaps intended as a semi-regular – although Phil Buckman's portrayal is frighteningly akin to Ted (Keanu Reeves) in his and Bill's eponymous filmic adventures, with just a dash of the *Beavis and Butt-head* irreverence.

1.20

'Fortysomething'

Written by Sy Dukane and Denise Moss
Directed by Rick Beren
First UK Transmission: 09.09.94

Skyline: Lights go on in various buildings.

Synopsis: After forgetting Roz's name live on air, the forty-one-year-old Frasier decides he's losing his marbles as well as his memory. This is compounded further that night when he forgets how to play a particular tune on the piano. Martin suggests he should stop fighting middle age – after all, when he hit that part of his life he did no end of daft things, such as dyeing his hair black and buying a Harley Davidson. 'You may think it's tough being middle-aged,' he says as he wraps up his talk, 'but think about me. I got a son who is middle-aged!'

Frasier, Martin and Daphne go clothes shopping, and while his father argues with his health-care worker over underwear, Frasier is flattered by the attentions of Carrie, a twenty-two-year-old psychology student currently working as a sales assistant in the store. She persuades Frasier to buy some trendy but smart clothes, guessing he's between thirty-four and thirty-six and probably an architect. After Carrie has gone to serve another customer, Martin points out she's probably on commission and flatters all her customers, but Frasier thinks there is more to it.

Carrie turns up at KACL the next day with his trousers – much to Roz and Bulldog's amusement. Carrie asks him out, but he refuses, feeling that, at his age, it would not be appropriate – much to the astonishment of Roz and Bulldog.

Later Frasier begins to have second thoughts: maybe things could work between the two of them. So he resolves to head back down to the store and find Carrie . . .

Guest Cast: Carrie (Sara Melson).

Where Everybody Knows Their Name: Bulldog (Dan Butler) makes his final appearance in the first season, but his popularity has ensured that he will return in the next run for even more episodes. Good.

Who's On The Line?: Rachel (Reba McEntire), whose husband keeps his ex-wife's ashes in an urn on the bedroom dresser. Until the end of the scene, that is – then they visit the inside of a vacuum cleaner!

Subtitles: The Short Blond Man With One Wet Shoe; It's This Or An Alfa Romeo; Stanley Barrister Must Be Really Really Rich; I Wonder If That Alfa Romeo Showroom Is Still Open.

Full-on Moon: Daphne offers us her philosophy on life, by pointing out three things she has learnt not to answer honestly: 'How do I look?, Do you like my hair? and Was it good for you too?'

Eddie Takes The Biscuit: In an attempt to get affection, Eddie burrows at Niles's shoes until Dr Crane is forced to scratch him behind the ears.

Frasier Has Left The Building: Daphne victoriously displays all of Martin's new underwear to Eddie.

On The Couch: A little too similar to 1.11, 'Death Becomes Him', where Frasier is obsessed with his own mortality. Here he's equally obsessed with getting old and wonders if a May-to-December-style relationship with Carrie may be the answer to his woes. Of course it's not, and it's the lack of novelty in this one that makes it a bit 'so-what?'. Carrie is nice enough, but hardly the sort Frasier normally seeks solace in, even if she is a psychology student. However, it does have a delightful moment when, after Bulldog has been flirting outrageously with Carrie before running off to get his show ready, Carrie asks Frasier, 'Is he gay? He seems to be overcompensating.' A look of delight crosses Frasier's face as he explains, 'I look forward to running that theory past him.'

Nevertheless, overall, a bit too derivative of the aforementioned earlier show and something of a damp squib.

1.21
'Travels With Martin'

Written by Linda Morris and Vic Rauseo
Directed by James Burrows
First UK Transmission: 16.09.94

Skyline: The light atop the Space Needle glows.

Synopsis: Planning his vacation, Frasier shows Roz his extravagant plans for a week of luxury away from his flat and his father. Roz tells Frasier that she plans to take her mother away on holiday with her, to Ireland. Racked with guilt, Frasier decides that he too should invite Martin along with him, and let his father decide where they will go. Unfortunately, that means a week in a Winnebago cruising the highways of America on a non-stop round trip to Mount Rushmore.

Both of them privately regret their decision to holiday together, Martin persuading Daphne to join them so that he doesn't have to spend a week alone with his son. Although initially dead-set against the idea, Niles agrees to come when he discovers that Daphne is going: the idea of a week cooped up in close confines with her has an obvious appeal.

Things go about as smoothly as could be expected, until Martin decides that he wants a photograph of them all standing next to a stuffed bear. The cost of this tacky memento is ten dollars, in Canadian money. When Daphne discovers that they've driven into Canada while she was asleep, she lets out an almighty scream – she hasn't got her Green Card yet and, if she leaves the USA before it is granted, she will be deported.

Guest Cast: Border Guard (Don Amendolia), Marvella (Pamela Gordon).

Where Everybody Knows Their Name: Hester and Martin had always wanted to take a trip like this one.

Subtitles: The Whoopin' Cranes; The Hole In The Head Gang; Checkpoint Charlie.

Culture Vultures: When you're trapped on a runaway Winnebago, surrendering yourself to the manly pursuit of all things outdoors, there isn't much room for being cultured. Even the ever-prissy Niles relents: 'I'm inspired. I'm going to put on a baseball cap.'

Full-on Moon: Daphne on her choice of holiday destination: 'I just grab a fresh pair of knickers, and see where the wind takes me.' Niles apparently finds this coarse honesty attractive. At least, we think it was her coarse honesty – it could just have been her knickers. And to break Niles's concentration, Frasier takes extreme, but very amusing, measures . . .

Out Of Sight: Maris won't allow strangers to carry her make-up bag. This is because one day a porter dropped it and broke three vials of rare lambs' placenta. She is currently visiting one of her sisters; this one lives in Dallas.

Eddie Takes The Biscuit: . . . and saves the day. When the border patrol guard begins to suspect that something is up (Daphne says nothing but 'sure', the only word she can pronounce in an American accent), Martin calls Eddie out of hiding and explains to the guard that they haven't got a rabies certificate. Frasier, seeing an opportunity to get rid of the dog, suggests that the guard just take Eddie and they will go on their way. Martin's police connections mean that Eddie is spared the dog pound, however, and Eddie is none too pleased at Frasier's willingness to ditch him. Assailed by angry barking, Frasier retorts, 'They would have returned you eventually!'

Frasier Has Left The Building: A black-and-white image of a sleeping Daphne being videoed by Niles – he wants to remember this inspiring vacation as much as anyone. Daphne, however, wakes up and stares, shocked, into the camcorder lens. The camera pans away and we see a very angry Frasier.

On The Couch: Towards the end of the episode, Martin explains his fear of spending time with his son: 'When we're alone together, I just don't know what the hell to say.' The major recurring theme of the show is back with a rather sad vengeance. Frasier is desperate to get on with his dad, and Martin feels the same about his son, but the two of them are so irreconcilable that such a thing is impossible. More accurately, whenever the two of them make an effort to bond, it is doomed to failure. In the relaxed moments at the end of the show, they just open up and genuinely share a joke (about making Daphne believe that this time they've driven her into Mexico). The two of them have enough in common, but they're so busy trying too hard to get along that they never notice that they already do: one of the fundamentals of the show's comedy.

This episode is notable for being the first not to feature any of the usual trappings of *Frasier*: no radio show, no Roz (beyond the opening scene), no Maris, and no high-society high-jinx. Removed from all this, the Crane clan must fend for themselves with only each other for company. And you can imagine what that's like. A jolly episode, with Daphne's border-jumping the highlight, this is a refreshing little interlude.

Oh, and we think Niles looks dead cute in his reversed baseball cap . . .

1.22

'Author, Author'

Written by Don Siegel and Jerry Perzigian
Directed by James Burrows
First UK Transmission: 23.09.94

Skyline: The elevator goes up the Space Needle.

Synopsis: Frasier meets a panicked Niles at Café Nervosa: it seems the younger brother is meeting his publisher there to discuss his idea for a book. The problem? Niles has no idea what book he's going to write. When Mr Tanaka, the publisher, sees the banter between the brothers, he suggests that a book written by them both on sibling relationships would be a great idea. Clutching at straws, Niles announces – to a delighted publisher and a horrified brother – that that was exactly what he brought Mr Tanaka there to discuss.

Reluctantly, Frasier agrees to write the book with Niles. After using Frasier's call-in show to gather anecdotes about sibling rivalry and support, the brothers receive a call from

Tanaka. Blithely, Niles announces that they have already written three chapters, though in truth not a word has yet been committed to paper. Tanaka says that he wants the chapters faxed over immediately, as he has a serialisation deal to bash out with *Reader's Digest*. Fudging, Niles and Frasier get themselves a few days' grace to get some of the book written.

Choosing to follow in the footsteps of Ira and George Gershwin, the good doctors lock themselves in a hotel room, promising themselves not to emerge until they have finished their work. Trapped alone, with only a laptop and a mini-bar for company, Niles and Frasier soon find themselves at each other's throat, too busy with their own sibling rivalry to write about anyone else's.

Guest Cast: Sam Tanaka (Mako).

Where Everybody Knows Their Name: Let's give a warm welcome to Luck Hari, the longest running of the various waiting staff at Café Nervosa. Hester Crane gets a couple of mentions, and Moose is once again credited as Eddie.

Who's On The Line?: Laura (Christine Lahti), whose sisters shave their heads in sympathy with her disastrous perm, and Donald, who hasn't spoken with his brother in twenty years.

Subtitles: It Was Probably Lake Smith; The Mother Lode; George And Ira.

Out Of Sight: Maris runs a sherry-tasting club, where things can get a little raucous. Apparently.

The Buddy Show: Martin tells the sad and sorry tale of Mitch Gossitt, his first partner, in order to show his sons that arguing with each other will only cause irreparable damage. Goss and Martin were posted on a seventy-two-hour stake-out, spent in a car with only each other for company. After this time, the two of them had wound each other up so much that Goss requested a transfer. A short while later, Goss was stabbed in the course of duty. Martin was unable to make it to the hospital before he died, and he has ever since regretted that they fell out.

Daphne is devastated by the story, and retires to the kitchen to cry her eyes out. Once the rift between Niles and Frasier has been closed, Martin joins her. Devious as ever, Martin explains to Daphne that Goss never existed – it was just a cheap excuse for him to get a bit of peace and quiet.

Frasier Has Left The Building: Eddie bounces up and down, trying to get at the muffins perched on a kitchen worktop. (Earlier, when he isn't quite ready to make up with Niles, Frasier offers his unwitting brother a muffin that Eddie has licked.)

On The Couch: Surprisingly for an episode so prickly with brotherly barbs, this is one of the weakest of the season. The best scenes are those of Niles and Frasier's self-imposed confinement in the hotel room. Tired and ratty, and as the dawn of their deadline breaks, they get into an all-out schoolyard scrap. The finest line is delivered by Frasier as he straddles Niles's chest, thumping his head against the mattress: 'You stole my mommy!'

As entertaining as the revelation of the childhood basis of the rivalry is, it is always better to see them casting good-natured bitches back and forth about their grown-up society connections. Their adult pursuit of position is childish in itself, and it's that duality that makes it funny. When they become simply immature, all the series' characteristic sophistication is drained away.

Featuring no significant input from Martin, Daphne or Roz, the episode falls a little flat. And that's a shame because Hyde Pierce and Grammer put their all into their dialogues – it's just unfortunate that those dialogues lack the series' usual sparkle.

1.23
'Frasier Crane's Day Off'

Written by Chuck Ranberg and Anne Flett-Giordano
Directed by James Burrows
First UK Transmission: 30.09.94

Skyline: Nothing happens.

Synopsis: Frasier fails to stifle a sneeze as he wishes Seattle good health at the close of his show. A concerned Gil Chesterton wanders in, asking if Frasier has caught a dose of the flu that's doing the rounds. Gil offers to fill in for him if Frasier would like a couple of days off, but Frasier politely declines. After Gil has left, Frasier explains to Roz that Bonnie Weems lost her slot because she let Gil replace her in a similar situation. Gil went down a storm with the listeners, and now Bonnie has been banished to a graveyard slot in the middle of the night. Frasier isn't prepared to let the same thing happen to him.

The next day, a still-ill Frasier finally realises that he has no choice but to take the day off. Gil steps in and is, unfortunately, scintillating. A panicked Frasier begs Niles to take his place on the radio show, figuring that his dry, pernickety brother can't possibly do a better job than Frasier. But oh, how wrong he is . . .

Where Everybody Knows Their Name: Gil Chesterton (Edward Hibbert) plays an obviously big role in this, his first episode, and mention is made of other station staff: Bonnie Weems, and Millie in Traffic. There is also a replacement station manager (see 1.09, 'Selling Out') who is a cat lover. A first mention for Marta, who is responsible for the foul-smelling herb poultice that Niles offers Frasier to help him recover. And we learn that Martin and Hester Crane once went to Mexico – and he got the sickest he's ever been.

Who's On The Line?: Blake (Steve Young) receives an apology from Frasier for suggesting he close his eyes and imagine he is on a tropical island. Frasier didn't know he was on a carphone. Gil deals with Louis (Gary Trudeau), who has forgotten that today is his tenth wedding anniversary, while Marsha, who is in love with her husband's brother, is Niles's first caller. Howard (Steve Lawrence) and Lois (Eydie Gormé) have reached an impasse where they are unable to say

'I love you' to each other. Niles fixes that, cementing his mastery of the airwaves.

During Frasier's dream, he is about to answer a call from Sonia when the trap Gil and Niles have prepared for him goes off.

There's a string of poor souls who have to suffer the drugged-up Frasier: Robert (Tommy Hilfiger) gets cut off for saying his name twice; Janice's (Patricia Hearst) problem is too boring for Frasier to even listen to; and Frasier gets a little too involved in a role-playing situation with Marjorie (Mary Tyler Moore).

Subtitles: Spring Is In The Air; Frasier Crane's Day Off; I Go To Pieces; Radio Daze.

Strange Bedfellows: Frasier manages to convince Roz that the midnight–4 a.m. slot would be ruinous to her love life: 'Those are your peak hours.' And the joke continues of Niles never really recognising Roz, until now, when he has to . . .

Full-on Moon: Daphne offers to care for Frasier while he is ill; she is used to tending her brothers' football injuries. These weren't acquired through playing the game: 'They got hurt beating up drunken Dutchmen in the stands.' Later, she offers Frasier some of her homeopathic tea ('It'll flush out your system. It'll also make your hair more shiny and manageable').

Eddie Takes The Biscuit: Frasier offloads the vile herb poultice by stringing it round Eddie's neck. Eddie, however, returns it a few minutes later.

Frasier Has Left The Building: The third of this episode's dream sequences. While Frasier natters away in the studio, Eddie sits in Roz's place in the booth next door. Suddenly, Roz wakes up and shakes the nightmare from her head.

On The Couch: A great episode, most notable for Grammer's portrayal of Frasier's various stages of illness. A string of increasingly self-pitying, grumpy incidents, culminating in a wonderful doped-up sequence when he regains temporary control of his radio show. While he's high on all sorts of drugs, the little touches of his performance (such as laughing at some spasmodic motion of his hand) are great fun.

David Hyde Pierce also puts in a great turn, as Frasier's brother gets his chance to be the radio personality – and enjoys the change, because his fear-of-intimacy group are apparently getting too close. For all Niles's deriding of Frasier's job, he really does seem to be revelling in it – and doing it very well. Niles announces on air that Frasier is a Freudian, and he is a Jungian – 'So there'll be no blaming mother today,' he chides. It is not interesting, merely proper, to note that Frasier is therefore not a psychiatrist, as he so often describes himself. Those who follow the work of Freud are known as psychoanalysts. There's something for your next dinner party.

Niles's protective measures against catching Frasier's flu are also very funny (handkerchief over the mouth, alcohol to clean his hands). The other regulars also get decent looks-in, what with Daphne's increasing impatience with Frasier, Martin's tales of his own wild illnesses, and Roz's desperate plea to get Frasier back before Gil can steal the time slot.

If this episode fails anywhere, it is with Gil himself. It never takes the chance to really explore how good a presenter he is, and so leaves us still with the impression that he's a bit creepy, a bit smarmy, and even more pretentious than Frasier. A missed opportunity, we feel.

1.24
'My Coffee with Niles'

Written by David Angell and Peter Casey
Directed by James Burrows
First UK Transmission: 07.10.94

Skyline: The elevator goes up the Space Needle.

Synopsis: The whole episode is just as the title suggests – a chat between Frasier and Niles in Café Nervosa (we also get to see the exterior of the café for the first time) with various interruptions from the other regulars.

While Niles tries to find out whether Frasier is truly happy, as it is exactly one year since he moved back to Seattle from Boston, the brothers' conversation covers topics as diverse as homosexuality, Daphne, shoes, German food, sex with Roz, Martin, and – of course – coffee. Their train of thought is often derailed, however, by the problems of the others in their life.

Martin is in a foul mood, for no obvious reason, and is giving everyone a hard time. Is it time, as he thinks, for him to move out of Frasier's apartment? Meanwhile, Roz thinks she's met Mr Right . . . again. But was she ready for her conversation to turn to conversion?

And of course the big question: is Frasier happy?

Where Everybody Knows Their Name: Luck Hari's waitress gets an enlarged role, and we hear mention of Frederick, as Frasier pictures himself as an old man, buying a funny dog and moving into Frederick's apartment. Yoshi finally gets his wish, and is allowed to build a Zen garden in the grounds of Maris's house. For a while, Niles thought that Maris had really got into the idea of relaxing there – until he discovered her there wittering away on her mobile phone. Moose receives a credit as Eddie.

Subtitles: My Coffee with Niles.

Culture Vultures: Niles seems bemused to discover that $400 shoes aren't the key to true bliss.

Strange Bedfellows: Andy Winslow, a new employee in the station's news department, has agreed to meet Roz for coffee. Roz is mortified, however, when he starts to try to convert her to Christianity. It's not that he's religious, Roz argues. 'I am ecumenical,' she cries. 'I embrace men of all faiths.' To which Frasier tartly mutters, 'If only it stopped there.' The real problem Roz has is that she hoped that this one could have been the one man who could have given her life meaning – but it's not to be, and she finds herself 'back in Roz's world'. So she goes home to try to attract the cute new handyman servicing her building, by wearing a negligée and ripping out her taps!

Full-on Moon: Daphne's dialect comes under fire in this episode. She refers to an umbrella as a 'bumberchute', a word that Martin finds annoying and ridiculous. Niles, though, warms to calling it a 'bumberchute', telling Daphne that he's 'always had an ear for your tongue'. Martin later gets some mileage out of extracting the Michael from her psychic abilities.

Out Of Sight: The episode opens with Niles giving a worried and frightened Maris directions over the phone. He explains to Frasier that 'she wandered into the kitchen by mistake. I had to talk her back into the living room.'

The real reason for Niles marrying Maris is questioned by Frasier: did he do it for her money? Niles, affronted, proclaims that he did it for love. The money was, however, a 'bonus'.

We also learn that Maris has an auto-harp!

Eddie Takes The Biscuit: Martin arrives at Café Nervosa, escaping from a nasty rainstorm, to be told that dogs aren't allowed. He stares into the middle distance, waves his arm around, and says, 'What?' Eddie, it seems, has graduated to guide dog status.

The soaked Eddie then leaps up next to Frasier, who growls, 'There's nothing like the smell of a wet dog to work up the appetite for supper.'

Frasier Has Left The Building: Having finally received the perfect cup of coffee, Frasier sits alone and enjoys it – until he discovers that still something else is wrong with it.

On The Couch: This jolly and unusual episode is the perfect end to the first season. A sequel of sorts to the first episode,

'The Good Son', this one once again takes stock of the situation Frasier has found himself in. Is he, as Niles seems so desperate to find out, happy with his life? It seems that he is.

It's absolutely packed with typically good lines and, although it is based around a conversation between the Crane brothers, still finds time to spotlight each of the other regulars. Martin, rightly so, gets the next biggest slice of the cake, as we discover exactly why he is in such a bad mood – everyone has forgotten his birthday, but he has been unable to say anything about it. Niles and Frasier are rightly appalled at their insensitivity, and once Martin has gone again their thoughts turn to their relationship with him. Frasier tells a painfully sweet tale of how he fell asleep on the couch one night, only to wake to find Martin stroking his hair. 'Tough as nails on the outside,' Niles comments of Martin, in possibly the best-delivered line of the episode, 'but on the inside one giant spike.'

Luck Hari as the waitress also excels in this episode. Although she has little to do, her increasing anger with Frasier's fussy complaints about one coffee after another is a delight to watch. She also manages to appear wonderfully knowing and sympathetic (like all good waiting staff should) when she finally brings the perfect coffee to Frasier at the close of the episode. 'Now. Are you happy?'

Of course we are.

Season Two

2.01

'Slow Tango in South Seattle'

Written by Martin Weiss
Directed by James Burrows
First UK Transmission: 30.06.95

Skyline: Fireworks explode over the skyline.

Synopsis: The female population of Seattle have gone mad for a book called *Slow Tango in South Seattle*, by Thomas Jay Fallow. Frasier can't see the appeal: he really isn't interested in trite, romantic pulp. Until, that is, he discovers that the book is based upon his affair with his music teacher, Clarice Warner. The affair happened when Frasier was seventeen, and it was his first time with a woman. The next time, he admits sullenly, was six and a half years later (presumably during his final year at Harvard). Rather than being affronted that his private life is now public knowledge, Frasier is rather more angry that his name was missed off the acknowledgments list.

He decides that he must confront Fallow and express his disappointment. Niles, however, suspects that the real cause of Frasier's disgruntlement has nothing to do with going unacknowledged: rather, he is still feeling guilty over leaving Miss Warner without saying a proper goodbye. Agreeing that this may be the case, Frasier decides to hunt down his old flame and make amends for walking out on her.

Arriving at Clarice's house, Frasier mistakes her mother for Clarice and proceeds to remind the scatty old woman that they once had an affair. She seems somewhat taken with the idea, but Frasier is far from pleased when he discovers that he's got the wrong woman.

Guest Cast: Clarice Warner (Constance Towers), Mrs Warner (Myra Carter), Thomas Jay Fallow (John O'Hurley), Clarice's Date (David Sederholm).

Where Everybody Knows Their Name: Three of the on-air talents at KACL make an appearance. Gil Chesterton (Edward Hibbert) makes cutting, food-related jibes at the revelation of Frasier's affair. Amber Edwards (Susan Brown) interviews Fallow on air. Bulldog (Dan Butler) has something to say about his own first time with a woman: it was a prostitute, a present from his father. All he wanted was a bike. Lilith and Frederick get mentioned by default when Martin discusses Frederick's conception, while Frasier knows Thomas Jay Fallow from *Cheers*. Frasier's reference to sex at Harvard may well be a reminder of his first wife, Nanette, whom he married at that time. Moose still gets his credit for portraying Eddie.

Who's On The Line?: Steve (James Spader) is considering having a baby with his wife, but is worried about how it will affect their sex life.

Subtitles: Slow Tango In South Seattle; He Was Not Yet A Man, Yet Oh So Much More Than A Boy; The Tears It Takes A Summer Wind To Dry . . .; I Feel Older Since His Shadow Left My Door.

Culture Vultures: Martin is worried that Niles may have had an affair with Miss Warner as well. He is pleased to deny this: 'While Frasier was getting his Rachmaninovs, I was actually studying music.'

Strange Bedfellows: Falling for his sensitivity and dubious talents, Roz expresses a typically healthy interest in meeting Fallow.

Full-on Moon: Daphne is enjoying reading the book, but gets a little too much into it. As Frasier sits alone in the lounge, finishing the novel (and flipping past a six-page metaphor), Daphne wanders in and smacks him over the head with the hardback. She is, it seems, less than impressed at Frasier walking out on Clarice.

Out Of Sight: Niles is worried that Martin has no photos of him and his wife in his room, so provides him with one. In it, Maris is wearing jodhpurs, which confuses Martin: he thought she didn't ride horses. Niles replies that she wanted to, but 'her little quadrupeds are so tight, she's incapable of straddling anything larger than a border collie'.

Maris, too, is enraptured by *Slow Tango*. Niles thinks it may be having an effect on her: he saw her 'cooing over the college student who skims the koi pond'.

Frasier Has Left The Building: Mrs Warner and Frasier are together at the piano. She sidles up the seat towards him several times, each time Frasier moving further away until he eventually falls off the end.

On The Couch: A reasonably routine episode, with little that stands out. The finest performance comes from Carter as Clarice's mother: her excitement at the prospect of this forgotten affair is wonderful. At first, you think she's just going to be given a typically dull old-lady role, but her sparkle as she warms more to the idea of getting to know Frasier again is great fun.

The biggest criticism to make of this episode is that the whole thing is a little predictable, down to the tiniest thing. Of course Clarice will forgive Frasier, and of course she'd have another young boyfriend. It's mildly disappointing to see the series seem to forget itself for a week, and become a bit of a no-brainer.

In the final analysis, 'Slow Tango' is not a bad episode, but it is by no means a good one.

2.02

'The Unkindest Cut of All'

Written by Dave Hackel
Directed by Rick Beren
First UK Transmission: 07.07.95

Skyline: The light atop the Space Needle glows.

Synopsis: Frasier's nightmare comes true: a whole army of 'miniature Eddies' come to haunt him. The Cranes' neighbour, Mrs Greenway, arrives at their door with a box full of puppies; she claims that Eddie fathered them by her dog Phoebe. It is now up to Frasier to get rid of them, but Daphne seems less than keen to see them go.

At KACL, Frasier continues his crusade to be rid of the puppies, but with little success. Finally, a family seems sure to take the last of the blighters away but, while Frasier's back is turned, Daphne takes steps to make sure that little Basil stays.

The whole turn of events leads Frasier to ask his father why Eddie hadn't been neutered, as they had agreed. Martin is simply reluctant to put Eddie through that, so Frasier decides that he must take matters into his own hands and take Eddie to the vet himself. But Martin arrives at the surgery just in time to stop Frasier from putting Eddie through the operation. While they argue, Eddie is frightened into making a break for it. Eddie is lost and alone in Seattle – will Frasier and Martin (with the dubiously useful Niles) ever find him again?

Guest Cast: Dorothea Greenway (Jo de Winter), Father (Joel Anderson).

Where Everybody Knows Their Name: Betty from Accounting warns Roz about Frasier's quest to get rid of the puppies. And Moose gets a further credit as Eddie.

Who's On The Line?: Rita (Lily Tomlin) is overwhelmed at home. She's caring on her own for a large family – all of them very young – and, what with everything else in her very busy life, she sometimes thinks that she's going to crumble under the pressure. Asks Frasier, 'Have you considered getting a puppy?'

Subtitles: Sunday In The Park With Eddie; Catwoman; Un Peu De Pate Derriere Les Oreilles; Doctor! No!; The Stakeout.

Culture Vultures: Frasier demands that Daphne not ball his socks up, like his father's, but carefully iron them and hang them on a sock divider. He doesn't want the cashmere to be bruised.

Further cashmere calamities later. When Eddie turns up, he is cold, wet and shivering. Martin immediately reaches for Frasier's jumper to wrap around him. He goes ballistic, before realising that his father's dog is more important than a one-hundred-per-cent cashmere pullover. He turns his anger at the misuse of the jumper into disgust at his father's fashion sense: 'It's meant to be worn with the collar up,' he says, rearranging Eddie's new outfit.

Strange Bedfellows: Frasier desperately tries to get Roz to take a puppy, holding one up in front of her stony face. She's not going to melt, though . . . or is she? 'Oh, you're adorable,' she squeals, holding the puppy, kissing him, and squeezing him against her cheek. She giggles at him, kisses him again, and tells him that she loves him. And then passes it back to Frasier, completely cold again. Frasier asks, 'How can you just toss him aside after such a tender display of affection?' Roz stares at him, before replying, 'I can do it with men, too.'

Full-on Moon: Daphne claims that the family who are going to take away Basil 'had a dark aura', although she was probably just making excuses for keeping him. She later has a psychic flash of Eddie sitting with Frasier – he is in fact resting on a park bench staring at a KACL advertisement for Frasier's show. Daphne also used to select her dates back home by whether or not her mother's spaniel liked them.

While Martin panics about the missing Eddie, she makes tea. When he tells her that he doesn't like tea, she tells him to shut up and drink it, because it's the only thing she knows how to do in an emergency. 'That's a real comfort coming from a health-care provider,' says Martin.

Out Of Sight: Niles escapes the house this episode, because Maris is hosting the Women's League Senior Yoga Group, and he doesn't like the idea of 'old money and body stockings'.

After Niles's harrowing experiences in the hunt for Eddie (he got lost in the park, saw a raccoon, and mistook a bush for a threatening old man), he whimpers, 'I want to go home now, and hold my wife. That is, if she'll let me.'

The Buddy Show: Martin would rather go to Duke's than take Eddie to the vet. Who can blame him? When Eddie later runs away, Martin's buddies at the precinct put an APB out on him. Martin tells us about three ex-colleagues here – first a squad psychiatrist known only as 'The Squirrel'; then Nick, who discussed bowel movements in great detail; and, most important of all, 'Canteen' MacHugh, so called because he could go hours without needing to use the toilet because his bladder was so big. As big as a . . . oh, you get the idea.

Eddie Takes The Biscuit: Far too many to list in their entirety – this is an episode about the dog, after all. The best moment, however, has nothing to do with Eddie's usual antics. Frasier and Niles are trying to trap him so that they can take him to the vet. Niles tries to comfort Eddie into thinking that the operation is nothing to worry about, but Frasier warns him not to say too much. He has learnt the word 'B-A-T-H', after all, and Frasier's worried that he might have learnt more English than that. The brothers Crane, therefore, communicate in French while they try to nab the dog.

Frasier Has Left The Building: Martin, Frasier and Niles have finally got Eddie to the vet's. As they wait, they keep their manhoods covered under cupped hands. When the dog is taken away by the nurse (none of them are prepared to take him to his doom), they all cross their legs.

On The Couch: The first half of this episode is a fluffy, cute-animals romp, while the second is a much more serious examination about respect between the Cranes. Thankfully, the change in mood doesn't jar. Highlights of the puppy storyline include Roz's aforementioned duplicity, the puppies staring at Frasier, and Daphne's overwhelming desire to keep them. On the other hand, Martin's worry that Frasier is taking decisions away from him and that his son may no longer respect him are beautifully played out in a script that, typical for the series, never descends into the usual sugary 'I love you, Pop'/'I love you too, son' American formula.

2.03
'The Matchmaker'

Written by Joe Keenan
Directed by David Lee
First UK Transmission: 14.07.95

Skyline: A helicopter rises up from the skyline and departs.

Synopsis: The Crane household is woken up in the middle of the night by the smoke alarm. Daphne soon calms the panic by admitting that she was having a cigarette in her room – something she occasionally does when she's feeling a bit low and depressed. Frasier asks Daphne exactly what's wrong, and she tells him that she's feeling bad about her love life – or rather, lack of one. They talk so far into the night, sharing cigarettes, that Frasier sleeps through and misses an important meeting with the new station manager the following morning.

The next day, Tom Duran, the new manager, pops into the studio to introduce himself to Frasier. He makes an impression on Frasier, and the good doctor invites him to dinner at his apartment on Saturday night. Secretly, he plans to introduce him to Daphne and thereby solve her problems. Unfortunately, Tom has other ideas. As Roz discovers, Tom is gay and thinks that Frasier has asked him on a date. Roz, angry with Frasier for having suggested that her morals are somewhat loose, does nothing to correct the misconceptions of either party.

So, Saturday comes, and chaos reigns . . .

Where Everybody Knows Their Name: A terrific introduction for KACL's new station manager Tom Duran (Eric Lutes). A nameless reference to Diane, and another embittered mention of Lilith. In an effort to cheer Daphne, Frasier embarks on the story of his relationship with Diane (as seen in *Cheers*). Of course, the story ends badly – not something Daphne really needs to hear. To rescue the situation, Frasier tells of his marriage to Lilith, presumably in an effort to prove that things can work out for the best. Or can they? 'I took my poor, battered heart and offered it to Lilith. Who put it in her little Cuisinard and hit the purée button.'

Who's On The Line?: Just James from Tacoma.

Subtitles: Manhunt; The Perils Of Refinement.

Strange Bedfellows: Roz, ill-advisedly, reveals to Frasier that she owns a little black book of all her dates. She plans to offer up a couple of names to Daphne. 'You do not have to donate one of your boyfriends to Daphne,' Frasier contends, before adding, 'One hates to break up a collection.'

Nevertheless, Roz carries on regardless. Her suggestions are Sven Bokman, an aerobics instructor; Gunther Deitrich, a model ('A German narcissist?' quips Frasier. 'There's an appealing combination'); and a tennis instructor called Brick. There follows a wonderful exchange, highlighting Niles and Roz's deep-seated antagonism: 'Why not just lather Daphne up, and hurl her over the wall of a prison yard?' Niles snipes. 'Excuse me,' says an indignant Roz, 'but I've dated all these guys.' Niles smiles, as if she's made his point for him. 'Well, where did you think I came up with the imagery?'

Frasier then goes on to dig himself deep into a hole, trying to avoid suggesting that Roz's standards are somewhat low. Unsurprisingly, Roz takes offence and storms away, saying, 'I can't stay. The fleet is in.'

Full-on Moon: Daphne, it seems, is used to being set up for blind dates. 'My girlfriends in Manchester used to set me up all the time, and it was always with some gangly bounder with a boarding-house reach. And he wasn't going for the Colman's Hot Mustard, if you know what I mean.'

Another psychic flash for her, as she takes Tom's coat. She senses that he has just gone through a messy break-up. Not unreasonably, he suggests that Frasier told her that. But this can't be, because she senses something else: 'There was a bitter dispute about ownership of opera recordings.' Only Frasier, and those used to his ways and those of his friends, would not immediately have their alarm bells rung by this comment.

Out Of Sight: Once all the confusion has been cleared up, Tom still suspects Niles is gay. 'This Maris guy he keeps mentioning is a woman?' he asks. Frasier considers this for a moment, before replying, 'Well, the jury's still out on that one.'

The Buddy Show: A brief mention of Duke's, when Martin tells Tom he knows some great bars.

Eddie Takes The Biscuit: It is he who exposes Daphne's smoking habit, carrying the packet into the lounge.

Frasier Has Left The Building: Tom has left, and Daphne and Frasier sit up again, smoking for comfort. But Frasier then notices the Surgeon General's health warning on the packet, points it out to Daphne, and they both stop. So, that does work, then!

On The Couch: If there's one criticism to level against this episode, it is that the stereotypical portrayal of Tom's homosexuality seems a little heavy-handed in this usually deft and subtle show. A love of the theatre and the opera, a willingness to move quickly on a first date, an interest in men in uniform – all of these are the hallmarks of a scriptwriter checking his *Big Book of Clichés* for a helping hand. But without this, the episode would fail totally, and, since 'The

Matchmaker' is one of the finest episodes ever, we should excuse it.

A prime concern, it would seem, of the denizens of the Usenet newsgroup alt.tv.frasier (an Internet discussion forum for fans of the show) is discovering the sexualities of the main stars. This is not unreasonable: someone new to the show would see the ever-camp performance of Grammer and the prissy, retentive portrayal by Hyde Pierce and assume just what Tom does of Frasier and Niles – that they're gay. As if in answer to everyone's question, along comes this episode and presents us with Tom, a character through whose eyes we can really see 'The Perils of Refinement' for what they are.

While the highlight is the farce of the second half, this doesn't mean that all the best material is saved until then. The scene in Café Nervosa in which Roz's morals are brought into question is stuffed to the brim with choice lines, and Peri Gilpin does a marvellous job at being greatly affronted (see above).

The pièce de résistance of the episode, if not the entire series, is the dinner party at Frasier's apartment. It's dramatic irony a gogo as everyone rushes round thinking one thing of Tom, while he's thinking exactly the opposite of them. And they're all wrong. And only we know the truth. But Brian Rix was never this erudite. The script is chock-full of lines so cleverly judged that they never slip over the edge from being marvellous double entendres into becoming crude innuendo: Frasier encouraging Niles to let someone else 'have a crack' at Tom; Tom believing all the Crane men are gay; Tom being impressed with the view from Frasier's lounge, only to be told that it's better from the bedroom; Martin's innocent description of the people at his favourite bar, Duke's, to a very interested Tom as a 'great crowd – lot of young cops'. Every one is a painfully funny delight.

Simply perfect, from beginning to end.

2.04

'Flour Child'

Written by Christopher Lloyd
Directed by James Burrows
First UK Transmission: 21.07.95

Skyline: Lights go on in various buildings.

Synopsis: Frasier's BMW breaks down and he, Niles and Martin are getting a cab back to his apartment. Their journey is somewhat delayed, though, when the driver (Arleen) goes into labour and the three of them must aid with the delivery. The whole miracle of birth inspires Niles to wonder whether it is time he became a father.

At the suggestion of Frasier, he carries a bag of flour around with him for a week: he is never to let it out of his sight, and treat it just as he would a real baby. The only problem is that Niles lets one mishap after another happen to his 'flour child', but they never seem to put him off the idea of fatherhood.

Meanwhile, Clarence, a guard at KACL, is in hospital for a kidney transplant. Frasier had signed his card thinking it was his birthday, and had put in a tactless message about getting 'nearer to death'. The race is on to steal the card from the hospital before Clarence can read it.

Guest Cast: Arleen (Charlayne Woodard), Clarence (Aaron Heyman), Mary (Linda Porter), Patient (Alvy Moore), Mother (Robin Krieger).

Where Everybody Knows Their Name: Frasier tells the story of holding the newborn Frederick for the first time, while he listens to Lilith warn him, 'If you ever come near me again, Frasier, I'll drop you with a deer rifle.' There's also the first reference to Maris's latest employee, Nguy, whose name Frasier can never pronounce. And another credit for Moose as Eddie.

Who's On The Line?: Maggie (Amy Madigan) has problems with Gavin, her new man. They've dated only twice, and he seems to be getting terribly clingy. While Frasier recommends that she talk it over with him, Roz obviously disagrees and is asked to suggest something else. She reckons Maggie should dump him – advice she takes, much to the annoyance of Frasier.

Subtitles: Special Delivery; Flour Child; No Guts, No Glory.

Culture Vultures: Niles panics when Arleen's waters break because he doesn't want his calfskin shoes to get wet – they might pucker.

An amusing little line comes when Niles arrives to meet Frasier at Café Nervosa, carrying his new sack of flour. 'May I join you?' he asks. 'Or should I say, may we?'

'Mais oui!' quips Frasier.

Full-on Moon: While discussing parenthood, Daphne launches into an imagined conversation between her at age fifty and her mother. This carries on well after she starts to leave the room, leaving a bewildered Frasier and Niles behind her. 'I wonder how many more people she's got in there with her,' ponders Frasier.

Out Of Sight: 'Under the thumb' just doesn't come close to describing Niles's role in his marriage. When considering being a father, Niles says, 'I like to know what I want, before Maris tells me.'

Frasier examines the label on Niles's 'child': 'Bleached. One hundred per cent fat free. Best when kept in an airtight container,' he reads, before commenting that it seems to be taking after its mother. When realising that Maris is approaching forty, Niles also wonders if he shouldn't have some of Maris's eggs frozen. Frasier's response is, of course, entirely obvious . . .

Eddie Takes The Biscuit: A *Cry In The Dark* moment, as Eddie eats the 'flour child'.

Frasier Has Left The Building: An intrigued Daphne picks up and cradles the bag of flour, before getting into a friendly tussle with Martin. The two of them end up throwing handfuls of flour at each other, which is a little unsettling if you think about it.

On The Couch: A very funny episode which also manages to deal sensitively with the frightening responsibilities of parenthood. This is probably the first time we really see how delicate and thoughtful Niles can be, particularly when he is at the hospital, gazing into the room full of newborn babies. For a moment, we realise exactly what he feels he is missing out on.

But then, we've also seen how dangerous a parent he can be. In the course of the episode, he manages to skewer, drop, bang, drown and burn his 'baby', before finally letting it get savaged by Eddie. As clumsy and unconcerned as he is about the bag of flour, it is touching to see him get so much into the idea of role-playing being a father.

2.05

'Duke's, We Hardly Knew Ye'

Written by Linda Morris and Vic Rauseo
Directed by James Burrows
First UK Transmission: 28.07.95

Skyline: The elevator goes up the Space Needle.

Synopsis: Niles comes to Frasier with a request for him to go halves on an investment in a new mini-mall being built by a company called Meadow-Wood Properties. Though initially reluctant to take the risk, Niles eventually persuades Frasier that it would be worth his while to put money into the project.

Later, Martin surprises his sons by inviting them to Duke's, his old hang-out, for a beer. Taken aback as they are, they agree to go along to see how the other half lives. Once there, they are taken to the bosom of Martin's friends and ex-colleagues and soon find themselves actually enjoying the experience. Until, that is, Martin decides to make a toast to Duke's, and all its patrons, and makes a spiteful attack against Meadow-Wood Properties who are to tear the bar down to make way for a mall.

Racked with guilt, can Frasier and Niles find it within themselves to own up to Martin that it is, in part, their money that is paying for the destruction of Duke's?

Guest Cast: Joe (Jack Wallace).

Where Everybody Knows Their Name: We finally get to meet the infamous Duke (John LaMotta) among Martin's ex-force buddies, and we also see Leo (Bill Gratton) for the first time. Frasier has to read a trailer for Amber Edwards' *Book Chat*, since Roz is outside wrestling with the chocolate machine.

While they reel from the bombshell of the invitation to Duke's, Frasier and Niles realise that not even Hester was ever asked to go to Martin's bar – and she 'could be quite the old rummy'.

A couple of mentions of Lilith in this episode. First, when Frasier arrives at the bar, all Martin's friends let on that he has told them all about their break-up – in great detail. Later, when asked if he can live with the guilty secret of being one of the investors in the mall, Frasier points out, 'I married Lilith. I can live with anything.' Also, when he discusses how easy it is to become attached to bars, he is clearly alluding to Cheers back in Boston.

Who's On The Line?: No full calls this episode, but we see Frasier saying goodbye to a Lorraine at the opening of the show.

Subtitles: Scent Of A Woman; Where Nobody Knows Their Name; Sleepless In Seattle (You Know We Had To Do It Eventually).

Culture Vultures: A great little scene, with Frasier and Niles trying to decide where to go to celebrate their investment. They reel off a list of Seattle's best restaurants, every one of them not quite right for the occasion. 'How do we live?' wonders Frasier, without apparent irony.

Strange Bedfellows: Roz, Frasier and Niles meet for coffee. Frasier begins to think that being responsible for the tearing down of Duke's might actually be seen as a public service. 'Men with guns will have one less place to go and liquor up,' he decides. But Niles points out that 'there's always Roz's'. Roz then asks, 'What do you say about me when I'm not around?'

There's another great bit in this scene, where Roz likens Frasier's situation to cheating on someone and then keeping it a secret from them. She goes into a somewhat overdetailed example, telling an obviously true story of the time she cheated on someone who was meant to be in Portland, but came back early to find her in bed with the cheatee.

Full-on Moon: Daphne has a date this episode, with a man called Derek. This is their third date, and Frasier and Martin point out that it is usual for young couples to move on to sex at this juncture. 'It takes more than three dinners to get bangers and mash with Daphne Moon,' she says, shocked at American mores. Later, we see her arrive home very late after a fourth date with Derek. She describes him as 'the perfect gentleman', and says that they ended their evening with a romantic walk in the park. As she turns to go to her room, we see that she has half the park smeared over the back of her outfit.

Out Of Sight: Martin introduces Niles to his drinking mates: 'He married money!' This is greeted by cheers and slaps on the back. As Frasier points out earlier, why would Niles want to invest in Meadow-Wood? 'You and Maris are already wallowing in money like a couple of yuppie hogs.' Roz thinks Maris uses her money to emasculate Niles, which he never refutes.

The Buddy Show: This time, we actually meet a whole load of Martin's friends. We also hear a story about Mickey Dougan, and his part in Martin's very bad joke about taking his police horse, Agides, into Duke's.

Frasier Has Left The Building: The Duke's crowd are in Frasier's apartment, drinking and smoking and hanging out. Frasier rushes around, spraying air freshener.

On The Couch: 'Duke's . . . is where he goes to escape the stresses, strains and petty annoyances of everyday life,' explains Niles. Frasier agrees: 'In other words, us!'

And so we bid a fond farewell to one of the series' silent stars: Duke's. This is a really sweet episode, with a couple of lovely scenes between Grammer and Mahoney as they examine their relationship once again. Martin's acceptance of change is touching, as is Frasier's need to understand what motivates his father's love of the bar, especially after Martin reminds him that, in the year or so they've been together, Frasier has already tried to get rid of his favourite chair (see 1.19, 'Give Him The Chair!') and even Eddie (2.02, 'The Unkindest Cut of All'). The two of them singing 'Danny Boy' is one of the highlights of the series' more dramatic moments, and Frasier describing an offer of a beer from his father as 'a validation' is so demonstrative of his insecurity with their differences. Great stuff.

2.06

'The Botched Language of Cranes'

Written by Joe Keenan
Directed by David Lee
First UK Transmission: 04.08.95

Skyline: A cloud passes above the skyline, and it rains.

Synopsis: It's raining in Seattle – not an unusual occurrence, but one that is getting on Frasier's nerves. When a caller phones in to ask for advice on how to spice up her life, Frasier suggests making changes, one of which could be to move to a different city. The next day, the show is inundated by callers who want to complain about Frasier's suggestion that Seattle is a bad place to live. Although he initially doesn't want to, Roz persuades him to apologise to the city on air. He does so, but doesn't realise that he's still on air when he spits out that the general populace of Seattle are a bunch of snivelling whiners.

There's only one way now that he can save face, and avoid being suspended by the station manager: to accept an invitation to be guest speaker at a benefit dinner for St Bart's Hospital, where Martin had his hip sorted. An unfortunately timed trip to the toilet, though, spells disaster, and Frasier manages to make faux pas after faux pas . . .

Guest Cast: Sister Joselia (Helen Geller).

Where Everybody Knows Their Name: A mention of Derek Mann (the newspaper critic from 1.04, 'I Hate Frasier Crane'), as he points out Frasier's alleged hatred of Seattle to his readers. Father Mike (George Deloy) makes an appearance, filling in for the lost Bishop at the benefit. Betsy at KACL's switchboard is having a bad day dealing with the listeners' complaints and Tom Duran may have to take Frasier off the air for a while. Meanwhile Bulldog (Dan Butler) is peeved that Frasier has broken his record for the number of phone complaints (Frasier's got 50, Bulldog 35) – Bulldog set up the record when he did his piece on female umpires: 'Finally, a chest worth protecting.' And a credit for Moose as Eddie.

Who's On The Line?: Edna (Alfre Woodard) starts the trouble. As a receptionist at a pest-control company, she is bored with having dealt with the same kinds of calls every day for fifteen years. Later, Connie (Sandra Dee) is giving

Frasier a piece of her mind over how she feels about his Seattle-bashing.

Subtitles: He Will Be The World's First Four Legged Leprechaun; Let A Smile Be Your Umbrella; Man Overboard.

Strange Bedfellows: Roz, trying to persuade Frasier to apologise for his comments, says that even her boyfriends are upset. 'Well,' mutters Frasier, 'we can't afford to lose a demographic as large as that.'

We also discover that Roz wanted to be a nun when she was younger. Her protestations that she changed her mind because she didn't like the idea of working at the weekends don't quite wash with anyone except Father Mike.

Full-on Moon: Grammie Moon's hip, we learn, was forever popping out of place, which is information, in a rare moment of impishness, Martin uses against Daphne in a practical joke.

Out Of Sight: Maris attends the dinner, but she is too busy trying to corner the head of the museum board for us to see her. Niles gives an amusing horse-race-style commentary of his wife trying to keep up with the reluctant chairwoman.

Eddie Takes The Biscuit: Eddie, poor thing, is forced to sport the latest in unfashionable rainy-day dog coats. Martin thinks it was bad enough he got neutered (see 2.02, 'The Unkindest Cut of All') without this . . .

Frasier Has Left The Building: After the disastrous events of the evening, Frasier writes out a cheque to St Bart's, watched over by Sister Joselia. She isn't happy with what she sees, even after Frasier adds a zero, so Frasier simply hands the chequebook and his expensive watch over to the sister.

On The Couch: An episode that puts Frasier firmly back in the spotlight, and is predictably good for that. His fervent belief that he has nothing to apologise for, along with his incredulous anger at those who would disagree with him, is classic stuff. The highlight of the episode, though, has to be his speech at the dinner. Unaware that it has just been announced that the Bishop has been lost at sea, he strolls on and wonders where he is, saying that he's 'sure he'll drift in' sooner or later. Following the advice to simply be confident whatever reaction he gets, he just blunders on thinking that no one is appreciating his humour. Exemplary foot-in-mouth material.

2.07

'The Candidate'

Written by Chuck Ranberg and Anne Flett-Giordano
Directed by James Burrows
First UK Transmission: 11.08.95

Skyline: The light atop the Space Needle glows.

Synopsis: The Crane brothers are horrified to discover that their father has appeared in a television advert for Holden Thorpe, the right-wing candidate seeking election success as a Congressman. In the advert, Martin waves his stick and points out that as a cop, 'I used to carry a gun. Now I carry a cane. I'm voting to elect Holden Thorpe. He's running because I can't.'

Later, at Café Nervosa, realising they cannot criticise Martin for his beliefs, Niles tries to get Frasier to publicly support his liberal-minded opponent, Phil Patterson. Frasier is going to vote for Patterson, but fears that to endorse him publicly would alienate a percentage of his listeners. However, at KACL, Thorpe gives Frasier a hard time on his show, and this makes Frasier's mind up for him.

Back at Frasier's place, everything is ready – Frasier is going through his lines, Phil Patterson's smiling, the director is checking the lighting and Niles is in everyone's way. The new Phil Patterson endorsement advert is ready to be made. During a brief break, Frasier and Phil talk on the balcony, and Phil reveals he was once abducted by aliens to take part in a galactic peace conference. The director is ready but on 'Action', Frasier finds it difficult to get through the speech. He goes into the kitchen and tells Niles what Phil has said, but his brother says it might be a one-off aberration, created by stress and overwork. Mollified, Frasier does the advert.

The next day at the station, Bulldog gleefully tells Frasier and Roz that the story is out about Phil Patterson and his aliens. Determined to prove that Phil is still the right man, Frasier goes on air, telling his listeners that whether Phil believes in little green men is irrelevant, it's his policies that matter. Trouble is, Bulldog was talking about a couple of Guatemalan illegal aliens living in Phil's house . . .

Guest Cast: Phil Patterson (Boyd Gaines), Director (Jack Tate), Boy (Christopher Walberg).

Where Everybody Knows Their Name: Bulldog (Dan Butler), a loyal supporter of Thorpe, makes another appearance while Luck Hari's waitress makes her only appearance this season. Chopper Dave gets a handful of mentions but is never actually seen in person.

Who's On The Line?: A caller named Susan, plus Congressional candidate Holden Thorpe (Sydney Pollack), who challenges Frasier to an argument and then hangs up. Among Thorpe's most popular catchphrases is 'Cancer aside, tobacco is good for the economy.'

Subtitles: Andy Warhol Said It Best; Citizen Crane; Let's Just Keep This Under Our Space Helmets; The Fault Lies Not In Our Stars But In Ourselves; One Person Speaking Out Can Make A Difference.

Strange Bedfellows: Chopper Dave buzzed Roz's place once with his helicopter, when she was sleeping with a Vietnam veteran, who started having flashbacks.

Full-on Moon: Daphne's uncle (we're never told which one) was a political writer for a tabloid. His biggest headline was

'High-ranking Minister caught wearing women's clothing'. 'You turned to page two to find out it was Margaret Thatcher but by then you'd already bought the paper!'

Out Of Sight: Maris has sent her servants down to Phil Patterson's campaign headquarters to lick envelopes. Maris herself cannot do this as she cannot produce saliva.

The Buddy Show: Duke calls Martin to say he's seen one of his adverts, and that the second one is currently showing on Channel 14.

Frasier Has Left The Building: Roz is plucking her eyebrows at Café Nervosa when the little cookie-selling boy annoys her.

On The Couch: An excellent episode, displaying *Frasier*-style farce at its best without a doubt. Frasier's marvellous pro-Patterson address to camera takes on a whole slew of new meanings after the revelation about Phil's apparent abduction. And if that wasn't hysterical enough, his on-air rant about Phil and the aliens is beautifully punctuated by Roz, initially bemused and then alarmed, when she realises Frasier's aliens are different from Bulldog's.

In fact, although one can sympathise with the Crane brothers' angst over the extremism of Holden Thorpe, the liberalisation of them (and Maris, bearing in mind her background) smacks of convenience for the sake of this one episode. They don't really strike us as particularly centre-left, and, although very funny, Frasier's conversation with the waitress in Café Nervosa about the coffees he won't drink is very forced and too politically correct for a snob like Frasier. For the record, he won't touch a Kenyan blend because they still poach elephants, a dark-roast Brazilian because of the rainforests or Salvadorian because of their human-rights violations. He goes for the Hawaiian.

And the funniest nonpolitical moment is Roz, grabbing Bulldog's tongue after he's been particularly lascivious and smacking it. Brilliantly inspired physical comedy.

2.08

'Burying A Grudge'

Written by David Lloyd
Directed by Andy Ackerman
First UK Transmission: 18.08.95

Skyline: The light atop the Space Needle glows.

Synopsis: Frasier returns home, having not had a very good time at work – he and Roz have been arguing – to discover that Eddie has found a new toy to play with in the park: an old Barbie doll. Martin blames this on Frasier for having Eddie 'fixed' (see 2.02, 'The Unkindest Cut of All') and wants to know why Eddie won't play with slightly more butch toys. Niles is on his way to the hospital to see Maris after her operation and asks Martin and Frasier to accompany him for moral support.

At the hospital, Dr Sternstein assures Niles that everything has gone well and Maris is convalescing. Frasier meanwhile has found a room containing Martin's old partner on the force, Artie Walshe. The boys are fond of Artie, who was around as they grew up (Fraser has fond memories of a young Niles asking for a salade niçoise at a weenie roast) and are aware that he subsequently fell out with Martin, but no one knows why. They tell Martin, but he could not care less. Artie never visited him when he was shot, so why should he see him just because he's having a stomach operation? Frasier manipulates Martin into visiting Artie, however, although the reunion is not pleasant.

Back at the apartment, they get the story behind the falling out. Artie spread a rumour throughout the department that Martin cried at the end of *Brian's Song*, a television movie about a cancer-struck ball player they were watching at Duke's. Martin always claimed he had pretzel salt in his eye. However, people around the department started leaving Kleenex on his desk and called him 'Boo-Hoo' Crane. In retaliation, Martin 'let something slip' about the size of Artie's wife's butt. 'It's enormous. It looks like she's shoplifting throat pillows!' If that wasn't enough, Martin resents the fact that Artie can never leave an argument without having the last word.

Frasier receives a telephone call and, despite his protestations of disinterest, Martin is clearly worried that it is bad news from the hospital. Although it is actually about Martin's car, Frasier lets Martin believe it was Artie, thus proving Martin still cares.

As a result, they head down to the hospital so that Martin and Artie can rebuild their friendship before it's too late . . .

Guest Cast: Artie Walshe (Lincoln Kilpatrick), Dr Sternstein (Paul Kent), Nurse (Lynne Adams).

Where Everybody Knows Their Name: Hester Crane's presence is suggested a couple of times when Martin talks about the old days with Artie and the other cops.

Who's On The Line?: Linda (Betty Comden), who is on a carphone with her husband Walter (Adolph Green) driving. They are lost and have phoned in for directions to the antique market from Cherokee and 14th . . .

Subtitles: Quick! Get Manila On The Phone; No Guts, No Gravy; Albuquerque Is Approximately 136 Square Miles; Well, We've Come This Far Without A Bedpan Joke . . .

Strange Bedfellows: Roz has her eye on Eli, a nineteen-year-old intern in the photocopy room.

Full-on Moon: Daphne once had a mole removed 'just south of Manchester' (and she's not talking about British geography . . .).

Out Of Sight: Maris is in hospital having a facelift. According to Niles, she's not used to hospitals, bar the usual childhood ailments – tonsils, adenoids, force-feeding . . . She later tells Niles over the phone that she is convinced she is gaining weight from the glucose in the IV and wants a nutrasweet drip. She also plays havoc with the nurses and, to make her feel more at home, Niles places her pearl-handled revolver under her pillow, then sleeps in a spare hospital room across the corridor.

The Buddy Show: Apart from the story behind Martin and Artie's falling out, we learn that they used to watch movies at Duke's, and Artie bought a small boat to teach Martin fishing. They once caught an old slipper, which Artie immediately threw on to the barbecue because he believed you should always eat what you catch. Artie's wife, with a butt the size of Albuquerque (allegedly), is called Loretta.

Eddie Takes The Biscuit: By his traditional hard stare, Martin knows that Eddie is accusing him of stealing his Barbie doll – he wants it back, even though, according to Martin, all the poodles in the park apparently laugh at him.

Frasier Has Left The Building: Eddie is playing with his new GI Joe until Martin turns his back, whereupon the dog retrieves his beloved Barbie . . .

On The Couch: An excellent episode, spotlighting Martin, which avoids so many of the usual sitcom clichés about people in hospital making amends (to spoil it, we have to tell you that Artie does not die) before they pass on. Possibly because the viewer is expecting this final dénouement, the show takes on a special meaning as we understand a little more about how Martin Crane ticks, and see just how obstinate and petty he can be over something so trivial as a movie. That said, we all know his situation because everyone does it – rows over something pathetic, the resentment builds and the need not to make up becomes more important than the original falling out. Frasier guides his father brilliantly along the path to enlightenment, and gives him the opportunity to talk to Artie just as they used to. Some lovely manipulation by Frasier there, especially during the phone call about the car, and he also gets the best moment of the episode for humour when he sees the photograph of Loretta beside Artie's

bed and sees just how large her behind is. We, thankfully, are
spared this sight . . .

2.09
'Adventures In Paradise' (Part 1)

Written by Ken Levine
Directed by James Burrows
First UK Transmission: 25.08.95

Skyline: A streak of lightning crosses the sky.

Synopsis: After a show, Roz and Frasier flick through *Seattle
Magazine*, reading about the 'hottest' people in the city
(neither Frasier nor Niles features). Frasier takes a fancy to
one Madeline Marshall, so Roz rings her and fixes a date on
Frasier's behalf.

On their first date, Frasier takes Madeline to a French
restaurant he likes, but they are distracted when the owner of
the establishment discovers that his unmarried daughter is
pregnant. Hearing the exchanges going on in the kitchen –
and witnessing the terrified clumsiness of the young waiter
who is clearly the father – Frasier is asked to intervene by the
girl's mother. Frasier indeed sorts the problem out, much to
Madeline's pleasure.

Two weeks later, they are still together (and driving Roz
mad, as she is going through a dry spell right now) and
Madeline asks if they can go away. They agree to go to Bora
Bora the next day. But on returning to his apartment, Frasier
is plagued by doubts. Is it too soon to go away together for a
week? The family persuade Frasier to go.

He and Madeline arrive at their chalet on Bora Bora. As
Madeline heads to the shower, Frasier goes to the verandah,
where a very special surprise awaits him . . .

Guest Cast: Etienne (Pierre Epstein), Mother (Kirstan
DeVere), Yvette (Jessica Pennington), Busboy (Rick Schatz).

Where Everybody Knows Their Name: Hester Crane not only gets mentioned herein, but we get quite a bit of depth added to her meeting with Martin. She was a psychiatrist often called in by the Police Department to run up a profile of a murder suspect. She and Martin met over the chalk outline of a victim. 'One look at her hair silhouetted against that flashing blue light of the coroner's wagon and I was a goner,' explains Martin. 'She drew a little smile on the head of the outline and I drew a pair of eyes and before you knew it, we were laughing like a couple of kids!' Frasier decides his father is a bit of a ghoul for that, but Martin sighs. 'I was joking. We couldn't draw on the outline,' he says. 'They hadn't moved the body yet.' A marvellous and much-expected expansion on what we know about Frasier's mother. This episode also features the first appearance of Madeline Marshall (JoBeth Williams), a brief return for Bulldog (Dan Butler) and, at the climax of the show, a scene-stealing one word from Lilith Sternin (Bebe Neuwirth).

Who's On The Line?: Chester (Art Garfunkel) who is fighting with his wife because his life is going nowhere.

Subtitles: Busman's Holiday; Let's Get Away From It All; People Who Live In Glass Houses.

Culture Vultures: Frasier is initially impressed with Madeline without even meeting her simply because she's single, a patron of the arts, and has an MBA from Stanford ('Well, if you have to go to school on the West Coast . . .'). What a snob. But then, you already knew that.

Full-on Moon: Daphne's mother gets very worried if she doesn't hear from her daughter regularly, so Daphne is writing a letter to her. Presumably to set Mrs Moon's mind at rest she is telling her about serial killers. Daphne can blow perfect smoke rings, a skill picked up from her grandfather, who used to smoke a stogie all day, then take out his teeth, still with the cigar clenched in them, and chase the kids around the room. Then when his mood changed, they'd have to run for their lives.

The Buddy Show: One of Martin's buddies from Customs has got him some confiscated illegally imported Cuban cigars. Martin, Niles and Daphne spend much of this episode enjoying them enormously.

Eddie Takes The Biscuit: Eddie thinks stealing Frasier's socks is a game. A better one is returning mismatching ones, however!

Frasier Has Left The Building: Roz is still ploughing through *Seattle Magazine* and then phoning people up.

On The Couch: Working on the assumption that any episode in which Lilith appears (even if it is just for one brief snatch) is immediately a classic, this one cannot fail. JoBeth Williams as Madeline seems the perfect match for Frasier and, after so many false starts, it looks as if he has finally found someone to love.

In fact, much of the episode is standard Frasier fare (that's no bad thing, of course . . .), although wonderfully punctuated by the sequence in the French restaurant and Daphne's attempts to teach Niles the art of cigar-smoke-blowing.

But it's those classic words 'To Be Continued' that put the gilt on this one – just knowing there is more of Lilith to come . . .

2.10
'Adventures In Paradise' (Part 2)

Written by Ken Levine and David Isaacs
Directed by James Burrows
First UK Transmission: 01.09.95

Skyline: Fireworks explode over the skyline.

Synopsis: Lilith introduces Frasier and Madeline to Brian. Within seconds, Lilith and Frasier are each trying to get one over on the other and so, to get over the embarrassment, Brian suggests they all dine together that night. Later, back in their chalet, Frasier is beginning to obsess with Lilith, and Madeline tries to be understanding and patient, even when Frasier starts listening at the wall between the two chalets. He is convinced they are making love next door. 'I don't hear anything,' points out Madeline. 'Exactly,' says the experienced ex-husband. Madeline decides to have a shower before she and Frasier settle down for the night. While she's there, Frasier begins imagining making better love with Madeline than Lilith is with Brian and starts faking orgasms. Eventually he is jumping on the bed, slamming it against the wall and shrieking out in ecstasy. If it wasn't bad enough that Madeline sees him doing this, Lilith and Brian are watching through the door – they were still out together.

On his next radio show, Frasier rather obliquely tries to apologise to Madeline over the air, which Roz thinks ought to do the trick. It does because Madeline rings and agrees to dinner at Frasier's. Roz then gives Frasier a bill from the Bora Bora hotel for the bed he wrecked.

Niles is taking Daphne and Martin to the opera where Maris has a tiny part, which he bought for her at a benefit auction. She is playing Ulric, the hunchback drawbridge operator, and they head off to see this masterpiece, just as Madeline arrives. A delighted Frasier takes a moment to dispose of Eddie, at which point Lilith turns up. Deciding she's had enough of dealing with Frasier's ex-wife, Madeline leaves and when Frasier returns, he is horrified to find Lilith there. She explains she has come to ask for his blessing – Brian wants to get married in Las Vegas as soon as possible, and Frasier has to face the fact that Lilith has successfully moved on in her life without him . . .

Where Everybody Knows Their Name: Chopper Dave gets a very brief mention. We also have the first appearance of Lilith's fiancé, Brian (James Morrison), a seismologist with MIT. 'How perfect,' proclaims Frasier to Lilith, 'Brian being a seismologist and you having so many faults!' Madeline Marshall (JoBeth Williams) bids her farewells this episode.

Lilith (Bebe Neuwirth) is in fine form, and there are under-standably a few mentions of Frederick, who adores his new father-to-be. Sam Malone (from *Cheers*) is briefly referred to, and then there's that little cameo from Diane Chambers (Shelley Long) at the end.

Who's On The Line?: Vic (Kevin Bacon), who is having a problem with women. Frasier passes him over to Roz, who, upon discovering Vic's a former male model who now works at a law firm, is eager to help in any way she can . . .

Subtitles: A Brief Recap Before We Continue; Paradise Lost; What Number Sunblock Must She Use?

Full-on Moon: Our Daff once dreamt of being a ballerina. Bless her.

Eddie Takes The Biscuit: Eddie watches Frasier and Madeline being passionate on the sofa. Naughty, naughty . . .

Frasier Has Left The Building: Frasier is running around the Bora Bora chalet trying to crush a bug . . .

On The Couch: 'My God, woman, I'd drive a stake through your heart but I don't think anything could kill you!' To try to list everything that is fantastic, great and indeed marvellous about this episode would take a book in itself. The high points have to be Frasier putting Eddie 'back where he belongs' and actually heading for the balcony, before changing his mind and putting him in Martin's room; Frasier's reaction on finding Lilith in the apartment where Madeline was moments before; and Martin's reaction to learning that Lilith is getting married again – but not to Frasier.

But without a doubt it is once again the Frasier-and-Lilith discussion scene that steals the show, as Frasier realises he's still on his own. Of course he'll give Lilith his blessing, but he's still very jealous. Only Lilith could say, 'Brian has been a dutiful suitor for some time and I'm convinced, to within an acceptable margin of error, that he loves me,' and make you know she's head over heels in love.

Twenty-five minutes of glorious comedy, this episode is *Frasier* at its best and we haven't even mentioned the superb twist ending . . .

2.11

'Seat Of Power'

Written by Steven Levitan
Directed by James Burrows
First UK Transmission: 08.09.95

Skyline: The elevator goes up the Space Needle.

Synopsis: Daphne is curiously keen on walking Eddie, despite the fact that the little chap is exhausted. It transpires that this is because she has seen a man playing frisbee in the park and wants to see more of him. Martin is concerned with more down-to-earth things – the toilet still isn't working properly and he asks Frasier to fix it. Frasier suggests calling a plumber but Martin thinks that's a waste of money and says he'll do it himself. Resigned, Frasier and Niles settle down to fix it because although 'we've conquered the intellectual world, in the world of nuts and bolts, we're at the mercy of tradesmen'.

Later, Frasier is attempting to follow the manual and fix the ballcock, while Niles is talking to Maris on the telephone, and coping with the fact that she is becoming aroused by the thought of Niles engaged in manual labour. Eventually they believe they have fixed it and, literally flushed with success, they see their happiness go down the pan as the toilet starts overflowing on to the floor.

Sometime afterwards 'the plumber's been called, the wine is chilled, suddenly my life makes perfect sense again'. Niles is happy. Until the plumber arrives – it is Danny Kriezel, who bullied Niles throughout their time at John Adams Junior High. Frasier points out that Danny hasn't recognised Niles, but Niles suggests that's maybe because he isn't stuffing his head down the toilet, flushing it and yelling, 'There goes Crane, down the drain.' Frasier remembers that Danny's older brother Billy was responsible for much of his fear at school (see 1.04, 'I Hate Frasier Crane'), particularly his fear of enclosed spaces from when Billy shoved him into a locker wearing a girl's field hockey uniform. Frasier tells Niles that their lifestyle is the best revenge, but Niles remains sceptical – good living is rarely a common revenge plot in opera.

However, in the bathroom he indeed begins to flaunt his lifestyle at an uninterested Danny – but then Danny actually has the better lifestyle, and certainly has a better Mercedes than Niles. Frasier arrives just in time to stop Niles flushing Danny's head down the toilet and instead persuades his younger brother to talk to Danny, to take this opportunity to put aside their differences and discuss the past rationally. Niles does this but Frasier suddenly finds himself confronted by his own nightmare – Billy Kriezel has arrived and natters away about how he once shoved a nerdy kid into a locker wearing a girl's field hockey uniform. Frasier must now try to follow the advice he gave Niles and not shove Billy's head down the toilet . . .

Guest Cast: Danny Kriezel (John G. McGinley), Billy Kriezel (Mike Starr).

Who's On The Line?: Elliott (Macaulay Culkin), who claims to be a forty-three-year-old businessman who is always being accused of sounding like a teenager. After Frasier apologises for making the same mistake, Elliott yells, 'Hah! Gotcha, Doctor Doofas . . .'

Subtitles: Heir To The Throne; If You Want It Done Right . . .; The Circle Of Life.

Strange Bedfellows: Roz has spotted a guy sitting behind her at a Seahawks game (they both have season tickets) and they've talked, but he hasn't asked her out yet. Roz thinks there may be something wrong with the back of her head. Frasier thinks that just maybe he's there to watch football.

Eddie Takes The Biscuit: Eddie stares Frasier down into giving him a scone. He also has a darn good drink from the toilet bowl.

Frasier Has Left The Building: Daphne, using the telescope to spot her man with the frisbee, wants to go out but Eddie cannot be found to provide an excuse. In the end, she goes alone.

On The Couch: It's almost as if they gave this writer a list of 'traditional' Frasier elements and got him to write a script without actually seeing an episode. Roz is man hungry. Eddie stares at Frasier to get his own way. Niles was bullied at school. Frasier hands out advice but never follows it himself. Martin is down to earth while his sons are too prissy to be mundane. Maris is bossy over the cellphone. And as a result of trying to cram all these clichés into one episode, and threading them around a rather tedious story as well, we are presented with possibly the least good episode (we hesitate to say 'worst' because there is no such thing really: 'worst' implies 'bad' and even at its lowest ebb, *Frasier* will always stand head and shoulders above other American sitcoms). It's difficult to put a finger on any single thing that doesn't work with this, and it's almost too easy (but very tempting) to say 'everything'. The Kriezels are uninteresting – in particular, the fact that Danny is a bully because of his father is just too normal to be a Frasier 'twist'. There's just something about this episode that simply fails to sparkle.

To look at its good points, though, there is a delightful moment when Frasier displays his multipurpose tool and Niles is immediately attracted by its turquoise inlay and Martin just shakes his head in despair. Or Niles's description of 'good living' as the ultimate revenge in opera: 'Ludwig, maddened by the poisoning of his entire family wreaks revenge on Gunthur in the third act by living well', and so forth. A very amusing moment, actually. Then there is Niles and Danny discussing their past and Niles pointing out that his case was a valise not an attaché case. 'Let's face it,' says Danny, trying to justify his bullying, 'when you turn up at school wearing a tweed blazer with elbow patches and carrying a valise, I mean I think the guilt here is fifty fifty!' Best of all is the 'circle of life' discussion, wherein the Cranes defend their place in society: 'By hiring a plumber, that plumber can afford, say, a Dolly Parton album. Ms Parton can then finance a national tour which will of course come to Seattle, allowing some local promoter to make enough money to send his cross-dressing teenage son to us for one-hundred-and-fifty-dollars-an-hour therapy!' And the ending is rather cute, a bit of a 'buddy' episode, as, working together on the toilet, Frasier and Martin bond in the same way that Niles and Frasier did earlier.

See, even the least good has some nice touches!

2.12

'Roz In The Doghouse'

Written by Chuck Ranberg and Anne Flett-Giordano
Directed by James Burrows
First UK Transmission: 15.09.95

Skyline: Lights go on in various buildings.

Synopsis: Roz has an accident at work (she trips over Bulldog) and badly sprains her ankle. This means she cannot get up from her bed now, so Frasier visits her there. And passes some work on to her to do. Bulldog also arrives, full of charm, although Roz is convinced he'll try to take advantage of her – 'You know what it's like in the jungle,' she says to a departing Frasier. 'They always go after the sick and the lame.' But no, what Bulldog does want is for her to leave Frasier's show and work for him. She's the best producer at KACL and he needs her . . .

When she tells Frasier this, he is immediately sceptical. He and Niles both assume that she and Bulldog slept together but this makes Roz angry – they didn't, and she feels it's about time she worked for someone who genuinely saw her worth. Frasier is still convinced that Bulldog is just working his way around to getting her into bed and Roz storms out (well, hobbles, really), claiming, 'The only mental disorder you've ever cured is insomnia!' 'Well, I'm surprised you had time to listen,' retorts Frasier, 'what with being so busy with your ultra-demanding producer tasks. Answering phones. Pushing buttons. My God, a cockatoo with a strong beak could do what you do!' Roz quits and goes to work for Bulldog.

Frasier goes through a variety of inappropriate new producers, while *The Gonzo Sports Show* goes from strength to strength with Roz and Bulldog's banter proving popular with everyone, even Gil Chesterton. All the time, however, Frasier is convinced it's just a matter of time before Bulldog reveals his true colours . . .

Weeks later, it still hasn't happened, and Daphne suggests it's time he swallowed his pride and apologised to Roz. 'It's not the same as Dad being wrong,' Frasier protests. 'Or your being wrong. I have a degree from Harvard and when I'm wrong, the world makes a little less sense.' Nevertheless he agrees to go to Roz's and apologise. He is unaware that Bulldog and Roz are there together, working out what they're going to do on the next show . . .

Guest Cast: Weird Bruce (Garett Maggart), Ed (Edward F. Gallick).

Where Everybody Knows Their Name: A riotous return for Bulldog (Dan Butler) in his biggest role yet, plus an all-too-brief return for Gil Chesterton (Edward Hibbert) who at least delights in not being able to invite Frasier to his party. And a mention of Maris's always unseen handyman Yoshi, who is guilty here of drunkenly destroying the Crane topiary.

Who's On The Line?: Marie (Carly Simon), who is pondering whether to go out with an older man. And when Bruce is in charge, he manages to lose a couple of manic depressives and cuts off Francesca (Rosie Perez) in mid-flow, which is unfortunate as she has a major fear of abandonment.

Subtitles: Bed And Bored; Niles Meets The Goatboy; You Can't Teach An Old Bulldog New Tricks.

Out Of Sight: Maris is unable to have any pets because 'she distrusts anything that loves her unconditionally'. The irony of this statement by Niles is not lost on anybody. Except him, of course.

Frasier Has Left The Building: Bulldog's new producer is Ed, who appears to have died during the broadcast.

On The Couch: A superb episode which leaves you forever wondering if Roz is right and Bulldog is being professional, or whether Frasier is right, and Bulldog is carefully waiting for the moment to strike. The fact that they're both wrong and right gives this one a marvellous dénouement and leads to one of the greatest closing lines of an episode ever, when Frasier smiles at Roz and says 'I'm listening . . .'

It's very nice to see Bulldog get a full episode to himself and this one really marks him down as a leading character (although it still takes until the fourth season before Dan Butler's credit moves to the title sequence rather than the end). The potential his character has for being more than just a sex-maniac sports jock is exploited fully here and with just the right amount of airtime. Like a good whisky distilled over a long time, the character of Bulldog has finally matured to the point where it can be savoured.

2.13

'Retirement Is Murder'

Written by Elias Davis and David Pollock
Directed by Alan Myerson
First UK Transmission: 22.09.95

Skyline: Nothing happens.

Synopsis: Martin is obsessed with a twenty-year-old case, the Weeping Lotus, he never solved while on the force (see 1.04, 'I Hate Frasier Crane', and 1.06, 'The Crucible'). He promised the victim's mother back then that one day he'd see the villain put away.

Frasier and Niles take him to a basketball game, but it still doesn't distract Martin's mind and he goes home to carry on trying to solve it. That evening, the boys return from a meal to find Martin still puzzling, and Daphne fills them in on the details, after Martin turns in for the night. Helen was murdered, the bullet entering her on a downward trajectory. As she lay dying, she wrote HELP in the dirt. A detective Shelby was the vice cop in charge of the case and the suspects include two ex-boyfriends, Clive Brisbane, the world-famous monkey trainer (his alibi was that he was at a racetrack and lots of people saw him), and Robatighe the logger, who was busy murdering someone else at the time.

Frasier begins to study the photographs and then it hits him. What if Brisbane murdered Helen by sending one of his trained monkeys to do it. The perfect alibi. They plan to wake Martin up and tell him, but Frasier realises that would not be fair. He has worked for years on the case and for Frasier to solve it would be adding insult to injury. Frasier rearranges the photos so that, by logical step-by-step deduction, Martin will come to the same conclusion. Awoken by the noise, Martin wanders over and indeed looks at the photos. Sure enough, it dawns on him . . . he's solved it.

The next day Frasier and Daphne await Martin's return from the precinct. He arrives, but downcast, saying the other guys thought he was mad. Martin is angry with himself: how could he have thought anything that stupid was the solution? Now he's a laughing stock. Frasier confesses it's partly his fault and explains how he arranged the photos to lead Martin to the same conclusion. Martin thanks him for his help, but it was still he who went to the police with the story . . .

A knock at the door and in come Martin's buddies from the force – he was right and the murderer has confessed everything. Martin, Daphne and Frasier are overjoyed. Martin refuses to take all the credit and makes Frasier tell his friends how he deduced the killer.

So Frasier begins to explain how the monkey did it – and then wonders why everyone, including Martin, is looking strangely at him . . .

Guest Cast: Al (Hale Porter), Sonics Fan (Randy Kovitz).

Where Everybody Knows Their Name: A return appearance for Martin's cop buddies Frank Collins (Ron Dean) and Leo (Bill Gratton). And a brief appearance by Bulldog (Dan Butler), who meets Niles for the first time and, commenting on his similarity to Frasier, laughs, 'Some gypsy put a curse on your family?'

Who's On The Line?: Marjorie (Mary Steenburgen), whom Frasier is helping to cure her vertigo.

Subtitles: Retirement Is Murder; Strangers In A Strange Land; Use A Monkey, Go To Jail.

Culture Vultures: 'What's the one thing better than an exquisite meal?' Frasier asks Niles as they return home from an excellent meal out. 'An exquisite meal with one tiny flaw we can pick at all night,' replies Niles. In this case it was the fact that the restaurant did not have any good cognacs.

Strange Bedfellows: Roz explains to Bulldog just why she has yet to succumb to his charms. 'When I do finally give in, I want us to enjoy it all the more. That is, if I'm not too distracted by the fact that every man on Earth has died.'

The Buddy Show: Lots of Martin's friends from the precinct come round to celebrate his successful closure of the Weeping Lotus case. Just why it's called the Weeping Lotus remains unclear. Lotus we can follow – geishas are often referred to as Lotus Blossom and it is suggested that Helen was not as innocent as one might want to think (Shelby the detective was a vice cop, after all). And that in turn prompts the questions: 'What was Helen doing to get a bullet wound of the sort implied here? And why is she Weeping?'

Eddie Takes The Biscuit: As soon as Frasier declares he's going out for a walk, Eddie is there, leash ready. He likes the rhododendrons on the north side of the park, apparently.

Frasier Has Left The Building: Frasier returns to find Daphne dead on the sofa, shot by Eddie.

On The Couch: A knockout show, in which once again Martin's chum Frank Collins gets to see Frasier failing miserably to deduce who the criminal is (see 1.16, 'Can't Tell A Crook By His Cover'). The killer was of course not the poor monkey at all, but Frasier's enthusiasm as he begins to suspect the monkey of any number of crimes that evening is suppressed hysteria at its very best. Daphne's initial sharing of the credit quickly evaporates as she twigs that the police don't think the monkey did it, but for Frasier it's too late. He is humiliated.

An excellent script masks the fact that no one ever actually says anything about the monkey between Frasier's initial deduction and his final explanation, so you can never be sure whether that was the story Martin relayed to the department or not. You suspect it isn't, but, as always with *Frasier*, you can rarely predict which way the story will go. Maybe it *was* the monkey.

A couple of nice observations during this episode: Niles has 'shy kidneys' and cannot use public urinals; and we see the beginning of the running gag where people think Niles is called Miles (Bulldog does it here). Oh, and a note to American sitcom writers: you're wrong – 'knocked me up' has exactly the same connotations in Britain as it does in Seattle.

2.14

'Fool Me Once, Shame On You'

Written by Christopher Lloyd
Directed by Philip Charles MacKenzie
First UK Transmission: 29.09.95

Skyline: The elevator goes up the Space Needle.

Synopsis: Niles is becoming increasingly agitated by rude people in Café Nervosa. People don't thank him for holding doors, or they bump past him. Roz joins him and Frasier with a video tape Frasier needs to return – an Angie Dickinson movie, naturally, rented for Martin's amusement – and Frasier puts it in his briefcase, which is subsequently stolen. A man who says he's a priest walks by with an identical case, so Frasier accosts him – trouble is, he really is a priest and it really is his case.

Frasier is back at home, phoning round trying to cancel his credit cards and not getting much joy. Eddie is staring at him and Frasier tells him to stop. 'I'm a humane man,' he explains, 'but right now I could kick a kitten through an electric fan.' Martin says Frasier is too trusting, but Frasier is sure this is a one-off – he's not going to change his life philosophy just because of one miscreant.

At the studio, Frasier puts out a plea for the thief to return his stuff (a dry-cleaning ticket inside the case means he's now lost his blue suit), and a man indeed calls and arranges to meet Frasier at Café Nervosa to return the case, which he says he's found (but minus the wallet).

Frasier and Niles wait in Café Nervosa, Niles angrily telling a woman customer not to push in front of him at the bar, until she smiles and he ends up buying her coffee. Niles is convinced Frasier is being taken for a ride, a point proven when the man fails to show up, but instead steals Frasier's car using the spare keys inside the briefcase.

A breakthrough occurs the next day when a woman, Denise, phones up after a night of passion, apparently with

Frasier. Realising the thief is using Frasier's name now, Frasier plays along with Denise, who is calling to cancel a date with 'Frasier'. Now he knows where the thief will be, Frasier goes down to meet his impostor . . .

Guest Cast: Phil (Nathan Lane), Heather (Joan McMurtrey), Priest (Bernard Kuby), Woman in café (Karen Person), Cop (James Willett).

Where Everybody Knows Their Name: The first appearance of the Café Nervosa waiter, played by Paul Cusimano.

Who's On The Line?: 'Nasty old Gertrude'. And Denise, taken in by Phil into thinking she has spent a passionate night with Frasier. No one is credited with supplying the voice of Denise, which is a little odd.

Subtitles: A Brief Case Of Love.

Culture Vultures: Frasier, in requesting that the thief return his stuff, points out that 'the double-breasted navy blue suit was meant to be worn with French cuffs and medium heel wing tips. You may be sick, but there's no reason why you shouldn't be stylish.' To make matters worse, when Frasier finally apprehends Phil, the thief, wearing this suit, Phil has taken up the hems – with staples!

Full-on Moon: If anyone has wondered just why we all love Daphne, this speech encapsulates everything that is wonderful, naive and dozy about her. Frasier and Martin are arguing about the general goodness, and otherwise, of mankind in cities today. 'This whole thing reminds me of when I first moved to London, and I was very mistrusting of people back then. I was convinced the way to stay out of harm's way was to walk the streets with my eyes cast down, never meeting anyone's glance. But finally I decided that was no way to live. One day I just lifted up my chin and took it all in. The change was amazing – there were sights I'd never seen, sounds I'd never heard. A tiny old man came up to me with a note in his hand. He needed help. I realised this was no city full of thieves and muggers. There were people here who needed me.

I took his note, read it, and to this day I can remember just what I said: "That's not how you spell 'fellatio'." ' A speech we feel should be printed in all guide books for London. If nothing else, it might increase the tourist trade a bit around Old Compton Street.

The Buddy Show: Charlie, a police buddy of Martin's, is keeping an eye out for Frasier's BMW.

Frasier Has Left The Building: Niles bumps into the attractive woman he bought the coffee for and she nicks his watch.

On The Couch: Quite a nice idea, but an episode with better one-liners than story. The idea of stealing someone's identity is hardly original, but it is carried off well here, simply because Phil is so totally unlike Frasier both physically and mentally. It stretches credulity a bit, when so many people seem to recognise Frasier by his voice, that Denise or Heather would assume that Phil was Frasier, but that's by the by really. The story is more of a morality play about trust and the decency of humans (well, all right, so it isn't, but let's pretend) and the juxtaposition of Frasier wanting to love everyone and getting irritated by the inconvenience of losing his case and the things he must do as a result is fun – not least because it gives us the wonderfully un-PC gag about the kitten and the electric fan.

Niles and Roz still aren't on the best of terms at the beginning of this episode, but by the end, they have found a level pitch they can co-exist on. The concept of Roz being part of the 'inner circle' only becomes a major force after this episode – sure we've seen her go out with the gang, or with just Daphne, but she still calls Martin 'Mr Crane' up until this point. It's a little milestone to have got past, but a nice one.

Oh, and it is established here that Café Nervosa is on the corner of Pike and 3rd.

2.15
'You Scratch My Book . . .'

Written by Joe Keenan
Directed by Andy Ackerman
First UK Transmission: 06.10.95

Skyline: A cloud passes above the skyline, and it rains.

Synopsis: Daphne has been reading the latest book by Dr Honey Snow, a self-help psychotherapy sort of thing. Frasier is naturally very dismissive of such trite rubbish, believing that it consists wholly of hugs, and nothing more than a belief in all-round goodness. Niles is similarly dismissive, and far more interested in selling his raffle tickets for Maris's opera group (see 2.10, 'Adventures in Paradise' (Part 2)). The first prize is the lead soprano Mrs Fitzgibbons coming to your home and performing 'Ride of the Valkyries'. Niles also has a new broker, Wendell, who is doing him some good on the stock market, and Daphne invests $500 on Wendell's forecasts and then asks Frasier to head down to the Book Nook, where Dr Honey Snow is doing a signing. With nothing better to do, he does so, along with Roz.

Honey Snow wants to meet Frasier and when he sees her, he has no problem hugging her tightly – she's a blonde nymphette with large breasts. Unsurprised at Frasier's sudden willingness to read her books, Roz departs.

Later Niles brings a cheque around to Daphne – Wendell's investments paid off, and Daphne is now $200 richer. She immediately hugs and kisses Niles and invests her winnings. Frasier is going to dinner with Honey, which Niles is appalled by. But Martin understands, saying any man alive would want her to analyse his dreams. 'Analyse them? She could star in them,' murmurs a smitten Frasier.

Honey arrives and flatters everyone and asks Frasier to write an introduction for her new book. Niles is delighted: he can't wait to see how Frasier gets out of having his name used to promote such twaddle. 'Just think,' Daphne says, 'by next fall, there'll be half a million copies in print, with your name right on the cover.' Niles grins evilly. 'I've got *my* Christmas shopping done!'

Two weeks later, Frasier is still trying to write the introduction, while Niles reads some of the ridiculous statements in the book: 'You don't need to be a star to twinkle' is bad enough, but Niles just adores 'Time is a concept known only to one of God's creatures – Man. Just for today, be a sunflower'. 'Frankly, I find it laughable that you're even considering putting your name on 500,000 copies of this piffle,' he says, then corrects himself. 'Not even piffle – this is piffle-lite!' Daphne then returns and Niles gives her another cheque from Wendell. A delighted Daphne rewards him with another round of hugs and kisses. When she's gone, Frasier points out that he too bought shares but they went down, which he finds bizarre. Niles confesses that the first winning was real but subsequent ones have been fraudulent. 'Niles, you are giving a woman money in exchange for physical affection. We're talking about the world's oldest profession. I admit this is sort of the Walt Disney version!'

At Honey's, Frasier finally tells her that he cannot write the introduction to her book, because he simply didn't like it. Honey is overjoyed at his honesty. Frasier, however, doesn't know when to stop . . .

Guest Cast: Dr Honey Snow (Shannon Tweed), Fan (Laura Waterbury).

Subtitles: Are There Any More Like You At The Institute?; You Scratch My Book . . .; Shrink Rap.

The Buddy Show: When he was a cop doing traffic duty, Martin used to see a gorgeous redhead who could flirt her way out of any ticket. His partner (Artie Walshe, perhaps?) was never taken in by her, however, which leads to Frasier noting that this is the famous 'Good cop, horny cop' routine.

Eddie Takes The Biscuit: Rolling on his back, Eddie appears to have little trouble finding his 'inner puppy'.

Frasier Has Left The Building: Niles, Daphne, Martin and a very alarmed Frasier try to appreciate Mrs Fitzgibbons's rendition of 'Ride of the Valkyries'.

On The Couch: While the Honey Snow story is a rather predictable bit of nonsense, the best moments in this very good episode concern Niles and his money-making broker, Wendell. Once he realises he's on to a winner with Daphne, he cannot help but ensure she makes cash, even when she really loses it. The ensuing argument between Niles and Frasier – because Niles points out that Frasier is lying to get physical affection from Honey Snow – is marvellous, especially as, having reached a stalemate, Frasier finally and desperately declares Niles is wrong because 'your woman is . . . English!' Niles just looks at his brother and quietly says, 'Frasier, you've lost this one.'

There's another nice running gag at the start of this show as Frasier keeps saying of various situations that he cannot do anything because 'I have my reputation to think of'. One by one the others in the show end this statement with 'Oh? What's the big deal?' Poor Frasier.

If anything lets the show down, it's the fact that, however desperate he is, Frasier has usually gone for brains over beauty and, for the relationship to have lasted the minimum two weeks it does here, there is little indication given that Honey Snow is in any way a pleasant person. Indeed, crap psychobabble aside ('Handshakes are just hugs for scaredy-cats' – I ask you!), there is very little beyond her being a Pamela Anderson clone that Frasier would normally go for. Either the sex was magnificent, or her best conversations with him all take place off screen.

2.16
'The Show Where Sam Shows Up'

Written by Ken Levine and David Isaacs
Directed by James Burrows
First UK Transmission: 20.10.95

Skyline: Lights go on in various buildings.

Synopsis: Sam Malone, baseball hero, is in town, claiming that he's coming in to see about a job with the Mariners. He comes to dinner at Frasier's place, where they catch up on old times, and Sam meets Martin (who he thought was dead) and Niles (who he thought didn't exist). He gets on well with Daphne, much to Niles's annoyance, so Frasier fills Niles in – Sam is a sexual compulsive and has been receiving treatment. Martin is completely bowled over to have such an important baseball celeb in his home and insists on Sam sitting in his chair. The phone rings – it's a woman called Sheila who, Sam confesses, is someone he was due to marry. Yesterday. When they're alone, Frasier and Sam talk about Sheila and how bad Sam feels about leaving her at the altar, but he suddenly wondered if he was ready for commitment. Frasier talks to him, and Sam realises he's made a mistake. He resolves to call Sheila and go ahead with the wedding.

The next day at Café Nervosa, Frasier, Niles and Roz are waiting for the happy couple, but when Sam brings Sheila in and introduces her, she says she's very tired and would rather head to the hotel to freshen up before dinner. After they've gone, Frasier tells the others that he and Sheila slept together three months ago – three months after she and Sam got engaged.

Frasier goes to Sheila's hotel room and she is apologetic. She too is a sexual compulsive but is getting over it and really wants her marriage with Sam to work. Frasier agrees never to tell Sam about their tryst, but then Sam returns. He's pleased that Frasier is there because he has a confession to make to

Sheila – he slept with someone else after they got engaged. Sheila, impressed by Sam's honesty, then decides to confess an equal sin to Sam, and Frasier realises he's about to get caught out . . .

Guest Cast: Sheila (Tea Leoni).

Where Everybody Knows Their Name: With Sam Malone (Ted Danson) in town, well, it's time to play Catch Up With the *Cheers* Characters here. Obviously we already know about Lilith, but, like Frasier, we've been intrigued to know what happened to our Boston pals. Sam tells us that Rebecca married Don, that plumber she fancied. He became very rich after inventing a low-flow toilet system, and then dumped her. Rebecca is now back at the bar, but drinking there, not working. Woody and Kelly had a little boy who, thankfully, did not inherit their intelligence genes. Norm is as one might expect, still propping up the bar, but after reading an article about a flesh-eating bacterium, Cliff hasn't left his mom's house. No mentions of Carla or Diane. And of course, we later discover that Sheila has been working her way through the *Cheers* regulars, including obviously, Frasier, but also Paul and even Cliff!

Subtitles: Martin Rises From The Dead; A Dirty Little Secret.

Strange Bedfellows: Unsurprisingly, Roz is immediately attracted to Sam and offers to show him around Seattle if he gets lost. He says he has no problem with the city, but tends to get lost in his hotel room . . .

Full-on Moon: Daphne spends most of this episode making unintelligible little giggly noises every time Sam so much looks at her. Fab.

Out Of Sight: Maris was delighted to discover that, when Niles was sweating all through their wedding, it wasn't nerves but just a congenital heart murmur. What a sweetheart, eh?

Frasier Has Left The Building: Having dropped Sam off at the airport, Frasier is driving home, still unable to get over the fact that he slept with a woman who had previously slept with Cliff!

On The Couch: What an amazing episode – everything you needed to round off *Cheers* and still provide Frasier viewers with one of the best episodes yet. From a purely trivial side, this episode finally addresses the fact that, when he was propping up the Cheers bar, Frasier never mentioned he had a brother and claimed both his parents died when he was in his early thirties. If Martin is annoyed at that (the explanation being that he and Martin had rowed on the phone just before he told Sam about his home life), he is even more disgusted to realise that Sam had been led to believe that, rather than a cop, Martin Crane had been a research scientist. Frasier's argument was that as he was dead, the truth hardly seemed to matter.

The other great moment in this episode is the revelation that Frasier slept with Sheila – more often than not, great disasters in the series are signposted beforehand, so the viewer can get maximum squirming time, but here it is just thrown in as a shock ending to a scene, and works all the better for it.

2.17
'Daphne's Room {a.k.a. A Room With A View}'

Written by Linda Morris and Vic Rauseo
Directed by David Lee
First UK Transmission: 27.10.95

Skyline: A helicopter rises up from the skyline and departs.

Synopsis: Frasier, against the advice of his father, steals into Daphne's room to retrieve a book that he was lent by the station manager. While there, he cannot resist having a little nose around, finding, among other things, a photo of Daphne with Prince Charles and a bottle of pills. Before he can leave, Daphne returns and Frasier is caught red-handed. He slips the pills into his pocket and makes his exit in shame.

After apologising profusely, Daphne forgives him. The only problem now is that he realises he must get the pills back into the room before Daphne has to take one later that evening. Daphne announces to Martin that it is time for his exercises, and Frasier sees his chance – but Martin refuses to exercise, and (after a lengthy game of cat and mouse) Frasier is caught again. This time, though, Daphne is in the shower and it seems that Frasier can do nothing to make sure that she doesn't quit her job and leave.

Where Everybody Knows Their Name: Since the book is a history of English theatre focusing on Sir Henry Beerbohm Tree, we can only assume that it belongs to Tom Duran, the gay KACL station manager (see 2.03, 'The Matchmaker'). And Niles makes a dig at both of Frasier's failed marriages.

Another of Maris's functionaries gets a namecheck: this time it's Nadia, her 'hatchet maid', who is refusing to let Niles talk to her on the phone.

Subtitles: To Boldly Go Where No Man Has Gone Before; Indiana Crane and the Disposal of Doom; Peace at Any Cost.

Culture Vultures: When Daphne announces that she plans to have her room decked out in a pink-and-yellow colour scheme, Frasier laments that 'she's really determined to keep me out of there'.

Strange Bedfellows: Two fascinating facts for your Roz fact file. She can sense when a man has recently had sex, and she would have sex for a Mercedes. Neither terribly surprising, really.

Full-on Moon: More family history revealed. It was a 'rite of passage' for seven of Daphne's brothers to sneak into the bathroom and catch a glimpse of her naked. The eighth brother, Billy, the ballroom dancer, snuck a peek at another brother, Nigel, instead.

Out Of Sight: As Maris requested, Niles did nothing to celebrate her fortieth birthday. Maris has, therefore, gone into a sulk. Martin suggests buying a present for her in recompense but perfume makes her come out in a rash, she can't eat candies because she's hypoglycaemic, and she's allergic to roses. When he suggests just grabbing her, bending her over and giving her a huge kiss, Niles says, 'She has abnormally rigid vertebrae. She'd snap like a twig.' Frasier wonders what all the fuss is about – after all, it's not the first time she's turned forty. Oh, and we discover that an entire branch of her family tree were slaughtered by the Huguenots.

Eddie Takes The Biscuit: When Martin announces that Eddie will do whatever he says, Frasier grabs his tail to stop him running when called just to prove his father wrong.

In the rugby-scrum chaos at the end of the episode, when everyone piles into Daphne's room, Eddie stares at the returning Daphne; there's a guilty look on his face, and a bra in his mouth.

Frasier Has Left The Building: Daphne, in her room again, checks every last corner and cupboard to make sure that she is alone. She finds Eddie buried under a pile of towels on the bed.

On The Couch: Another episode in a farcical vein, and one that works terribly well. Niles's rant about having to be restrained when thinking of entering Daphne's room is brilliant; Grammer puts on a great show when Frasier is caught as Daphne is about to take a shower; Niles desperately trying to find any excuse to follow Frasier when he is going to see Daphne – all of it marvellous. It's full of some of the best lines the series has seen, too. This is an episode where the women come top again: Roz's few lines are perfect; Daphne's mocking acceptance of her position as a 'servant' with no privacy really puts Frasier in his place; and all the discussions about buying Maris's forgiveness are great. And – at last – Niles sleeps with his wife!

NB: Although the episode's correct title is 'Daphne's Room', UK listings magazines referred to it as 'A Room With A View', hence the dual title.

2.18
'The Club'

Written by Elias Davis and David Pollock
Directed by David Lee
First UK Transmission: 03.11.95

Skyline: Fireworks explode over the skyline.

Synopsis: Niles arrives at Frasier's studio with good news: he has been invited to lunch at one of Seattle's most exclusive establishments, the Empire Club. An opening has arisen in the membership, and Niles has decided to go for it. Frasier is initially a little jealous, but he soon receives good news – another member of the club has been indicted in a finance scandal, so there are now two vacancies. It seems the Crane brothers are both about to have a dream come true.

They arrive at the club, and things seem to be going well, until they are told that the indicted member has had the charges against him dropped. There is now only one membership up for grabs, and Frasier and Niles begin to fight dirty to get it.

The next day, Niles receives a call telling him that he has been passed over for membership: Frasier is in. Racked with guilt, Frasier decides that he can't possibly accept his place in the Empire Club, so heads over to tell them to give his place to Niles. But there's been a mix-up, and a hot-headed Niles has no idea . . .

Guest Cast: Mr Drake (W. Morgan Sheppard), Mr Spencer (Mitchell Edmonds), Wentworth (Jim Norton).

Where Everybody Knows Their Name: Again, the episode of *Cheers* where Frasier once went out on a window ledge in an effort to get Lilith's attention ('The Girl in the Bubble', Part Two) is brought up. When Niles uses this against him at the club, Frasier responds by telling everyone the story about an anarchist-loving Niles who mooned President Nixon.

Who's On The Line?: Sid (Gary Sinise) lacks confidence when using the telephone, to the point where he has to read out everything he says from a prepared script.

Subtitles: The Crane Scrutiny; He Ain't Heavy . . . He's My Brother.

Culture Vultures: The whole episode is one long snob-fest, with the brothers cooing after the promise of a place in the Empire Club. Their rapture at the softness of the club's leather chairs is something you must see to believe.

Strange Bedfellows: Roz thinks she can pull a few strings to get Frasier closer to membership. She apparently knows Walter Strickland Snr, which both mystifies and awes Frasier. How did she get to know Mr Strickland? 'The less you know, the happier you'll be.'

Full-on Moon: Daphne's Uncle Harold was famous for naming parts of his body after members of the royal family. He had quite a happy life, Daphne says, until 'Aunt Kate caught him introducing the Prince of Wales to a cocktail waitress'.

Out Of Sight: As they prepare to leave for the cocktail party at the club, Frasier asks Niles where Maris is. She is apparently waiting in the car, 'practising her vivacious giggle'. At the party, she leaves the brothers to it while she subtly tries to sabotage the wives of the other candidates by swamping them in hors d'oeuvre.

Eddie Takes The Biscuit: Martin wastes Frasier's imported prosciutto by offering it to Eddie if he will perform new tricks.

Frasier Has Left The Building: Eddie sits and begs at Frasier, who offers him a piece of the ham. He begs again, and an exasperated Frasier offers him the whole plateful of prosciutto.

On The Couch: An entertaining episode that, despite the focus on the brothers, still has plenty for the other cast members to get their teeth into. One of the best sibling-rivalry moments of the series comes when Frasier is told that he has got into the club. He explains to Niles that he can't be happy about it, knowing that his brother has lost out. Niles graciously leaves Café Nervosa, wishing Frasier congratulations. Once he has gone, Frasier starts whooping for joy and offers everyone a coffee. Just as Niles walks back in.

It is a strange fault of the series, though, that Frasier and Niles are never as funny when removed from the real world of the series and put somewhere else (a similar thing is evident in 1.22, 'Author, Author'). It is their snobbery that creates their comedy: when they are surrounded by similar snobs, or even bigger snobs, we begin to lose sympathy for them. Nevertheless, their sniping at each other can be very amusing.

2.19

'Someone to Watch Over Me'

Written by Don Seigel
Directed by James Burrows
First UK Transmission: 10.11.95

Skyline: A streak of lightning crosses the sky.

Synopsis: Frasier and Roz have done it again – their show has been nominated for a prestigious SeaBee Award for the second year running (see 1.18, 'And The Whimper Is . . .'). Frasier continues to glow in adoration when his number-one fan, Kari, phones to tell him how wonderful he is. He's really quite touched by this, until he begins to suspect that Kari is a bit touched herself: she manages to sneak a home-knitted scarf into his briefcase, and a note into his jacket, before sending a bunch of congratulatory balloons to his apartment. She tells him that she will be looking out for him at the SeaBee Awards ceremony, and Frasier begins to think that he needs some sort of protection.

The evening of the award comes, and Frasier sets out with his family and his new bodyguard, Cindy. But the paranoia is beginning to drive him to distraction. Who could the stalker be? It could be anyone at the ceremony. It could be the head of the nomination board. It could even be Cindy. Will Frasier get through the evening intact?

Guest Cast: Cindy Carruthers (Alyson Reed), Kari (Renee Lippin), Mrs Littlejohn (Rita McKenzie).

Where Everybody Knows Their Name: Bulldog (Dan Butler) is on fine form. He's received a nomination too (his fourth since 1991) and, when he arrives at the ceremony, makes moves on Cindy. Her initial reaction (to strangle him and threaten him with death) turns him on, until it looks like she might really mean it. We also hear about KACL's Leo the Happy Chef, who also had a stalker who eventually managed to break into his house.

Who's On The Line?: At the beginning of the episode, Frasier is assuring Brian that there's no such thing as a born scatterbrain, which Brian suspects he is. All Brian needs to do is be a little more focused and concentrate on one thing at a time. Frasier can't follow his own advice, though, as he suddenly breaks away from the call when he hears about the SeaBee nomination.

Later, Frasier decides to suffer more glowing praise from Kari, rather than help a compulsive shoplifter from Bainbridge with their problem.

And Madman Martinez (John Lithgow) phones in with a fake problem, in order to get free advertising for his second-hand-car dealership.

Subtitles: Getting A Bit Loopy; Krakatoa, West Of Java (The Movie Was Wrong); Someone To Watch Over Me; The Lady In Red.

Culture Vultures: Frasier and Niles announce with glee, and in unison, that they are going to see a performance of *Der Fliegende Holländer* (Wagner's *The Flying Dutchman*).

Strange Bedfellows: Roz intends to wallow in the nomination – in the back seat of her limo with her date, regardless of what this does to her hair. That is, until the pimple arrives and she has to head to the awards dateless . . .

Full-on Moon: Daphne has a psychic flash about Cindy when they meet – her grandfather, she senses, had a steel plate in his head. Cindy's only response is to ask Frasier whether Kari had a noticeable accent.

Out Of Sight: Tragedy strikes Maris. She can't make it to the awards because her manicurist has been taken critically ill, and she won't be seen in public without perfect nails. Besides, she is still probably feeling a little jealous of Frasier – isn't she, she asks Niles, important enough to need a bodyguard too?

Eddie Takes The Biscuit: A difficult time for Eddie this episode, as he is terrified by both Cindy and the voice of Kari.

Frasier Has Left The Building: Frasier (dishevelled after inadvertently getting into a scrap in a car park) and Roz (her face covered in hair to hide a spot that looks like a 'biblical plague') step up to the podium to accept their award.

On The Couch: Roz is, without doubt, the funniest thing in this episode. She goes on a crash diet to lose weight in time for the awards, only to get to the day and find a huge spot has erupted on the end of her nose. Her increasingly bizarre efforts to do something about it (putting a cold tea bag on the spot, hiding behind a programme while she waits for Frasier at the ceremony) are great, but the final solution – to sweep her hair down over her face – is the best.

Otherwise, this episode suffers from being a tad predictable. Of course Frasier is going to suspect his own bodyguard and, of course, Kari will turn out to be harmless when we meet her. Although it has some funny moments, this episode's entertainment seems to be at the expense of its intelligence. And ours.

2.20
'Breaking The Ice'

Written by Steven Levitan
Directed by Philip Charles MacKenzie
First UK Transmission: 17.11.95

Skyline: The light atop the Space Needle glows.

Synopsis: Roz is in a dilemma: she accidentally said 'I love you' to a man, and he didn't return the favour. This sets Frasier wondering. He has never heard his father say those words to him, though he hears Martin tell both Eddie and his friend Duke that he loves them. A worried Frasier stands by as Niles agrees to accompany his father on an ice-fishing trip to Canada, and soon realises that his one chance to hear Martin say 'I love you' may rest on his accompanying them.

When they arrive at the lake, things go from bad to worse, as Frasier's mood steadily gets darker and darker. They lose the keys to Niles's car, stranding them in their cabin for the night. Their only relief is Martin's bottle of Jim Beam, which could well prove to be the key to Frasier's salvation . . .

Guest Cast: Ranger (Rick Cramer).

Subtitles: Roz Doyle And The Temple Of Doom; I Only Have Ice For You; Proof That Hell Really Does Freeze Over.

Culture Vultures: When Martin first suggests to Frasier that he take Duke's place on the fishing trip, Frasier tries to get out of it by offering to take his father to a performance of *The Iceman Cometh*, arguing that it follows a similar theme to the fishing trip.

Niles's excitement at the fishing trip is blissfully funny. He describes himself as 'a man of the Great Al Fresco', and reassures everyone that he'll be able to keep warm as he's dressed in layers – 'Polo, Eddie Bauer and Timberland'.

Stranded in the cabin on the frozen lake, Martin and his sons turn to whisky and drinking songs to get them through the evening. Frasier suggests a great aria from *La Traviata*, but Niles insists that the piece comes from *Rigoletto*. Once the argument is resolved, they even manage to get their father joining in and enjoying it.

Strange Bedfellows: Roz has accidentally said 'I love you' to a man. He was licking a certain spot behind her ear, and she meant to scream 'I love that' but it came out wrong. When he didn't repeat the words back to her, Roz knew that she was in trouble. But, she reasons, surely 'it's just polite' to tell someone you love them if they say it to you.

Full-on Moon: Daphne remembers the times her brothers' friends would go out fishing. She would watch them returning, ruddy and 'so masculine – I just couldn't wait to pan-fry their kippers.'

We also hear about a nameless aunt of Daphne's 'who used to say "Goodnight, Mr Vanderpump" to a hat rack'.

Out Of Sight: Is Niles not frightened about spending a night in the snowy wilds? Apparently not: he has seen the rehearsals of Maris's interpretative dance troupe, and now 'the wilderness holds no terror'.

While wondering if their father could tell them that he loves them, Frasier asks Niles whether it would be nice to hear Maris say 'I love you'. 'I imagine it would be,' is his response, 'but let's stick to attainable goals.'

The Buddy Show: Though he is unheard, Martin's old pal, the owner of his favourite (now demolished) bar, Duke, calls to cancel their fishing trip.

Frasier Has Left The Building: Daphne's peaceful weekend alone comes to an end as the Crane boys arrive home. Martin and Frasier file in, carrying half a dozen fish each, and they are greeted with a peck on the cheek. A sheepish Niles follows behind, his one measly fish hanging from a hook. Daphne kisses him anyway.

On The Couch: For an American sitcom episode revolving around the theme of familial love, 'Breaking The Ice' manages never to wallow in schmaltz or sugary sweetness. Of course it all ends happily – Martin tells both Frasier and Niles that he loves them, and they return the sentiment – but Martin has to chug a lot of whisky and look away from his sons before he can say the words. Also, by giving those three words their suitable gravitas, the episode avoids the trap of using them as horrible, saccharine, throwaway lines. The final scenes in the cabin are really quite affecting: both touching and funny.

David Hyde Pierce shines in this episode, as a Niles desperate to get closer to his father. Throwing himself into the fishing trip wholeheartedly, he quickly learns all he can about the lake, and the fish in it. His constant fact-dropping really gets on Frasier's nerves, but it shows how far he is willing to go to make a connection with his father.

2.21

'An Affair To Forget'

Written by Chuck Ranberg and Anne Flett-Giordano
Directed by Philip Charles MacKenzie
First UK Transmission: 24.11.95

Skyline: Fireworks explode over the skyline.

Synopsis: Just another day at KACL. Frasier receives a call from Gretchen, a woman with a thick European accent, who is convinced that her fencing-teacher husband, Gunnar, is having an affair with one of his pupils, although she has no evidence. Before Frasier can attempt to help, Roz butts in and suggests a foolproof way of finding out whether he has been unfaithful. Offer him two choices for dinner: if he picks the fattening one, then he doesn't care how fat he gets and is happily married; if he picks the low-fat meal, then some-thing's up. Gretchen rings off, promising to do just that.

Back home, Frasier is talking to Niles and discovers that Maris has taken up fencing lessons with a Bavarian instructor, and is often working at them way into the night. Frasier becomes immediately suspicious and the next day, when Gretchen calls the show again, he digs for more proof that Gunnar is having an affair with Maris.

Convinced now that Maris is cheating on Niles, Frasier heads over to her house to confront her about it. Once he's there, Marta shows Frasier into a room where she says 'Missy Crane' is inside a sensory-deprivation tank. Frasier then proceeds to tell Maris that he knows she is having an affair and that she should come out of the tank and talk to him about it. When she is not forthcoming, Frasier whips the door of the tank open, only to discover that Marta has got her pronouns mixed up and 'Missy' is actually a deeply shocked 'Mister' Crane.

Now Niles's honour has been impeached, he decides that the only thing to do is confront Gunnar and fight for his wife. Let the swashbuckling commence!

Guest Cast: Gunnar (Brian Cousins).

Where Everybody Knows Their Name: More mention is made of Lilith's infidelity, and also a series of articles she wrote with Frasier – ironically about the keys to a successful marriage. (She got half of them in the divorce settlement.) We also hear again about Hester's affair with Stan Lawlor (see 1.08, 'Beloved Infidel').

This is another appearance for Marta (Irene Olga Lopez), who is familiar with the German tongue. She worked as a maid for an emigrant German family shortly after the war. Surely not . . . Well, it would explain why she can bear to work for Maris.

Who's On The Line?: Apart from the distraught Gretchen (Glenne Headley), the only other caller we hear about is a man who has just discovered that his girlfriend is his long-lost sister. Frasier, however, doesn't want to hear about his problem: he's more interested in Gretchen's call. He tells Roz to tell him to 'relax, we've all been there'.

Subtitles: Bavarians At The Gate; In Case You're Wondering, It's A Sensory Deprivation Tank; Get Out Your Dictionaries.

Culture Vultures: Alcoholic snobbery must prevail, even in the most desperate of situations. Niles arrives at Frasier's, devastated at his wife's apparent cheating, and Martin suggests that Frasier get him a brandy. But he's all out, and he proceeds to reel off a list of all the other drinks he has available.

Full-on Moon: Daphne reveals that she had an ancestor who was one of the mutineers on the HMS *Bounty*. She now has fantasies about some young lookalike of hers running along the beach of some tropical island, naked and heavily tanned. For a moment, Niles shares those fantasies.

We also hear about her brothers' interest in model kits – although she suspects they were only in it for the glue sniffing.

Out Of Sight: As you'd expect, there are plenty of Maris mentions this episode. Gunnar, in his unrequited love letters, calls her his 'little liver dumpling', and gives her a name that translates only as 'not quite human woman'.

We hear about the time Frasier confronted her over the political correctness of serving veal at the dinner table – this led to her trying to commit suicide.

And Martin bitingly comments, when he discovers that Maris is learning German, 'Just when you thought she couldn't get any cuddlier.'

Eddie Takes The Biscuit: He pitches in when Martin and Frasier are comforting Niles, and offers his own little lick of support. Niles's only response is to nearly sit on him, twice, later in the same scene.

Frasier Has Left The Building: Celebrating his still-happy marriage, Niles joins Maris in the deprivation tank, bringing her champagne and a rose.

On The Couch: As you'd expect from an episode that won the series an Emmy, this is prime *Frasier*. The absolute highlight is the confrontation between Gunnar and Niles. Gunnar speaks only German; Marta speaks German and Portuguese; Frasier speaks Portuguese and English; Niles speaks only English. The quick-fire translations from one end to the other are hysterical. The ensuing sword fight – a pastiche of every swashbuckling epic you've seen – is perfect, and even includes Niles swinging from a chandelier. Once again, *Frasier* marries impeccable physical comedy with a mercilessly witty script.

2.22
'Agents in America, Part Three'

Written by Joe Keenan
Directed by Philip Charles MacKenzie
First UK Transmission: 01.12.95

Skyline: A helicopter rises up from the skyline and departs.

Synopsis: Bebe Glazer, Frasier's agent, is back in town. She's affronted by the new contract Frasier has negotiated – he has been offered only an eight-per-cent rise, but Bebe thinks she can get him thirty to forty per cent. In order for her renegotiations to be a success, though, Frasier has to play along with her plan: he feigns an illness that keeps him away from work. But KACL know that the illness is fake. And Frasier knows that they know. And they know Frasier knows that they know . . .

As time drags on, Frasier begins to get increasingly worried that the gambit has failed and he is out of a job. His possessions are brought back to his apartment, and new people are being auditioned for his slot. Bebe tells him not to worry but, in a skewed effort to ease Frasier's mind, she phones the station manager Tom Duran and demands a decision by midnight. The long wait begins.

At five minutes to midnight, a desperate Frasier receives a call from KACL – they are going to open renegotiations in the morning. Delighted, Bebe and Frasier celebrate with a few bottles of champagne and, in the heat and excitement of the night, one thing leads to another . . .

Guest Cast: Mike (Tony Crane).

Where Everybody Knows Their Name: Of course, Harriet Sansom Harris is back as Bebe (complete with her trademark 'Wink!'), and on top form. Her performance on the window-sill of Tom Duran's office is breathtaking: spurned by Frasier after their night of passion and just before she must negotiate his new wage, she threatens suicide – but it's all a ploy to make Frasier look even more indispensable. Daunted by her craziness, Niles can offer only one piece of advice for Frasier on the topic of Bebe: 'She's the devil, Frasier. Run fast, run far.'

Eric Lutes as Tom Duran (see 2.03, 'The Matchmaker') makes his second and final appearance. And Bulldog (Dan Butler) is back, desperate for Frasier to save Bebe's life – his contract is soon to run out, and she's his agent too. We also hear the first mention of Ma Nature, a possible replacement show for Frasier's. At some time in the future Ma obviously gets a job at KACL.

Passing mentions for Father Mike, the Happy Chef and Nanette from *Pet Chat*, both of whom earn more than Frasier

– despite the fact that Father Mike has taken a vow of poverty.

Subtitles: Frasier Crane, Mambo King; It's Like Swan Lake, Only Deeper.

Culture Vultures: Hysteria hits the wine club, as the club president Reggie Belnap dies. Everyone is scrabbling for his position, and Maris is only just managing to keep on top of the competition. She has incriminating evidence against another contender, however. She has pictures of Matthew Pym's wedding, clearly showing that the champagne he served was not merely domestic, but from Connecticut.

Frasier's critique of daytime soaps is well scripted: 'Oh, Zirconia! Can't you see? Stone doesn't love you, he loves Placenta!' As Daphne points out, 'I don't think someone called Frasier should be pointing any fingers.'

Out Of Sight: After much argy-bargy, Maris receives the honour of presidency of the wine club. On her inaugural trip to a vineyard, though, disaster strikes as she tries out the stomping vat – she can't crush even one grape.

Eddie Takes The Biscuit: Frasier extricates himself from the sticky situation of having slept with Bebe and makes sure that it will never happen again. After he has bid a disappointed Bebe goodbye, Eddie just stares accusingly at him. 'Oh,' growls Frasier, 'like you never crawled under the wrong fence once in your life.'

Frasier Has Left The Building: Niles sits alone in Café Nervosa and explains to Bebe that Frasier is not there. Once she has gone, Frasier appears from his hiding place behind the counter.

On The Couch: Harriet Sansom Harris once again brings a sparkly edge to an episode and, as Bebe, wreaks yet more complicated havoc upon Frasier's life. Her tireless disrespect for other people is wonderful: treating Daphne as nothing more than a maid, completely blanking Niles, even fooling Frasier into thinking she has become suicidal. Her constant manipulation is frightening but, as she points out to Frasier, she's just the kind of person you want working for you.

2.23

'The Innkeepers'

Written by David Lloyd
Directed by James Burrows
First UK Transmission: 08.12.95

Skyline: The elevator goes up the Space Needle.

Synopsis: Gil Chesterton announces on air that Orcini's, one of the Crane boys' favourite restaurants, is to close (Niles was taken there by his grandfather for his eighth birthday and, even then, was quite happy to send the food back because it failed to meet his exacting taste). Niles and Frasier take Daphne and Martin for a last meal there only to realise that, with their touch, they could make it a money-spinner. The 'Happy Brothers' then buy the lease and put their skills to the test on the opening night.

However, neither is quite satisfied. For a start, the Cherry Jubilee lacks enough brandy (although neither realises the other is regularly topping it up) and they have different views on how to serve soufflé. 'When people hear the name "Niles Crane", I want them to think "big soufflé",' he tells Maurice, the temperamental French chef. Trouble is, within a short while, Maurice has quit, two of the staff are unconscious and the rest scarper when Niles lets slip that the Head of the Immigration Bureau is seated outside.

Faced with impending disaster, Frasier allots Niles to be sous-chef, Daphne his kitchen helper, Martin to serve drinks and Roz to wait at table. But just as he thinks everything is going to be all right, Gil Chesterton arrives with a party of restaurant critics, Niles chucks a toaster into the eel tank and Roz lights the Cherry Jubilee . . .

Guest Cast: Otto (Nathan Davis), Owner (Mike Nussbaum), Maurice (Jay Bell), Sous-chef (Alan Shearman), Waiter (Robert Lee Jacobs), Barman (Tom Hewitt), Brad (Diedrich Bader), Customer (Deborah Lacey).

Where Everybody Knows Their Name: Gil Chesterton (Edward Hibbert) 'the grand dame of Seattle', is responsible for warning Frasier that Orcini's is closing – he is also responsible for Frasier electing not to tell his patrons the truth about his staffing problems and thus is indirectly responsible for the disasters that ensue. Bulldog (Dan Butler) also heads to Frasier's eatery, along with his latest female friend who, he clearly suggests, is a . . . well, a lady of the night.

Subtitles: Les Freres Heureux; No Eels Were Harmed During The Making Of This Episode.

Culture Vultures: Frasier, rueful after Martin has criticised him once again, looks at the Orcini's menu and says he'd order the crab cocktail for his father 'but I'm afraid the irony would be lost on him'.

Strange Bedfellows: 'My typical date's idea of a gourmet evening,' explains Roz to Frasier, 'is take-out, make out and home by *Letterman*.' Roz is going out with Brad, who seems nice enough and probably isn't in a hurry to watch *Letterman*, although he is rather too quick to order bread and butter from the restaurant's new 'waitress'. Roz also gets a delightful revenge on Niles who, upon being asked if he's heard which thriving Seattle night spot is closing, just quips 'Roz? You're moving?' He subsequently realises he should never let Roz near his antique books again!

Full-on Moon: Daphne has an aunt who ran a teashop and at various points lopped a finger off with a cleaver, scalded herself, gagged over a grease fire, killed rats and brawled with labour racketeers. Par for the course where the Moon family is concerned, really.

Out Of Sight: Maris cannot go to Orcini's after she had a bad Christmas experience there. She was seated at a table adjoining that of an Italian soccer team, and said she was in the mood for a goose. 'And, perhaps inevitably,' says Niles, 'tragedy occurred.'

The Buddy Show: While on the beat, Martin remembers a corner restaurant that changed hands twenty times in ten years. Among its incarnations were Lin Fong's Lychee Palace, Tony's Meatball Hutch and A Little Taste of Yorkshire. Niles puts this down not to mistiming or bad placement but a tacky choice of names.

Frasier Has Left The Building: Bulldog, semi-clothed, staggers out of 'the grotto' and finds some wine and flowers among the wreckage, before returning to his date.

On The Couch: Knowing the *Frasier* production team's predilection for anything British, one can only assume that they opted to forget *Frasier* for a week and instead make *Carry On Restaurant*. Never reaching the level of out-and-out farce, if you replaced Frasier with Kenneth Williams, Niles with Charles Hawtrey, Daphne with Barbara Windsor, Martin with Sid James and Otto with Bernard Bresslaw, you've got the perfect saucy film. Trouble is, this is another case of taking the characters away from what makes *Frasier* work and putting them in a frankly ludicrous situation that lacks any credibility.

That's not to say that, on a strictly *Carry On . . .* level, this doesn't have moments of genius (indeed, Daphne's method of killing eels is one of the best scenes ever in a *Frasier* episode), but they are too few and far between. For the most part, it's a case of holding your breath and waiting for the next astonishing disaster to occur.

There are one or two traditional *Frasier* gems – both Otto and Maurice are great (Jay Bell looks as if he's genuinely trying not to laugh at David Hyde Pierce's amazingly OTT camp performance at one point), and Frasier's shrewd observation that the French don't have a word for 'lightheartedness' is pomposity at its best. But the true glory is the very last line . . .

2.24
'Dark Victory'

Written by Christopher Lloyd, Linda Morris and Vic Rauseo
Directed by James Burrows
First UK Transmission: 15.12.95

Skyline: Lights go on in various buildings (a touch of irony here, we feel).

Synopsis: It's the end of another long week for Frasier, and he is looking forward to heading home for his father's birthday party, to make up for the fact that he and Niles forgot it last year (see 1.24, 'My Coffee With Niles'). Before he leaves the studio, Roz receives a package containing cheese from her family's reunion in Wisconsin. She admits to Frasier that she's very upset that she can't be with them, so Frasier offers for her to come along to Martin's party to cheer herself up.

Roz, however, walks in on a less than cheery atmosphere. Daphne and Martin are arguing because the latter refuses to do his exercises, and Daphne is beginning to wonder whether she should just move out and get her own place. Niles, meanwhile, has a bone to pick with Frasier. Earlier that day, Frasier received a call to his show from a woman who was complaining that she thought she had reached the end of the road with her current therapist. Frasier suggested that she perhaps find another, only to discover later that she was one of Niles's patients.

Just when it seems things can't get any worse, the whole of Seattle is hit by a total blackout. Frasier is trapped with his extended family, and everyone is at one another's throat. Can even a game of 'I'm the dullest person' save the day?

Guest Cast: Curtis (Josh Adell).

Who's On The Line?: Caroline (Shelley Duvall) is the patient of Niles that Frasier suggests should find a new therapist.

Subtitles: What If He Had Taken A Really Big Breath?; There Is Nothing Wrong With Your Television (It's A Blackout).

Culture Vultures: After attacking her taste in furniture, Roz wheels on Niles and snaps, 'You won't even buy a chair unless some fey French aristocrat has sat his fat, satin fanny in it!'

Strange Bedfellows: Everyone is playing 'I'm the dullest person'. The idea is that everyone has a pile of pennies and each person in turn must say 'I'm the dullest person because . . .' and then name something they haven't done. If anyone else has done it, they give that person one of their pennies. A reticent Daphne has her arm twisted into going first. Bored and cranky, she says that she has never had sex in a lift, in a phone box, in an aeroplane, or on a merry-go-round. Before Frasier can finish suggesting she should take it seriously and try choosing something that someone else might have done, Roz drops a penny into Daphne's pile. Followed by three more.

Out Of Sight: Niles decides he should phone Maris to check she hasn't been panicked by the blackout (she had previously had to be drawn out from under the bed by the promise of a Prozac, after a particularly loud thunderstorm). Everything seems to be fine, though, until Niles tells her to take off her slumber mask. Then she really panics.

Eddie Takes The Biscuit: During the blackout, Martin asks Frasier if he's found Eddie. There is a thump and a growling yelp – it appears he has. Later, Eddie gets his head stuck in a ice-cream tub. For no reason, but it's funny in a cute kind of way.

Frasier Has Left The Building: 'Thanks for Calling': the first of what will become regular round-ups of the celebrity callers in the season. Kevin Bacon (Vic in 2.10, 'Adventures in Paradise', Part 2), Macaulay Culkin (Elliott in 2.11, 'Seat Of Power'), Sandra Dee (Connie in 2.06, 'The Botched Language of Cranes'), Shelley Duvall (Caroline in 2.24,

'Dark Victory'), Art Garfunkel (Chester in 2.09, 'Adventures in Paradise', Part 1), John Lithgow (Madman Martinez in 2.19, 'Someone to Watch Over Me'), Amy Madigan (Maggie in 2.04, 'Flour Child'), Rosie Perez (Francesca in 2.12, 'Roz In The Doghouse'), Sydney Pollack (Holden Thorpe in 2.07, 'The Candidate'), Carly Simon (Marie in 2.12, 'Roz In The Doghouse'), Gary Sinise (Sid in 2.18, 'The Club'), James Spader (Steven in 2.01, 'Slow Tango in South Seattle'), Mary Steenburgen (Marjorie in 2.13, 'Retirement Is Murder'), Lily Tomlin (Rita in 2.02, 'The Unkindest Cut of All'), and Alfre Woodard (Edna in 2.06, 'The Botched Language of Cranes').

On The Couch: A simply glorious episode that ends far too soon. It's packed with brilliant lines: the best being during Frasier's tour of the 'party' when he addresses and solves everyone's problems for them. This is a marvellous examination of what it must be like to be a professional counsellor and a perfect example of what it must be like to be Frasier. A great ending to a great season.

Season Three

3.01

'She's the Boss'

Written by Chuck Ranberg and Anne Flett-Giordano
Directed by Philip Charles MacKenzie
First UK Transmission: 05.07.96

Skyline: A shooting star passes overhead.

Synopsis: Terror stalks the corridors of KACL. The new station manager, Kate Costas, has arrived, and her first act is to fire Father Mike. Frasier goes in for his first meeting with the iron maiden straight after Father Mike, only to receive bad news himself. Kate tells Frasier that, while his ratings are good, they need to be better. He suggests playing classical music at the opening of his show – an idea that Kate thinks is too highbrow. She suggests he try spicing his programme by doing theme shows a couple of times a week. The idea appals Frasier, and he refuses. In return, Kate moves his show to the small hours of the morning, where Frasier must deal with the twin evils of truly twisted callers and a complete lack of sleep.

In revenge, Frasier spices up his night-time show by inviting callers to phone in about the topic of sex – he greets his first caller not with 'I'm listening', but 'What are you wearing?'. The next day, Kate and Frasier listen to a tape of the show in her office and agree that some solution has to be reached. Frasier threatens to walk, but Kate counters with a threat of legal action for breach of contract. It seems they are at a deadlock, until Frasier has a bright idea.

Where Everybody Knows Their Name: Say goodbye, if you will, to Father Mike (George Deloy), fired this episode. Bulldog (Dan Butler) and Gil Chesterton (Edward Hibbert) are naturally scared for their own jobs (in Bulldog's case, he even seems scared for his life).

When Frasier is accused of being worried about having a female boss, he counters that, 'If I had trouble taking orders from a woman, Frederick would never have been conceived.'

And, of course, this episode marks the first appearance of Kate Costas (Mercedes Ruehl), who will go on to play quite a big part in Frasier's life. The dirty girl.

Who's On The Line?: In his graveyard slot, Frasier receives a series of calls from bakers, one of whom is named Keith (Tom Hulce) and he thinks it's a great job. Mark (Matthew Broderick) works in a convenience store, and is worried because the image of him on the security camera 'is doing things I don't approve of'. Frasier falls asleep during a call from Phyliss (Carrie Fisher), who is suffering from insomnia. As he snaps back to wakefulness at the end of her call, having missed her entire problem, he simply suggests she sleep on it. Then there's also the longshoreman Frasier tells to come out of the closet and the nervous gay man to whom he recommends spending some time at the docks. And finally, Jill (Teri Garr) is Frasier's first caller to his spiced-up sex-themed show. She's wearing nothing, so Frasier decides to join her, stripping off in the studio. Frasier also tells Kate Costas about a caller who wondered why nobody liked her, but we'll never be entirely sure if this wasn't a metaphor he uses just to try to score points off his new boss.

Subtitles: Crass Appeal; A Long Night's Journey Into Day; Nocturnal Transmissions; While You Were Sleeping.

Culture Vultures: Frasier seems unprepared to admit that Kate is right when she tells him that Bartók's concerto is in C, not D.

Strange Bedfellows: Roz is peeved because her date with Dennis Abbot (by all accounts, a very rich man) will be ruined by her having to start work at 2 a.m.

Full-on Moon: Daphne says that her brothers always had difficulty taking orders from her, and she was always nagging them to do one thing or another – among those named here are Nigel, Reginald and the ubiquitous Billy.

Eddie Takes The Biscuit: Eddie gets into a fight with the Doberman from upstairs, and receives a nasty cut in his ear. The vet fits him with a plastic collar to prevent him from scratching the wound. Daphne, however, seems quite pleased with how things have worked out – she can put Eddie next to the television, and it improves the reception.

Frasier Has Left The Building: Martin and Daphne try to get a better picture on the television by popping Eddie on top, turning him this way and that.

On The Couch: Mercedes Ruehl makes a stunning debut as Kate Costas. Kate and Frasier almost immediately begin their heated sparring that will lead to so much trouble over the episodes to come. She is a delight to watch: cutting, intelligent, witty, and probably the only person in the show able to cut Frasier down to size. The resolution of the episode, where Kate and Frasier make it appear that they have each got their own way, is a clear signal of the clever relationship that will develop between them.

The little subplot about the breakdown of the security system around Niles's house is an amusing diversion. Maris is worried that they are now at risk, so Niles buys a gun. Although it is only a starting pistol, he still manages to cause enough chaos with it. Hyde Pierce does a marvellous little job of playing Niles the gunman.

3.02

'Shrink Rap'

Written by Christopher Lloyd
Directed by David Lee
First UK Transmission: 12.07.96

Skyline: A hot-air balloon rises from behind the skyline.

Synopsis: The episode opens with Frasier and Niles on opposite sides of a counsellor, discussing the problem that has brought them to his door. What follows is the story of another botched Crane Bros enterprise.

Frasier, increasingly frustrated by the short time he spends with each 'patient' on his radio show, has moved into an office in Niles's psychiatric practice. Martin thinks this is a ridiculous idea, citing other joint projects featuring his sons that have become disasters (specifically the events of 1.22, 'Author, Author', and 2.23, 'The Innkeepers'). And indeed, from the minute Frasier walks through the door to join his brother, the problems begin.

When Frasier sits in on one of Niles's therapy groups, the patients all seem more interested in what Frasier, not his brother, has to say. This leads to a screaming row, scaring off the group of patients and attracting the attention of Dr Schachter, the couples counsellor in the office next door. He suggests to them that he should go through their problems with them, to see if he can help.

It isn't long, though, before Dr Schachter comes to think that – for the first time in his career – he has found a couple who are truly irreconcilable. Frasier and Niles are, he decides, distrustful, competitive, bitchy and unpleasant. Is there any hope for the Crane brothers?

Guest Cast: Dr Schachter (Milo O'Shea), Mrs Kalish (Kristen Lowman), Mrs Kelly (Lesley Woods).

Where Everybody Knows Their Name: To really push home the point about Frasier not having enough time with his callers, Bulldog (Dan Butler) marches in as Frasier's show is ending, takes over the mike, and cuts off his last caller. We also see one of Niles's patients, Mr Carr (Don Sparks) for the first time, although, bizarrely, he receives no credit at the end of the episode.

Who's On The Line?: Jill (Blair Brown) is the poor unfortunate who was cut off by Bulldog. Frasier was trying to get to the heart of her recurring dream. She is visited by a young girl who appears at her bedroom window: she has something important to tell her, but Jill cannot hear what it is. While Frasier is listening to this, rapt, he fails to notice Roz at the window of his booth trying to signal to him that he's out of time.

Subtitles: Hmmm . . .

Culture Vultures: A name-drop for Enrico Caruso, a famous Italian tenor (the Pavarotti of his day), as Niles scorns Frasier's arrogance thus: 'Caruso wasn't so in love with the sound of his own voice.'

Full-on Moon: Daphne tells a story about her neighbours when she lived in London who used to have noisy sex, every detail of which she could hear. Niles, however, is retelling Daphne's story to Schachter and adds a lot of fantasy to the situation. She says that finally she decided to give her neighbours a taste of their own medicine and – in Niles's version – Daphne shows Martin, Frasier and Niles exactly what she did. Jane Leeves then brilliantly launches into a *When Harry Met Sally*-type rapture, shrieking and crying with pleasure. At one point she screams the most absurdly funny line in this episode: 'Just take me, you devil-spawn sex monkey!'

Frasier Has Left The Building: Frasier is moving out of Niles's offices. He and Martin emerge, carrying small bundles of possessions. Daphne follows, slowly lugging the filing cabinet.

On The Couch: An unusual, and very good, episode told mostly in flashback, through the twisted perspectives of the two brothers. The comedy really picks up, though, when we're back in the present and Dr Schachter decides to try a simple trust exercise on Niles and Frasier. In this, one brother must fall backwards and be caught in the arms of the other. It is obvious from their constant questioning – 'Is he in position?' – that this lack of trust is at the heart of their problems. But, once they've found out that Schachter's qualifications

come from disreputable Caribbean universities, Niles and
Frasier are immediately able to put their differences aside as
they sneer snobbishly at the other doctor's lack of education.

3.03
'Martin Does It His Way'

Written by David Lloyd
Directed by Philip Charles MacKenzie
First UK Transmission: 19.07.96

Skyline: Nothing happens.

Synopsis: Frasier's Great-Aunt Louise has passed away, and
he is asked to give her eulogy at the funeral service. But
Louise was an unpleasant old woman who never said a nice
word to anyone, and Frasier is having trouble finding one for
her. Niles, meanwhile, has been asked to dispose of her ashes
and can't think of anywhere suitable.

While mulling over missed opportunities, Martin has one
of his darkest secrets blown by Daphne – years ago, he
dreamt of writing a song for Frank Sinatra. It isn't long before
Daphne has dragged the shoebox full of lyrics out and shown
them to Frasier and Niles. They suggest that they could write
the music for one of the songs, and Martin could finally
realise his ambition. 'She's Such a Groovy Lady' soon takes
form, and the next day Martin mails it to Sinatra's people.

Soon, the day of the memorial service comes and Frasier
still hasn't got a eulogy prepared; nor has Niles thought of
somewhere to scatter the ashes. Frasier has been fruitlessly
looking through an old photo album for inspiration, and Niles
notices a photo of Louise at Wilson's Meadow. It was there
that she made Niles climb up a tree to retrieve his tangled
kite; she laughed as he fell out of the tree and broke his
collarbone. Niles realises that this is the only time he has seen
her happy, so decides to dispose of Louise's ashes there.

On the way to the memorial service, Martin, Frasier and Niles stop at Wilson's Meadow to scatter the ashes. Niles leaves the car to try to do so (but he can't get the lid off the urn), while Martin tells Frasier that his song has been rejected. Niles eventually asks Frasier for help with the ashes, and Frasier succeeds in opening the urn – but only by managing to spill the ashes over the brothers.

After this mishap, and with Frasier still no closer to writing a eulogy, can the day be saved?

Guest Cast: Minister (Tom Troupe).

Where Everybody Knows Their Name: Hester and Martin used to enjoy listening to Sinatra together.

Who's On The Line?: It's Ed, Roz tells Frasier, but Ed has gone. Frasier asks who else is in line, but Roz has just taken a big mouthful of a peanut-butter sandwich. Unable to speak, she mimes the caller's name. Roz points to her eye, then leans over to one side. Frasier correctly surmises that her name is Eileen (Mary Elizabeth Mastrantonio).

Eileen is worried because she keeps fantasising about other men when she has sex with her husband, particularly a certain radio psychiatrist. Indulging Eileen, Roz describes Frasier thus: 'Six foot one, granite jaw, the broad shoulders of a Marine . . . cobalt-blue eyes, chiselled cheekbones and . . . full, provocative lips.' Just for a second, Frasier really thinks Roz sees him that way.

Subtitles: In The Wee Small Hours Of The Morning; Try Holding It Under Some Hot Running Water.

Full-on Moon: Daphne talks about Grampa Moon's funeral. Before the service, her brothers had gone on a 'three-day bender' and 'they crawled to that funeral on their hands and knees . . . They had an obligation: they were the pallbearers.'

Out Of Sight: Niles is forced out of the house because Maris is hosting a meeting of her book club, and he makes the women feel uncomfortable. One of them has a problem saying 'Balzac' when he is around.

Eddie Takes The Biscuit: Eddie is found rubbing his back vigorously on the couch when Frasier arrives home. In a sharply delivered line, Frasier says, 'Dad, I thought we had an agreement. Eddie doesn't roll around on my sofa, and I don't throw him in front of a bus.'

Frasier Has Left The Building: A janitor sweeps up the last of Louise's ashes that Niles had poured out of his shoe during the service.

On The Couch: A brilliant episode, with a couple of wonderful scenes. Frasier and Niles helping Martin commit 'She's Such a Groovy Lady' to paper at last serves up some wonderful comedy. Martin screams out his 'doo-waps' in a viciously hoarse voice, while his sons desperately try to convert the noises into some form of music. The lyrics of the song are hilarious, and we defy anyone to find the words 'hi-dee-heydee' in any other piece of music.

Niles's background antics while Martin tells Frasier that his song has been rejected are pure *Airplane*-type humour: smashing the urn against a tree, jumping on it, all the while just visible from behind the headrest of Frasier's seat. And Frasier's final solution to the problem of the missing eulogy is great, the choir doing a marvellous job of interpreting the song that Martin has written.

3.04

'Leapin' Lizards'

Written by Chuck Ranberg and Anne Flett-Giordano
Directed by Philip Charles MacKenzie
First UK Transmission: 26.07.96

Skyline: Lights go on in various buildings.

Synopsis: Bulldog makes a fool of Frasier by putting in a crank call to his show. Bulldog as 'Mac' complains that he has to suffer an insufferably arrogant co-worker, and Bulldog soon reveals himself and tells Frasier that that person is him. The pranks continue, until Frasier decides to ask Kate Costas to do something about it. She, however, is reluctant to: Bulldog's listeners love it when he picks on Frasier, so she wants it to carry on for the sake of the ratings.

Deciding that his only chance is to get even, Frasier sneaks a lizard (which Bulldog is terrified of) into Bulldog's studio. But the joke goes horribly wrong when the lizard bites off Kate's fingertip and she ends up in hospital, swearing bloody revenge on the culprit. Frasier's guilty conscience gets the better of him, but how will Kate react to the confession?

Guest Cast: Nurse (Jodi Taffell).

Where Everybody Knows Their Name: Kate (Mercedes Ruehl) and Bulldog (Dan Butler) obviously have big roles in this episode (in fact, if you want a better look at how Bulldog runs his show, you'd be hard pushed to find one). We catch a quick glance of Nanette (and her dog, Spanky) from *Pet Chat*, just before Kate goes in to tell her that her show has been cancelled (see 2.22, 'Agents in America, Part Three'). We also meet Pete, Bulldog's producer (Michael Whaley), and Susan Rosen, Kate's PA (Annie Larussa). And there's a brief mention of Chopper Dave and Frasier's low opinion of his job. Maris's gardener Yoshi is briefly mentioned – though not by name – during the short exchange that marks Niles and Kate's first meeting.

Who's On The Line?: No real callers to Frasier's show – only Bulldog. And if you want to see rude, check out the way Bulldog handles his own callers, such as Jack (Billy Crystal) and Rob (Ed Harris).

Subtitles: Singing In The Rain; The Nose Knows; Leapin' Lizards.

Culture Vultures: Niles is excited because an exhibition of fourteenth-century Japanese netsuke figurines is about to open, but Kate rains on his parade when she tells him that there are no really rare pieces there.

Frasier returns from work, drenched to the skin by the thunderstorm outside. He is livid with the Seattle populace and their impolite behaviour when it rains – 'And,' he explodes, 'they wear brown shoes with white socks!'

Frasier and Niles remember the fun they had making anagrams out of the names of the board members of their wine club. Their favourite is 'Sidney Assbucket'.

The funniest moment in the whole episode has to be when Bulldog phones Frasier at home and tricks him into singing 'Three Little Maids' from *The Mikado* live on air.

Full-on Moon: Daphne enjoys hot chocolate through her nose (and just thinking of that makes her homesick). We also learn that Grammie Moon may have been somewhat duplicitous when it came to her husband's heart pills. No wonder he passed away . . .

Out Of Sight: Niles nearly mixes up his wife's tranquillisers with the ones meant for Eddie. He also tells of the time that a 'disgruntled servant' left a whoopee cushion on Maris's chair, but luckily she was 'too light to activate it'.

The Buddy Show: Duke's cousin Louie can reportedly make you 'laugh so hard, the beer comes out of your nose'. The boys on the force once replaced Martin's bulletproof vest with a bra.

Eddie Takes The Biscuit: He is given pills to calm him down when he is scared by the thunderstorm, and he ends up practically comatose, almost falling off his chair.

Frasier Has Left The Building: Everything seems to be quite normal. Frasier is wandering around his apartment with drink in hand, but what is that look on Daphne's and Martin's faces? Frasier slumps on to the sofa, and discovers that they've put a whoopee cushion under his seat.

On The Couch: There's a bit more exploration of Kate's character in this episode, and Ruehl gives a great performance – especially in the scene where Frasier comes to apologise for planting the lizard in Bulldog's studio. Tanked up on tranquillisers, she gradually slips into a fit of giggles and Frasier thinks he's in the clear. He tells her what he did, just when she is most unable to do anything about it. But she seems a little more lucid than Frasier suspected.

David Hyde Pierce really gets to exercise those wonderful facial muscles of his when he is trying to quietly unfurl a sweet from its wrapper in the studio, much to his working brother's annoyance. Eventually he stuffs the sweet – wrapper and all – into his mouth, only to make even more noise as he pulls the wrapper from between his lips.

This is a nice little episode, with some wonderful interplay between Frasier and Bulldog, and some great moments between Frasier and Kate that foreshadow the tempestuous times to come.

3.05
'Kisses Sweeter Than Wine'

Written by Anne Flett-Giordano
Directed by Philip Charles MacKenzie
First UK Transmission: 02.08.96

Skyline: The elevator goes up the Space Needle.

Synopsis: Frasier is hoping to become maître de chez of his wine club, and prepares to host an important meeting to impress the other members. Of course, Martin's barcalounger has to go, so he and Niles begin to carry it into Martin's room. On the way, though, Niles slips and the chair crashes to the floor, gouging a huge scratch into Frasier's parquet. Niles tells him not to panic, and calls for his favourite handyman, Joe DeCarlo. Frasier is worried that the work won't be done in time for the meeting that evening, but Joe assures him it will be done by midday.

Daphne and Joe are immediately attracted to each other and Niles begins to panic, thinking that he might lose his little goddess to Joe. Cornering Daphne in the kitchen, he tells her than Joe is notorious for sleeping with all the women he works for, and he persuades Daphne that going out with him is a very bad idea. When Joe eventually does ask Daphne out for the evening, she point-blank refuses.

Later that afternoon, Frasier arrives home from work to find not only Joe still working, but a fleet of electricians working in his flat. Joe explains that, when he plugged in his electric sander, a fuse blew and he realised that the apartment's wiring was defective. Frasier begins to panic again, but Joe reckons that the work will be done in just a couple of hours – in plenty of time for the meeting. But more problems soon arise . . .

Frasier's gas pipes are damaged, the water has to be cut off, and his guests are due to arrive in less than an hour. Will all the work be done in time for the meeting? And will Niles's sense of ethics get the better of him and persuade him to explain away his lies to Daphne?

Guest Cast: Painter (Kevin Weisman), Electrician (Kev O'Neil), Bruce (Peter Siragusa).

Where Everybody Knows Their Name: This is the introductory episode for Joe (Tony Carreiro), who will go on to spend a lot of time with Daphne.

Who's On The Line?: Marilyn (Brooke Adams) phones in complaining of homesickness. She tells Frasier that she is pining for her home state of Wisconsin – which is, of course, Roz's home too. The two of them then proceed to swap tales of all the people they both know.

Subtitles: Sip, Swish, Spit; The Clot Thickens.

Culture Vultures: Frasier's panic over the scratch in his floor is marvellous. No one's suggestions of a solution come close to making him happy, and his anger steadily increases. He finally blows his top when Martin tells him that sometimes he should just settle for things being less than perfect. 'It's that kind of advice,' snarls Frasier, 'that leads to shag carpeting!'

Out Of Sight: Joe is one of the few men who can satisfy Maris. 'Something,' says Niles, 'that's still, regrettably, on my "to do" list.'

One of Niles's tactics to drag Joe away from Daphne is suggesting he come over to his house and check out one of Maris's new plans – to annex Niles's library to make some more room for her hats. Maris and Niles have also taken to giving each other inappropriate presents as jokes: she gave him a bowling bag, he gave her a cookbook and at one point Niles reveals that he has been asked to pick some things up for Maris at the drugstore. That's why he's carrying $700 in cash.

Eddie Takes The Biscuit: Martin gives Eddie a warning that 'politicians are coming!', and the little dog hares after his master into hiding.

Frasier Has Left The Building: Niles and Frasier try to carry their father's chair back into the lounge, dropping it several times on the way. Frasier finally gives it an angry kick.

On The Couch: Daphne – finally! – meets someone she fancies. The first few scenes between her and Joe are wonderful, particularly the 'Honeybun'/'Sugar' exchange and the spark of static electricity that passes between them. Niles (whose ethical-dilemma-based nosebleeds make a return this episode – several times in fact) then attempts more than once to point out that it was simple electricity and nothing else. This provides some hilarious scuffling back and forth across the carpet and repeated poking of Frasier in an effort to repeat the effect.

Frasier's escalating frustration with the repairs to his apartment is great to watch too. Once again, it is Martin who saves the day with his down-to-earth manner and complete understanding of what the world is really like. All in all, a very fine episode with brilliant lines for everyone.

3.06

'Sleeping with the Enemy'

Written by Linda Morris and Vic Rauseo
Directed by Jeff Melman
First UK Transmission: 09.08.96

Skyline: The light atop the Space Needle glows.

Synopsis: Chaos reigns at KACL. Kate Costas has denied the station's support staff their usual five-per-cent rise, and they are up in arms. Unintentionally, Frasier gets caught up in the disagreement and soon becomes their spokesman in the talks with Kate. He knows, though, that for any threats they make to be effective, he must get the rest of the presenters at KACL on his side. With the support of the whole radio station, Frasier finally confronts Kate and makes his demands.

What should be a simple industrial dispute soon turns into a personal attack, as Frasier and Kate ask each other why they find it so hard to get along. Sniping turns to shouting and, before long, Kate and Frasier face each other across the desk. As they close in for the kill, they suddenly find themselves locked in a passionate kiss. Confused, they break apart, and Frasier hurries out.

This new setback muddles the negotiation process even more, and Frasier must return to Kate's office to settle the matter once and for all. Despite accusations of arrogance and manipulation, Kate and Frasier soon realise that there is a sheer animal magnetism between them. But they mustn't allow it to get in the way of the discussions over the pay rise – which in the end last a matter of seconds, so they can get down to much more serious business on Kate's desk.

Where Everybody Knows Their Name: Frasier hosts a get-together of KACL's on-air staff at his apartment, and everyone is there: Bulldog (Dan Butler), Gil Chesterton (Edward Hibbert) – who meets Daphne and Martin for the first time – Cheryl, and Floyd the Happy Chef, who has presumably assumed this mantle from Leo (see 2.19, 'Someone To Watch Over Me'). This episode also marks the return of Noel Shempsky (Patrick Kerr), who is initially chosen to lead the charge against Kate Costas (Mercedes Ruehl).

Who's On The Line?: June (Laura Dern) is calling in because her husband complains that she never pays attention to their conversations. Frasier, meanwhile, is too busy watching the commotion outside to listen to her.

Subtitles: Couldn't We Just Stop Eating Grapes; The Bloodless Coup; I Draw The Line At Blanche Dubois.

Culture Vultures: Frasier left his prized Mont Blanc pen in Niles's car. After Frasier accuses Gil Chesterton of being elitist, Gil counters with, 'Well, thank you, Mr Everyday People!'

Out Of Sight: One of Maris's houseboys once developed an appendix problem, so, at enormous cost to herself, she heroically sent him off . . . back to the border! Niles arrives at Frasier's, dishevelled and distraught – Maris has found a grey hair in her widow's peak, and blames him for it. He recklessly switched on the bedroom light while she was undressing.

Eddie Takes The Biscuit: Despite a moment of stubbornness, Eddie soon loses his place on Martin's barcalounger when Bulldog barks loudly at him.

Frasier Has Left The Building: Noel dreams of confronting Kate in her office and winning the pay rise on behalf of the support staff. When he emerges triumphant, he sweeps Roz into his arms and kisses her.

On The Couch: Oh, my. This episode kicks off possibly the finest two-parter *Frasier* has brought us. As surprising as their sudden attraction is to Kate and Frasier, it is much more so to us: brilliantly, there are no clues, no hints that the kiss is about to happen. And when it does, it takes our breath away. Tremendous stuff.

As if that wasn't enough, the episode is packed with typically good performances from the supporting cast. Gil Chesterton gets some cracking lines, and Bulldog's description of his date as a 'charity event' is cruelly funny. As a consequence of the episode being so KACL-centric, there is little to do for Martin, Niles and Daphne but, for once, we don't mind.

3.07
'The Adventures of Bad Boy and Dirty Girl'

Written by Joe Keenan
Directed by Philip Charles MacKenzie
First UK Transmission: 16.08.96

Skyline: A streak of lightning crosses the sky.

Synopsis: It is one day later. Frasier is anxious about the ferocity of his attraction to Kate, and is beginning to think that they should just slow down and cool off. After much agonising, he finally realises that he should tell her this.

Martin, meanwhile, has his own problem with a woman who is coming on too strong. Dierdre Sauvage, the romantic novelist who lives upstairs and wrote *The Rose and the Rapier*, is moving out and wants to try it on with Martin one last time. Martin desperately tries to avoid her but Frasier eventually throws him into the jaws of hell.

That night, Frasier is alone in the studio, filling in for Floyd the Happy Chef. Kate appears in the studio during a news break, and tells Frasier that she thinks they should slow down. Frasier is relieved to find that they are in agreement, and the two, now relaxed, begin to discuss the whole situation. Frasier says it makes him feel like a 'bad boy', while Kate thinks of herself as a 'dirty girl'. And with these words, the damage is done. Once again, their sheer attraction takes over and they collapse on to the studio desk in a passionate embrace.

Meanwhile, across the city, listeners hear the news report suddenly stop to be replaced by fevered cries of 'Yes! I'm a bad boy . . . ! You dirty girl!' Suddenly, the whole of Seattle knows about bad boy and dirty girl and what they were up to in the studio. Can Frasier's life really get any worse than this?

Guest Cast: Dierdre Sauvage (Pamela Kosh), Removal Man (Harris Laskawy).

Where Everybody Knows Their Name: After the bad boy/dirty girl incident, Bulldog (Dan Butler) approaches Frasier. Frasier thinks it's to take another potshot, but Bulldog merely hugs him and says that he's very proud of him.

Frasier must fill in for Floyd the Happy Chef because he's in rehab.

Who's On The Line?: Polly (Cyd Charisse) phones Frasier saying that she's lacking 'a certain spice'. Frasier suggests all manner of activities to give an edge of excitement to her life, but it soon becomes clear that she isn't aware that Frasier is filling in for the Happy Chef. Polly meant that she'd run out of cinnamon to use in the apple tart she was baking.

Subtitles: The Adventures Of Bad Boy And Dirty Girl; Dirty Girl, Sign In Please.

Strange Bedfellows: Roz complains when she has to work between eight and ten in the evening, because she's due to meet 'a successful, handsome doctor'.

When Frasier arrives in work the day after the on-air lovemaking, she tells him that he's not allowed to make any more snide remarks about her love life – 'I don't care if I start dating a lumbercamp.'

Full-on Moon: Frasier asks Daphne how she'd hypothetically react if she was told by a hypothetical man that he thought they were hypothetically going too fast. She launches into a long speech, complaining, 'not that it was too fast for you last night', before finally yelling, 'Well, you can just sod off, Trevor Mulgrew!' Hypothetically, of course.

Out Of Sight: Maris isn't coping well with bearing the Crane family name, once the bad-boy scandal gets out. To distance herself from the shame, she has added an accent to all her stationery, so that it now reads 'From the desk of Maris Crané'.

Eddie Takes The Biscuit: Dierdre's removal man shares a lift with Frasier and accidentally spills juice from his chilli dog on Frasier's suede shoes. What's going to get *that* out, Frasier wonders? Eddie runs over and licks the mark off the shoe. 'Dog saliva,' Frasier remarks. 'Nature's miracle solvent.'

Frasier Has Left The Building: Martin and Eddie try to sneak out of the apartment without attracting the attention of Dierdre. While they wait for the lift, they give shifty glances this way and that, checking for her presence. When the lift arrives, they back slowly into it, but Martin is unaware that Dierdre is already inside waiting for him.

On The Couch: Kelsey Grammer and Mercedes Ruehl have a barrel of laughs in this direct sequel to the previous episode: their playfulness as they toy with the phrases 'bad boy' and 'dirty girl' is spectacular. This whole scene is the highlight of the episode, their body language cleverly displaying their animal attraction for each other, while their intellects wrestle with the consequences. Of course, when it gets down and 'dirty' their intellects fail them and the fun really begins.

The short scene of Niles in his car, listening to the whole thing, is brilliant. What caps it all is the inspired silliness of the airbag pinning him to his seat when he runs into the car in front. Even Eddie is enraptured by the show that Frasier and Kate put on for Seattle.

This is, simply, one of the very best episodes – the kind of prime-example episode you'd show someone to persuade them that the show was funny. And anyone would be hard-pushed to not find it funny. Brilliant.

3.08
'The Last Time I Saw Maris'

Written by Ian Gurvitz
Directed by Philip Charles MacKenzie
First UK Transmission: 23.08.96

Skyline: A shooting star passes overhead.

Synopsis: Maris has gone missing, and everyone gathers together at Niles's house to comfort him. Martin uses his police connections to track her down and, finally, some charges to her credit card show up in New York. Niles suddenly realises that all Maris has done is gone on a shopping spree and is instantly relieved. But Frasier is less happy: he is concerned about Niles being under the thumb of his tyrannical wife, and begins to suggest he should stand up for himself.

When Maris does return, Niles does just that. Frasier's advice backfires, though, and Maris throws him out of the house and says that she's going to file for divorce. Deep in denial, Niles quickly tries to adjust to a bachelor life but, when he returns to the house to collect his things, he realises that he doesn't really want to leave.

Where Everybody Knows Their Name: Noel Shempsky (Patrick Kerr) has posted a petition begging the producers of *Star Trek* to introduce a new character based on Roz: 'The all-powerful space vixen Rozalinda, four-breasted queen of the planet Rozniak'. Roz is, of course, less than flattered.

Niles bids a fond farewell to his staff (naming Jean-Pierre, Marie and Bernard). Marta (Irene Olga Lopez) has just one question to ask him before he goes: 'Can we come with you?'

Frasier tells Niles exactly what he should say to her to save his marriage. It is a long monologue about standing up to your wife, and Frasier – shooting his advice in the foot – ends with the desperate threat, 'I will not let you treat me like this,

Lilith!' before he realises his mistake and corrects the wife's name to Maris.

Who's On The Line?: Vinnie (Paul Mazursky) has called in because he has left his pinkie ring at one of his many lovers' houses. Frasier, disgusted with his treatment of women, accuses him of knowing nothing about jewellery. 'A pinkie no more needs a ring than a neck needs a gold medallion.'

Subtitles: Thank God Gucci Was Closed; What Light Breaks Through Yonder Window; Denial Ain't Just A River.

Culture Vultures: When Niles storms out of Maris's house, he slams the door behind him for effect. Unfortunately it is a 'fourteenth-century Bavarian cathedral door' and he needs the help of two servants to slam it. 'What it lacked in spontaneity,' he notes, 'it made up for in resonance.'

Full-on Moon: In Maris's house, while everyone is wondering where she has gone, Daphne holds a poker in her hand and gets a 'vibration' from it. She sees Maris waving it at someone and shouting, 'You thief!' Niles reassures her that Maris had been waving it at a decorator who had tried to overcharge her.

Out Of Sight: Describing Maris to the police, Martin comes up with a superbly succinct portrait: 'Thin. Make that very thin. Caucasian. Very Caucasian.'

When they hear about the sales on Maris's credit cards, Niles thinks at first that the cards have simply been stolen. Martin reels off a list of the places the cards were used: Armani, Valentino, Cartier, Tiffany. Niles asks if they were used in any restaurants, and when Martin says that they weren't, he shrieks, 'She's alive!' It turns out that she is reliving her 'Saints alive, I'm thirty-five!' shopping spree.

The Buddy Show: A cop called Mike helps Martin track Maris down.

Eddie Takes The Biscuit: On the way back to the apartment, Frasier, Martin and Daphne stop for a bite to eat. They have left Eddie alone for three hours, and Daphne is certain he is going to need to relieve himself immediately. She's right: the minute they open the door, Eddie rushes into the lift, his lead in his mouth.

Frasier Has Left The Building: A beautifully wrapped gift lies on Roz's console. Excited, she opens it only to find a four-cupped bra inside. The pranksters all stand at the window of the studio, worshipping the almighty Rozalinda.

On The Couch: While the bizarre relationship between Niles and Maris has always been a source of laughs, in this episode it becomes more than that as we realise just how frightened Niles is of life without her. The most poignant moment comes just before Niles finally leaves, when Frasier suggests he sit down and be calm. Where should he sit? Niles wonders out loud, before going to every chair in the room and telling his brother and father what memories it holds for him. Although there is much comedy on the way, this episode's strength lies in its serious and sad tone. A gently moving, and very clever, episode.

3.09
'Frasier Grinch'

Written by David Lloyd
Directed by Philip Charles MacKenzie
First UK Transmission: 30.08.96

Skyline: The Space Needle is decorated with Christmas lights.

Synopsis: It's Christmas Eve, and Frederick is coming to spend it with Frasier – their first together since his parents' divorce. Frasier has ordered a ton of educational toys for his son's presents, while Martin has decked Frasier's halls with foul old follies.

Frasier and Niles meet for coffee, and Niles tells his brother that he is hopeful of a reconciliation between him and Maris before the end of the year. But when he tries to pay the bill by credit card, only to find that Maris has cancelled all his access to his money, he begins to think he may be wrong.

Back at Frasier's apartment, everything is ready – until Frasier suddenly realises that the mail-order company has sent him the wrong presents. Martin suggests that Frasier buy an Outlaw Laser Robo-Geek for Frederick, but Frasier is still determined to find something educational. He and Niles head down to the mall to see if they can find anything in time.

Luckily, they bump into a man who has been shopping at a place that sells only educational toys – but it is already closed. Seeing a quick buck, the man offers to sell what he has bought to Frasier for $1,000. Frasier offers him $300, and tells Niles to give him a cheque for the rest – knowing, of course, that the cheque can't be cleared because Maris has frozen Niles's assets.

It seems at last that everything is going to be all right. But as Frasier is saying goodnight to Frederick, his son tells him he's very excited because he's asked Santa Claus for an Outlaw Laser Robo-Geek and he's looking forward to receiving it. Frederick goes to bed, leaving Frasier alone with his father. Martin then talks to Frasier about his attitude towards Christmas gifts: Frasier just buys people what he thinks they should have, not necessarily what they would want. Six years' worth of discarded presents to his father show Frasier what he means. But maybe Martin has saved the day – just what is that waiting under the tree for Frasier?

Guest Cast: Marge (Becky Ann Baker), Ned (Klee Bragger), Jack (Tegan West).

Where Everybody Knows Their Name: Our favourite waitress (Luck Hari) makes a brief but welcome return, wielding a pair of scissors. Finally, Luke Tarsitano makes his only appearance as Frederick (who isn't allowed sweets by Lilith). And, with the greatest of respect, what an annoying little brat he is. (The kid in the toy shop who laughs at Frasier for wanting a Living Brain is a million times more charismatic, sadly.)

Bulldog (Dan Butler) and Gil Chesterton (Edward Hibbert) make a reappearance, trying to distract Frasier from reading his uplifting, educational Christmas parable to his listeners. Their tactics include wrapping him in fairy lights and tinsel, trying to set fire to his script, and – finally, and almost successfully – bringing in a stripper to bare her all.

A brief mention of Joe, in case we'd forgotten his relationship with Daphne: she is spending the holiday with him and his parents. And memories of Hester are invoked when Frasier sees the way Martin has decorated the apartment for the festive season.

Who's On The Line?: Bob (Ray Liotta) is phoning because he's tempted to take the wrong plane and, instead of spending Christmas with his family, spend the holidays on a tropical beach somewhere. Although Frasier tries to reassure him that everyone's in 'the same gravy boat' when it comes to family Christmases, he is quite sure that Bob is going to whoop it up on the beach.

Subtitles: If I Only Had A Brain; A Mall And The Night Visitors.

Strange Bedfellows: No mention of any particular man this episode, but a brilliant put-down from Frasier. Roz arrives at Café Nervosa, weighed down with shopping bags, complaining, 'I never know what to give the men in my life.' 'Since when?' Frasier counters.

Full-on Moon: Daphne is taking a plum duff to Joe's house. She has made it to Grammie Moon's special recipe, which basically involves soaking it in rum for hours on end. Grammie Moon always used to light the pudding at Christmas, and when she appeared with no eyebrows Daphne's family all knew it was time for dessert. 'To this day,' Daphne dreamily muses, 'the smell of burning hair puts me in the holiday spirit.'

Out Of Sight: To avoid difficult questions about his separation, Niles tells Frederick that Maris is in a coma. 'I thought the truth would just upset him.'

Eddie Takes The Biscuit: The poor wretch spends the episode dressed as a miniature Santa Claus. 'Dad, you have to get out more,' says a concerned Niles on seeing the dog. 'You've started doing old-lady things.'

Frasier Has Left The Building: Martin tries to take Eddie for a walk while the dog is still dressed as Santa, but Eddie resolutely refuses to move. When he takes the hat and coat off the dog, though, Eddie rushes out of the house, glad to be free at last.

On The Couch: Even a comedy as clever as *Frasier* isn't immune to the American schmaltz of Christmas. While a lot of the episode is sugary, at least it manages to poke fun at the usual American excesses: Frasier and Niles reacting badly to Martin's choice of decorations being a good case in point. If anything, the episode is let down by an overly sentimental ending. Would it hurt, just once, for a programme as honest as this to acknowledge that bad things can happen at the happiest times of the year?

At least, as a counterbalance to the inevitably happy ending to the Frederick plot line, we have Niles's quietly desperate belief that he can still save his marriage to Maris. But Niles's misfortune (and it is great, and getting greater) isn't dwelt upon, making more room for Frasier and Martin's quest for a happy Frederick. While it is doubtless entertaining, we have only one thing to say: Bah, humbug!

3.10
'It's Hard to Say Goodbye If You Won't Leave'

Written by Steven Levitan
Directed by Philip Charles MacKenzie
First UK Transmission: 13.09.96

Skyline: A cloud passes above the skyline, and it rains.

Synopsis: Frasier is preoccupied: he can't stop thinking about Kate and their time together. Could it be, he wonders, that he's really fallen for her? Deciding that this is the case, he resolves to tell her. But, before he gets the chance, Kate announces to him that she's leaving her job at KACL for one in Chicago – and she is leaving tonight.

That night, Frasier is due to meet another woman for a date, but he is still troubled by his feelings for Kate. He realises there is nothing left for him to do but go to Kate's apartment and try to catch her before she leaves. When he gets there, he tells her everything and is delighted to find that Kate feels the same way too. They decide that, even though they will be living in different cities, it is still worthwhile continuing the relationship.

With scant minutes left together, Frasier takes Kate to the airport and they say a brief goodbye. Just as Frasier is about to leave, it is announced that Kate's flight has been delayed indefinitely. She rushes back into the terminal and they spend the wait talking and getting to know each other better. Before long, though, they both begin to realise that they don't have much in common and that maybe they're not destined for each other after all.

Guest Cast: Tony (Vaughn Armstrong), Donna (Marnie Moisman), Flight Agent (Doug Tompos), Driver (Elvin Whitesides), Gate Attendant (Jane McFie).

Where Everybody Knows Their Name: A final, but memorable, appearance of Kate Costas (Mercedes Ruehl) marks the ending of one of *Frasier*'s better storylines. When Frasier reveals that he can't stop fantasising about Kate, his father tells him and Niles that it's perfectly OK: he used to fantasise about Hester all the time – wearing a cheerleader's outfit, lying near-naked in front of an open fire. This is all too much for the sensitive Crane boys. There are also a number of flashbacks to previous episodes featuring Kate and Frasier . . . enjoying each other's company.

Subtitles: The City With Broad, Bare Shoulders; It's Hard to Say Goodbye If You Won't Leave.

Culture Vultures: During the final talk with Kate, Frasier suggests something that they might do when they spend time together in Chicago – they could go 'antiquing'. A somewhat dubious Kate replies, 'I am not one of those people for whom "antique" is a verb.'

The Buddy Show: Martin is writing a letter to Murray Dingman, an old army friend. Niles watches him write over his shoulder, passing comment on his grammar and saying that it's wrong to end a sentence with a preposition. Martin scribbles something on a sheet of paper and hands it to Niles, who says that ' "off" is a preposition too'.

Frasier Has Left The Building: Daphne and Eddie are fast asleep and resting on Niles as he watches a movie on television. He needs to get to his glass of sherry, but to move his arm would disturb both of them. He reaches out with his foot and nudges the glass towards him: it gets closer and closer, before he finally knocks it on to the floor.

On The Couch: The final episode in the Kate Costas sequence sees a strange and moving parting of the ways. Both Ruehl and Grammer get to stretch their acting muscles to great effect. While Frasier is wrapped in melancholy over his thoughts for Kate, she is able to show little touches of vulnerability that we've rarely seen before. When they announce their feelings for each other, a complete transformation comes over Kate and she becomes much more girlish and giggly – surely the first sign that Frasier is about to stop finding her attractive. Their final goodbye is very touching: Frasier holds her hand for the last time and says, 'It's a pity, though.' To which Kate can only reply, quietly, 'Isn't it?'

On the funnier side, the little subplot – Niles trying to watch films he's always wanted to see – is great. His reactions when the endings of both films are spoilt by everyone are beautiful to watch.

3.11

'The Friend'

Written by Jack Burditt
Directed by Philip Charles MacKenzie
First UK Transmission: 20.09.96

Skyline: A helicopter rises up from the skyline and departs.

Synopsis: Niles offers Frasier two tickets for the best seats at a horse-racing meet. Niles doesn't want to go, and Martin's playing poker with his buddies, so it seems Frasier must find someone else to go with him. He is about to phone one of his friends instead when he realises that he actually doesn't have that many close friends in Seattle. A little worried about this, he dedicates his next show to the topic of making friends and invites Seattle to call in and reach out, both to Frasier and each other.

The rest of his show is made up of phone calls from nutcases and a tired and cynical Frasier finally realises his mistake. Roz brings through a bundle of faxes at the end of the show – all from nutters, except for one. Bob seems a nice enough guy and Frasier decides to call him and arrange to meet.

Frasier meets Bob at Café Nervosa and almost instantly they strike up a rapport. Swept up in his enthusiasm for this new friend, Frasier suggests that they go and celebrate with dinner. It is shortly thereafter that he discovers two unconnected things about Bob: he's in a wheelchair; and he is the most insufferable, annoying bore Frasier has ever met.

Frasier is then caught in a crisis of conscience. He doesn't want to have anything more to do with an increasingly familiar Bob, but doesn't want the other man to think his change of heart has anything to do with the wheelchair. But if Frasier doesn't act soon, Bob is going to move into his apartment block and make his life hell, for ever.

Guest Cast: Bob (Griffin Dunne), Ralph (Ben Mittleman), Patrons at Café Nervosa (Diane Behrens, David Jay Willis).

Where Everybody Knows Their Name: Luck Hari's waitress is just one of many horrified by Frasier's 'attitude' to wheelchair users.

Who's On The Line?: Frasier tells Seattle that he wants them to come up to him on the street and say hello, to become his friend. The first caller after this announcement is Gerard (Armistead Maupin), who wants to meet up with Frasier, and maybe even comb his hair . . .

Frasier also receives a call from George, who wants him to invest $5,000 in his French-fry vending machine. Among Frasier's faxes is one from Garth, who keeps dead, rotting squirrels in the boot of his car.

Subtitles: Maybe Just A Shampoo And Set; Butane And The Beast; The Squeaky Wheel Gives The Grief.

Culture Vultures: Spurned by Frasier in preference to his new friend, Niles takes his pool cleaner, Ralph, out for coffee. Niles tries to get the other man involved in choosing the fabric for his new sofa covering from a crammed book of swatches. All Ralph can offer is the comment, 'I live in my van.'

Strange Bedfellows: When asked how Roz gets rid of anyone she doesn't want to see any more, she replies that she simply says, 'I love you and I want to have your baby.'

Full-on Moon: Niles's reason for not wanting to go to the races is simple. The jockeys – 'diminutive, underweight figures in expensive silks, wielding riding crops' – remind him of Maris.

Eddie Takes The Biscuit: Martin warns Frasier that, if he doesn't do something quickly, he'll end up hanging around only those people who act exactly the same as he does. While he says this, he wriggles uncomfortably in his seat, rubbing his back against the chair. On the floor, meanwhile, Eddie is doing exactly the same thing.

Frasier Has Left The Building: Daphne is once again trying to get Martin to eat more healthily. She is preparing some fruit drink in a blender and, while her back is turned, Martin slips in a doughnut and some beer.

On The Couch: After the tumultuous episodes before it – Frasier's affair with Kate, and Niles leaving Maris – this episode is probably a little ordinary for its own good. Its weakness lies with Bob, who is too genuinely annoying a character for the viewer to do anything but agree with Frasier; and once the audience have lost the ability to distance themselves from Frasier's pomposity, a lot of the comedy is drained away.

Of particular note, though, is Niles's reaction to Frasier's choice to 'see other people' ('I've only been your brother for, hmm, thirty-eight years now') and the brothers' eventual making up. Niles's first line to Frasier on being reunited with his brother? Well, what else could it be but this: 'Are these wingtips too busy with these pants?'

3.12
'Come Lie With Me'

Written by Steven Levitan
Directed by Philip Charles MacKenzie
First UK Transmission: 27.09.96

Skyline: A hot-air balloon rises from behind the skyline.

Synopsis: Daphne wakes up on a beautiful morning to find Joe in her bed. Immediately, she jumps up and makes moves to get him out – if Frasier discovers that he has spent the night, he will be furious. Unfortunately, they are caught at the door and Frasier, who has suspected they are having sex for a while, finally has enough proof to confirm it to himself.

He decides that he needs to speak to Daphne about it. He is adamant that she cannot have sex under his roof, so Daphne comes to think that maybe she should move out. When Frasier says that he doesn't want her to, Daphne asks what choice she has.

That weekend Daphne goes away with Joe, and Martin and Frasier are left alone to fend for themselves. Before even the first morning is over, they are threatening to kill each other and they both realise that Daphne is the glue that keeps them together. If she does go, they will fall apart – but is it too late for Frasier to stop her leaving?

Guest Cast: Dirk (Tim Choate), Henry (Scott MacDonald).

Where Everybody Knows Their Name: Joe (Tony Carreiro) makes his first reappearance since his introduction, but only for the first few minutes of the episode.

Subtitles: They're Playing Do-Si-Do, But Not For Me; He Cried With His Boots On.

Culture Vultures: Niles is in agony this episode, as it seems his society friends have deserted him, relegating him to the B-list of party guests. His first hint of this comes when he realises that he hasn't been invited to the Hoedown for the Homeless.

Eddie Takes The Biscuit: When Frasier catches Joe and Daphne in an embrace at the door of his apartment, it is obvious that they have spent the night together, despite their embarrassed protestations. Frasier wonders whether anything else could happen to make the moment more awkward, just as Eddie scampers up with Joe's underpants in his mouth.

Martin gets Eddie to clean up some spilt sauce on the dining table, prompting Frasier to describe the dog as 'our own foul-breathed little Handiwipe'.

Frasier Has Left The Building: The situation is resolved – Frasier has agreed to let Joe stay in Daphne's room. The next morning, Daphne pours three glasses of orange juice, carefully picks them up in her hands and strides off towards her room. Laughing, she returns immediately, the Crane boys having fallen for her prank.

On The Couch: A great little episode that gets funnier as it goes along, the final scene being one of the cleverest the series has ever achieved. All the way through the episode, Frasier accuses Martin of being in denial over his weight – his father would prefer to think that his trousers have shrunk, rather than accept that he has got fatter. The only way Daphne can persuade Frasier into accepting that she and Joe have sex is by making him deny to himself that they do. (The fake explanation – that Joe was injured by a startled sheep while he was holidaying in the Falklands in the middle of the Argentine conflict – is hilarious.) And the only way Niles will be happy with his fall from grace within society is by accepting their shifty reasons for not inviting him to the hoedown and believing their half-baked assurances that it won't happen again.

The three Crane boys all sit around, ramming these points home to themselves, burying their heads in the sand. Then Martin offers round some cookies, explaining that they're half-fat – which, of course, means they can eat twice as many. A wonderful scene, which succeeds, thanks to a turn of three marvellous monologues.

And there's a nice reference back to Martin's Sinatra fixation (see 3.03, 'Martin Does It His Way') when he sings a tiny snatch of 'She's Such a Groovy Lady' in the kitchen.

3.13
'Moon Dance'

Written by Joe Keenan, Christopher Lloyd, Rob Greenberg, Jack Burditt, Chuck Ranberg, Anne Flett-Giordano, Linda Morris and Vic Rauseo
Directed by Kelsey Grammer
First UK Transmission: 04.10.96

Skyline: Party balloons float up from behind the skyline.

Synopsis: Niles is upset when he reads in the society page of the newspaper that Maris has gone on a three-week cruise with Pearson Broadwater. He is beginning to get the impression that his old world is moving on without him, so he decides to take action. He arranges a date for his club's winter dance, the Snow Ball, but suddenly realises that his date is likely to want to dance – and he doesn't know how. Daphne offers to teach him, and the two embark on an evening of ballroom-dancing lessons.

By the time that he has become a proficient dancer, Niles receives a call from his date saying that she has had to cancel. Niles can't bring himself to tell Daphne straightaway, but when he does she suggests that maybe she should go instead. Niles, of course, thinks this is a great idea.

Frasier returns from a short trip to visit Frederick, and his father tries to tell him all about what's been happening. But Frasier doesn't want to hear – he's officially still on holiday, and doesn't want to know about whatever little problems everyone has had while he's been away. Despite Martin's best efforts, Frasier will not listen. Then the doorbell rings and Daphne, dressed in a stunning red ball gown, rushes to the door saying that her date is here to pick her up. She lets the date in – and Frasier sees that it is Niles, clutching a long-stemmed red rose. They go, and Frasier is left very confused.

At the ball, Niles and Daphne have a wonderful time. When the tango comes on, Daphne takes Niles's hand and pulls him towards the dance floor. He protests that he doesn't know the tango, but when she says that it's a dance all about contact and passion he gladly goes along. Gradually, they whip up a storm on the floor, their dancing getting more and more excited and passionate. Daphne says, though, that she senses Niles is holding back and tells him that he should let go. He does just that: 'Oh Daphne, I adore you,' he says. 'I adore you too,' she replies.

Guest Cast: Lacey Lloyd (Christine McGraw), Andrew Lloyd (Hank Stratton), Conductor (Michael G. Hawkins), Claire Barnes (Nancy Stafford).

Where Everybody Knows Their Name: Frasier leaves at the beginning of the episode to spend a week with Frederick (which disgusts Roz, as she has to spend the week producing a show with a radio chiropodist). And there is a brief mention of Marta, whom Niles describes as 'my ex-maid and current mole', plus another serving of Café Nervosa's busiest waitress (Luck Hari). There is a mention of Hester and Martin being briefly separated – presumably as a result of her affair with Stan Lawlor (see 1.08, 'Beloved Infidel').

Who's On The Line?: Marlene (Jodie Foster) is the caller in the last thirty seconds of the show. Before she can even get to her problem, she has to calm an excited dog and get her husband to tend to their crying son. After that, she explains that she and her husband don't seem to find time to have sex any more.

Subtitles: He Was A Band Leader Married To Charo; Where Else Would Coroners Get Together?

Culture Vultures: A big surprise, as we discover that Niles can't dance. As he is learning, he voices all our feelings on the early stages of ballroom-dancing lessons: 'This is boring, yet difficult.'

Full-on Moon: Daphne used to help her brother Billy practise ballroom dancing. And she went to school with a boy called Niles, although she called him 'Niley'.

Out Of Sight: 'She never liked going anywhere alone,' Niles comments of Maris when he sees she's off on the cruise with Broadwater. 'Except bed.'

Niles never bothered to learn how to dance because Maris never wanted to: 'She dislikes public displays of rhythm.'

Eddie Takes The Biscuit: Martin spends the entire episode trying to prove to Daphne that Eddie is an intelligent dog. First of all, he dumps a towel over his head – the faster he shakes it off, the more clever he is. Eddie just sits there and makes no attempt to move it.

Martin is also trying to teach Eddie the names of all his toys. Eddie has particular difficulty telling Banana from Mr Pig.

Frasier Has Left The Building: Martin holds up a flash card with a picture of a banana on it. Eddie stares and stares at it, before finally dashing out of shot and returning with a banana. The camera zooms out, and we see the room is full of bananas.

On The Couch: This is one of those episodes that everyone must see. The moment when Niles declares his feelings for Daphne, and she appears to reciprocate, is heart-stopping. When they go on to share a tender kiss, the viewer really thinks that what seems to be happening is really happening. Then, when Daphne compliments Niles on his acting skills, the whole thing is as shattering to us as it is to him. Beautifully done.

3.14
'The Show Where Diane Comes Back'

Written by Christopher Lloyd
Directed by James Burrows
First UK Transmission: 11.10.96

Skyline: A shooting star passes overhead.

Synopsis: As his show finishes, Roz rushes in to tell Frasier that a woman has just barged into the building, determined to see him. Suddenly, at the window of the studio, a familiar face appears: Diane Chambers, Frasier's one-time fiancée from Boston. Inside, Frasier screams in terror.

Frasier immediately runs over to the offices of Niles to talk to him. Throughout their conversation Niles becomes more and more convinced that Frasier still has to resolve certain things with Diane – like telling her how he felt when she left him standing at the altar. Frasier, with Niles's help, soon realises that he has to confront Diane and tell her how he feels, so he invites her over for dinner.

At dinner, Diane manages to offend both Martin and Niles and they soon give up trying to make polite conversation with the woman. As the evening progresses, talk turns to her reason for being in Seattle: the performance of her new play, *Rhapsody and Requiem*, by a small theatre company. But each time the play is mentioned, Diane gets an uncontrollable twitch in her cheek. Asking for time alone with her, Frasier soon discovers that an important investor has pulled their backing out of the play. Diane asks if Frasier would be willing to stump up some money, which he does.

Both Martin and Niles begin to suspect that Frasier is falling for Diane again, and he does nothing to prove them wrong. Diane asks Frasier to go to the dress rehearsal of the play, and it is there that Frasier's feelings for Diane are finally resolved.

Guest Cast: Stan (Perry Stephens), Clark (Danny Breen), Darla (Judith Corber-Wexler), Ned (Googy Gress), Dr Franklin Crean (John Carroll Lynch), Mary Anne (Cali Timmins).

Where Everybody Knows Their Name: A second appearance for Niles's women-hating patient Mr Carr (Don Sparks). But of course, the real star here is Shelley Long, back as Diane, and on top form. When Frasier initially tells Niles that the 'scourge of my existence' is back in town, Niles thinks he means Lilith. But he normally gets some sort of signal if she has returned: 'dogs forming into packs, blood weeping down the wall'. Martin later tells Diane that Hester, who tried to interfere with her wedding plans to Frasier back in Boston (in the *Cheers* episode 'Diane Meets Mom'), has died.

We are reminded also of the whole of the Cheers gang, as Diane's play is obviously based around the Boston bar. We have Stan as Sam, Clark as Cliff, Ned as Norm, Darla as Carla, Mary Anne as Diane, and Dr Franklin Crean as you-know-who.

Subtitles: Interplay; Foreplay; Afterplay.

Out Of Sight: Diane remembers a dinner with Maris. She apparently ate everyone's serving of sorbet, then had to go and get a member of staff to massage her stomach. Diane laughs as she remembers the funny little woman, then realises she has said something insensitive. She asks Niles if she and he 'got married and lived happily ever after'. 'No,' says Niles. 'Can't say as we did.'

Frasier Has Left The Building: Eddie sits on the couch with a sock in his mouth, and Martin comes out and tells him off for stealing it. The screen fades to black, and we see Eddie caught in a spotlight (in a similar manner to a part of Diane's play, where three of the characters explain how their lives are tied to the bar, and to Diane, more out of habit than choice). A thought bubble appears above the dog's head, reading 'I can't help it. It's what I do.' Back in reality, Eddie snuffles under a sofa pillow and pulls out another sock.

On The Couch: A brilliant episode, with probably the best opening scene the show has had. Just after a jolly Diane appears, waving, at the window of Frasier's studio, the screen cuts to black. We then hear a scream build in volume and, as the camera pulls out, we see that the black was the darkness inside Frasier's wide-open mouth.

The episode is made up of a series of hilarious scenes: the first panicked conversation with Niles about Diane's return; the dinner party at Frasier's; and finally the exclusive preview of *Rhapsody and Requiem*. This is certainly the highlight: Frasier's increasingly angry reactions to seeing Diane parade Cheers and her life there across the stage are very funny. The play itself is a brilliant spoof on experimental drama, particularly the vignettes of Stan, Ned and Clark and their attachment to the bar. Just after Frasier has reassured his father that Diane has changed – that she no longer believes the world revolves around her – we see a play written about herself and her power over people. A marvellous contrivance.

The ending is suitably emotional, but one still can't help but notice the inappropriateness of Frasier being attracted to Diane (just as it seemed a little misplaced in *Cheers*). Nevertheless, Kelsey Grammer does a fine job of showing us exactly how his character feels.

3.15

'A Word to the Wiseguy'

Written by Joe Keenan
Directed by Philip Charles MacKenzie
First UK Transmission: 18.10.96

Skyline: Nothing happens.

Synopsis: Could this be the key to Niles getting Maris back? When she phones, in trouble with the police for a traffic violation, Niles is overjoyed – she needs his help, and he feels that this is the chance to prove himself to her. When Martin refuses to use his police contacts to help him, though, Niles turns to more nefarious methods.

Roz recommends to him Jerome Belasco, a man who can 'fix' things, and Niles and Frasier arrange to meet him. With one simple phone call, Maris is cleared of all charges. Niles immediately offers payment, but Belasco refuses, so Niles says that he will do any favour for him in return.

The next day, Belasco appears at Frasier's apartment to collect his favour. He wants Frasier to talk to his girlfriend Brandy during his show and tell her to marry Belasco. When Brandy does call in, though, Frasier hears a catalogue of misery about the relationship that makes him have second thoughts. In the end, all he can do is tell Brandy to leave Belasco for ever.

Guest Cast: Jerome Belasco (Harris Yulin).

Who's On The Line?: We hear the end of a conversation, with Frasier telling someone to avoid bingeing on food so that they can fit into some lovely new ball gown. It's then revealed by a somewhat distracted and embarrassed Frasier that the caller's name is Steve (Randy Travis).

And, of course, there's Brandy (Faith Prince), who tells Frasier that Jerome forces her not to get a job, that she thinks he's cheating on her, and that the sex with him is over faster than a vaccination. (Brandy, eventually, gets a job as Niles's receptionist, where she announces his job to all callers as 'per-sy-key-at-rist'.)

Subtitles: The Little Commodore; A Word To The Wiseguy; Doesn't Everyone Have Poi Ramekins?

Strange Bedfellows: Roz announces that she once went out with a man, called Phil, who had trouble with the police ('Notice the complete lack of gasps following that statement,' says Niles), and that's how she got to learn about Jerome Belasco.

Full-on Moon: When Belasco visits Frasier's apartment, Daphne tries to discern his exact line of work with her psychic abilities. She thinks he is an osteopath, because she can see him 'hovering over people with broken bones'.

Out Of Sight: Frasier reports that it's no wonder Maris has a pile of unpaid parking tickets – she believes her allergy to chocolate entitles her to use disabled parking spaces.

Frasier can see Maris being imprisoned only 'if they move the bars closer together', and later describes her to Belasco as 'ounces of fun'.

Maris used to call her father 'the Commodore', and he was the one who sorted out her problems when she stole a jewelled crucifix from the Vatican.

And Niles gets a pleasant surprise this episode – for the first time ever, Maris says 'thank you' to him.

Frasier Has Left The Building: All the way through the episode, Martin has been troubled by an unknown someone who is stealing his newspaper. Over the closing credits, we see that the thief is a young professional woman. As she tries to sneak off with the paper the lift doors open, so she craftily drops it to the floor to avoid suspicion. Niles, emerging from the lift, picks it up for her like the gentleman he is, and then gives it back.

On The Couch: Top marks to the scriptwriter for familiarising Niles with all the *Godfather*-esque lingo. His constant commentary on the dealings with Belasco is very funny. After a couple of episodes centred on the characters in the show, things go more or less back to normal this time out. Brandy is a scream, with a voice that could curdle milk, and the 'happy' ending is very funny. An all-round entertaining episode.

3.16
'Look Before You Leap'

Written by Chuck Ranberg and Anne Flett-Giordano
Directed by James Burrows
First UK Transmission: 25.10.96

Skyline: The elevator goes up the Space Needle.

Synopsis: It's 29 February, and Frasier is in fine spirits: the day is unseasonably warm and bright, and he begins to think it's the perfect day for taking a leap. He urges everyone around him to do something that they wouldn't normally do. Daphne is persuaded to finally treat herself to a new hair-do; Martin is urged to go to Montana for the birthday of an old police buddy; Roz is cajoled into declaring – on air – her instant love for someone she met on the bus. Frasier himself is due to appear on a telethon that night and pledges that, instead of his usual 'Buttons and Bows', he is going to sing a difficult aria from Verdi's *Rigoletto*.

On the other hand, Niles is dissuaded from having sex with Maris, no matter how much *crème fraîche* is involved. Frasier is worried that doing so would ruin any chance of serious discussion between them over their future. This doesn't sit well with an increasingly horny Niles – even a cold shower can't stop him thinking about sex with Maris.

As the day goes on, Frasier's advice begins to backfire on the band of leapers. Martin's flight nearly ends in disaster when a flock of geese are sucked through the engines;

Roz almost gets together with her man then discovers he's married; and Daphne's new hairstyle is a total mess. Panicked by everyone's misfortune, Frasier decides that he's not stupid or brave enough to try the aria, so he plumps for 'Buttons and Bows' once again. But, even then, is he safe?

Guest Cast: Pete (Murphy Dunne), Gary (Justin Gorence), Stage Manager (Benjamin Brown).

Where Everybody Knows Their Name: When Niles is getting excited, and a bit sickly, about the thought of having sex with Maris, Martin reminds him of the time he and Hester wouldn't discuss the Cuban missile crisis in front of him, because it gave him bad dreams. 'It's a two-way street,' Martin tells his son.

Subtitles: No, But I Hear Olag Cassini Takes That Bus; Huh?

Strange Bedfellows: Roz tells Frasier the story of meeting Gary on the bus. 'Suddenly,' she says, 'I smell Lagerfeld. And I look up and there he is.' 'Carl Lagerfeld?' teases Frasier. When she describes Gary over the air, she begins to gush before finally saying he is 'cute'. The shock to her system of being so gooey over a man leads her to think she's turning into Marsha Brady.

Full-on Moon: Martin does a very mean (take that any way you want) impersonation of Daphne talking about her hair, Princess Di and, of course, Grammie Moon's words of wisdom.

Out Of Sight: Maris has phoned Niles, suggesting they should 'get together' – and he knows she means '. . . for sex'. He begins to ponder dreamily on this, and even Frasier's advice to Niles to take a cold shower does no good – he still can't stop thinking about his wife. 'It stood to reason,' Frasier realises, 'being showered with coldness would only bring Maris more to mind.'

The Buddy Show: Being the end of February in a leap year, it is the birthday of Martin's old police friend Jimmy (he's sixteen, though he is, of course, really sixty-four years old). He really wants to go to the party, as they always have a competition over who has got the best scar. Now that Shark-Bait O'Reilly has died, Martin thinks he's in with a good chance of winning.

Eddie Takes The Biscuit: Frasier appears at the beginning of the episode, having taken Eddie for a walk. 'What are you doing with him?' asks a surprised Martin. 'We went for a walk,' Frasier replies. 'I was talking to Eddie,' says Martin.

As Martin and Daphne finish watching Frasier's hilariously disastrous rendition of 'Buttons and Bows', they suggest that they rewind and watch it again. Before they can, however, Eddie grabs the remote control and runs off with it.

Frasier Has Left The Building: Niles arrives at Frasier's, to console his brother on his embarrassment at the telethon. Frasier checks that Niles didn't have sex with Maris, and Niles reassures him that he stayed chaste. But, as Frasier moves off, Niles wipes the last bit of crème fraîche from behind his ear.

On The Couch: Ah, misfortune – the root of the best belly laughs. This episode is basically a series of very funny jokes about how good ideas can cause horrible pain. The best is, of course, Frasier's last-minute reversion to 'Buttons and Bows', the words to which he has suddenly and inexplicably forgotten. Martin's description of the plane crash, though, is brilliant – especially the part about not minding when the man next to him suddenly grabbed his hand.

Niles's desperate situation is also brilliant. When Daphne walks in, her hair in a nightmare state, mascara smeared by her tears, his cry of 'Will these infernal temptations never end?' is so wonderfully heartfelt. The moment when he finally realises that 'Niles gotta have it!' is bliss.

3.17

'High Crane Drifter'

Written by Jack Burditt
Directed by Philip Charles MacKenzie
First UK Transmission: 01.11.96

Skyline: Lights go on in various buildings.

Synopsis: Frasier is late for work: someone has parked in his space, and he has had to park several blocks away. This is only the first of many discourtesies piled against him. When he gets home, his new neighbour in the penthouse upstairs, the rock star Freddie Chainsaw, is playing his music too loud. (When Daphne tells him that his last album sold five million copies, a bitter Frasier comments, 'I'll just add that to my list of reasons to die.') He finally has to leave his own apartment just to get some peace, but even the usual haven of Café Nervosa isn't free from impoliteness.

Frasier and Niles try time after time to get to a table just as it becomes free, but each time they are beaten by someone else. Finally, they stand by a couple who are about to pay their bill. As they leave, they step aside to let them go – but someone quickly sneaks into one of their vacated seats. This is the final straw for Frasier, who grabs the man by his shoulders and pushes him out of the café.

The next day, this contretemps has made it to the newspaper's society pages, and Frasier is being hailed as a hero for his 'politeness'. Daphne was inspired to take action against someone who annoyed her. Someone had been taking her laundry out of the machine and leaving it, unfolded and wet, on the table. In revenge, she took her new red knickers and put them in with his white wash. And she's not the only one – all Frasier's callers are phoning in to say that they have taken extreme forms of revenge against people who have been impolite to them. Frasier begins to realise that his actions have prompted a wave of angry retribution across Seattle, and decides to meet with the man from the café and try to settle this with words. But the man announces that he is suing Frasier for assault.

Guest Cast: Video Store Clerk (Mark Benninghofen), Doug Harvey (John Cygan), Customer (Naomi), Curtis (Troy Blendell).

Where Everybody Knows Their Name: A return appearance for the waiter played by Paul Cusimano, who tells everyone that Niles's rented car is being towed away.

Who's On The Line?: Roz fills in for Frasier when he is late and begins to take a call from Lydia (Joan Allen), who is receiving obscene phone calls. Just as Lydia starts to explain her problem, Frasier crashes in, exhausted from running, and takes over from Roz. He leans into the microphone and pants heavily from his exertion. Lydia screams at a confused Frasier.

Before he goes on, Frasier apologises for being late, saying that there's 'nothing quite so inconsiderate as making someone wait'. The next call is from Brenda (Katarina Witt), who is having some sort of trouble with her sister. Just as she is about to explain, there is a clicking sound as Brenda's call-waiting kicks in, and she tells Frasier to wait a moment.

The day after the incident in Café Nervosa, Frasier receives a series of calls from people who have been inspired by his actions. Mitch (Jerry Orbach) has smashed the leaf blower that his neighbour uses early in the morning; Chris (Billy Barty) has stuffed rotten shrimp in someone's air-conditioning unit; Chuck (Eric Idle) has FedExed someone a package of one hundred scorpions; Rochelle (Jane Pauley) has set her neighbours' lawn on fire in revenge for their dog fouling her own; and there is a brief mention of 'Becky with a nail gun'.

Subtitles: A Little Something For All You Donald Crisp Fans; The Etiquette Lesson; No Actors Were Hurt During The Filming Of This Scene.

Culture Vultures: Niles's car has been scraped, so he has had to hire a new one. But the hire firm had run out of luxury models, and he has been lumbered with something he calls 'a hunchback'. When Frasier explains that they're called hatchbacks because of the design of their boot, Niles is amazed that 'they named the car after its most hideous feature'. A little later, when the 'hunchback' is under threat of being towed away, Niles won't lift a finger to stop it – he doesn't want anyone to know that it's his car.

Niles's apparent knowledge of zoology gets an amusing airing: when he greets Frasier after his new-found fame as a man of action, he describes him as 'the man who floats like a lepidoptera and stings like a hymenoptera'.

Frasier Has Left The Building: Daphne is in the lift, heading down to the laundry room with a basket full of clothes. Two men join her in the lift, both carrying rackets: one is dressed in tennis whites, the other in tennis pinks. As they leave, Daphne pulls her red knickers from the basket, twirls them around her finger, and blows over them as if they were the smoking barrel of a gun.

On The Couch: Frasier's tension in this episode is palpable: one bad thing after another winds him up and up, until the 'etiquette lesson' at Café Nervosa is inevitable. His ethical unease with the situation he subsequently finds himself in is just as real. Kelsey Grammer really does a fine job here. Niles's jealousy of Frasier's ability to stand up for himself is fun. It is this, of course, that leads him to take his own actions to save the day.

A great little episode, really digging the goldmine of Frasier's character to find some wonderful comedy.

3.18

'Chess Pains'

Written by Rob Greenberg
Directed by Gordon Hunt
First UK Transmission: 08.11.96

Skyline: The light atop the Space Needle glows.

Synopsis: Frasier has bought an antique chess set and wants to play with it as soon as possible. Niles declines, explaining that it would remind him too much of Maris, so Frasier turns instead to his father. After a little persuasion, Martin sits down for a game with Frasier, and he wins. This troubles Frasier – after all, isn't he the more intelligent one within the family?

To appease his competitive streak, Frasier challenges Martin to another game. Martin wins again; and he wins the next, and the next. Frasier, by this point, is driven to distraction and cannot sleep. In the dead of night, he sets off the smoke alarm to wake everyone. Since he is awake, Frasier suggests, maybe Martin would like a game of chess. His father begins to suspect that this is about more than just chess and tries to refuse, but when Frasier offers him $5,000 if he wins, Martin leaps to the board. This time, he loses, but still Frasier worries – did Martin let him win?

Where Everybody Knows Their Name: This episode marks the first appearance of Niles's nameless whippet (the 'actor' isn't named either). Martin, Frasier and Daphne all carefully try to avoid stating the obvious to Niles – after all, he has got the dog to fill the void in his life left by Maris's departure. But he seems to have filled the void a little too accurately: the dog is small, thin, quiet, sensitive, delicate, and it completely refuses to do anything he says – which is fine by him. (Even the subtitle – 'And She's Hypoglycemic' – rams the point home!)

There's also a very quick appearance by Luck Hari's waitress at Café Nervosa, and a reference to Frederick, who, Frasier fears, may one day beat him at chess.

Subtitles: Maybe It's Short For Nodule; And She's Hypoglycemic; Chess Pains.

Culture Vultures: Frasier's new chess set is a Jean-Francois Blanc design, from 1882.

Strange Bedfellows: Roz arrives at Nervosa distraught. 'Trouble on the dating front?' asks Frasier, not unreasonably. 'I'm not that shallow, all right?' she bites back. 'It's about my hair.'

Full-on Moon: Daphne tries to cheer up the defeated Frasier in the same way she used to jolly her brothers along when they lost a football match. She makes a little sock puppet and sings a song to Frasier, trying to get him to join in. Frasier just reaches out and clamps the puppet's mouth shut, saying, 'I would rather have a tarantula lay eggs in my ear than hear any more of this puppet show.' Daphne gets the point, and she and the puppet leave him alone.

Out Of Sight: Niles won't play chess with Frasier because it will remind him of the Thursday evenings he spent playing the game with Maris. Frasier can see that she would be a fan of the game: 'The king is stationary, while the queen has all the power.'

Eddie Takes The Biscuit: Daphne says that the relationship with a dog can be one of the most rewarding a person can know. Just at that point, Eddie jogs up – lead in mouth – desperate for a walk. Daphne tells him that, since he's always drinking from the toilet, it's about time he learnt how to use it.

Frasier Has Left The Building: Daphne and Martin play draughts, and Daphne wins. Martin picks up a sofa cushion and screams into it, echoing an earlier scene in which Frasier – who has just lost a game of chess to his father – screams with rage into a large cushion on the balcony.

On The Couch: In a series of brilliant scenes, Martin wins game after game of chess. It's a nice touch that the only moves we ever see him make are the final, winning ones. His victories are always effortless, despite the fact that he refers to the pieces by names such as 'prawns', 'tower thingy' and 'horsey guy'. The final battle, in the small hours of the morning, is fought using the most wonderfully bitter tactics –

particularly Frasier's sudden mention of a phone call from the cemetery where his father is to be buried one day.

Of course, the whole episode is about 'the son eclipsing the father', as Niles puts it. While Frasier thinks this is already the case, there is still this final battle of the chess games to be won. And then, when he does win, he naturally suspects that his father deliberately lost. Once he is convinced that the game was won fairly, however, all Frasier can do is say, 'I'm sorry I beat you, Dad.' A rather sweet ending to a very good episode.

3.19

'Crane Versus Crane'

Written by David Lloyd
Directed by Philip Charles MacKenzie
First UK Transmission: 15.11.96

Skyline: A streak of lightning crosses the sky.

Synopsis: Niles has been asked to testify against an old millionaire called Harlow Safford. Safford's son is convinced that the old man is not in a fit mental state to govern his own money any more, and wants control of his estate to be handed over to him. Not long after Niles agrees to take part in the proceedings, Frasier is approached by Mr Giroux, Safford's defence lawyer, and asked to at least try to talk Niles out of testifying against him. Though reluctant, Frasier agrees to spend an evening in Safford's company to make his own mind up about the man.

After a few hours with Safford, Frasier decides that, far from being in any way mentally unsound, the old man is simply living the kind of childlike, frivolous life to which he is entitled. When Frasier approaches Niles to tell him this, his brother accuses him of being jealous of Niles's upcoming fame (the trial is to be televised). The conversation soon turns into a bitter argument and Frasier decides to testify against Niles in the courtroom.

When the day of the trial comes, Frasier speaks first, but Safford's behaviour begins to deteriorate. Although it starts off as merely disruptive, it soon turns into sheer lunacy as he imagines the courtroom to be a train, and the people in it to be passengers. It seems that Niles was right, after all.

Guest Cast: Harlow Safford (Donald O'Connor), Mr Giroux (James Winker), Judge (Neil Vipond), Bailiff (Baron Kelly).

Who's On The Line?: Frasier discovers that Roz is giving advice to his callers once the show is over. He interrupts her telling Beth (Mrs Fields), a woman convinced her husband is having an affair, to hire a private detective. After Frasier chastises her for her interference, Roz promises never to do it again. As Frasier closes the door behind him, Roz picks up the phone to Bill and says, 'I'm listening.'

Subtitles: Second Opinion; If I Had Only Worn My Cotton Chinos; Another Reason To Keep Cameras Out Of The Courtroom.

Culture Vultures: Shortly after the episode opens, Niles and Frasier return from a performance of Wagner's *Parsifal*.

Full-on Moon: To back up Martin's argument that being old doesn't necessarily make you infirm, Daphne mentions her Great-Aunt Beryl. She lived well into her nineties, though she did lose her eyesight in her seventies and her sense of balance in her eighties. It seems that her testimony does little to back Martin up.

The Buddy Show: Martin is watching a tape of a boxing match which one of his police friends recorded for him from pay-per-view television. His friend can't get pay-per-view, but he does have a pirate aerial; he copied the match for him and biked the tape over to his apartment on the police station's account. As Frasier puts it: 'Another inspiring tale of our men in law enforcement.'

Eddie Takes The Biscuit: Eddie has an unerring sense of when Martin is eating junk food. He rushes in as Martin tries to settle down with a huge bag of crisps. Daphne shows him the way that she gets rid of Eddie when she doesn't want him around: she makes a high-pitched yelping noise, and Eddie runs and buries his head under a sofa cushion. Just then, Frasier and Niles return from the opera, singing one of the arias. Even more terrified, Eddie makes a break for Martin's room.

Frasier Has Left The Building: Niles, since he never got the chance to read his summation at the hearing, reads it now to the decidedly uninterested bailiff in the judge's chair. When Niles has finished, he slips some money into the man's hand – his payment for listening.

On The Couch: This episode's subject matter is, frankly, dull and – more importantly – weak. Its main fault lies in the fact that it undermines itself. We'd all love to believe Frasier when he makes his impassioned attack on society's view of normality, but Safford's mad outburst in the courtroom makes both him and us feel like fools. Although we've nothing against Niles, in this case we really don't want him to be right.

The many arguments between the brothers, though, are a source of a few good laughs. Their reconciliation at the end, where Frasier offers to be the judge so Niles can get the chance to read his summation, is both amusing and warm (though he doesn't go through with it). But, on the whole, this episode is not one of the best the series has ever served up.

3.20
'Police Story'

Written by Sy Rosen
Directed by Philip Charles MacKenzie
First UK Transmission: 22.11.96

Skyline: Party balloons float up from behind the skyline.

Synopsis: Driving at breakneck speeds, Frasier is stopped by an attractive policewoman. She is about to write him out a ticket when, thanks to Frasier's unsubtle hints, she realises that he is *the* Frasier Crane, from the radio. Because of this, and the fact that she notices from his licence that today is his forty-third birthday, she decides to let him off, warning him to drive carefully – she wouldn't want to see him get hurt, after all.

This little meeting plays on Frasier's mind: he is convinced that the policewoman liked him. He gets Martin to phone the station and find out more about her – and learns that her name is Maureen Cutler. When they discover that she is drinking that night at McGinty's, Frasier persuades his dad to accompany him (so he doesn't stick out like a sore thumb, obviously).

They get there and meet up with Maureen and, while Frasier is at the bar, Martin and Maureen begin to chat. Halfway through their conversation, Maureen's pager beeps and she has to go. Before she leaves, she gives Martin her number and tells him that she'd love to get together with him sometime.

Martin is now in a quandary: *he* finds Maureen attractive and would love to see her again, but how will Frasier feel about his father stealing the woman he likes?

Guest Cast: Charlotte (Jillie Mack), Maggie (Denise Poirer).

Where Everybody Knows Their Name: Maureen Cutler (Jane Kaczmarek) makes her first appearance as Martin's new belle. Luck Hari's waitress is asked by Niles to get Martin a plain coffee. She asks if he would like a biscotti, and Niles says that he probably would – but she is to call it a cookie so as not to frighten Martin. Martin, though, knows what a biscotti is, making him think he is being talked down to. And there's a brief reappearance of KACL's favourite busybody, Elizabeth (Bette Rae).

Subtitles: Sins Of The Father; Does This Mean You Won't Do My Taxes, Edna?

Strange Bedfellows: At the beginning of the episode, Frasier is speeding because he's giving Roz a lift to her date and she's running late. Unfortunately, he gets pulled over just at the point when Roz is on the back seat, pulling her jeans on. Maureen naturally assumes that she is a 'birthday treat' for Frasier.

Full-on Moon: Daphne gathers her friends at Frasier's apartment, thinking that Frasier is out. Although we don't hear Maggie talk much, Charlotte has a lot to say – and her accent is even more bizarre than Daphne's.

The Buddy Show: Martin gets his force chum Charlie to identify Maureen from the area Frasier was in when he was stopped.

Frasier Has Left The Building: Frasier is asleep on the couch as Martin arrives back home from his date with Maureen. He tries to quietly sneak past but Eddie rushes in and leaps on Frasier, waking him up.

On The Couch: An episode that, while funny, lets itself down by portraying Frasier as too daft and Martin as too selfish. Can we honestly believe that Martin would date the woman that Frasier is after, without there being any comic consequences (which there are not)? And Frasier's over-enthusiastic attraction to a total stranger is a little out of character – regardless of the nine months that have passed since the last time he had sex, with Edna from Accounting.

Nevertheless, the episode has its moments. The scene where Martin asks for Niles's advice over the situation is great, with Niles desperate to be able to tell Frasier that his dad has been asked out by Maureen. And the surprise party at KACL (with Edna in attendance) is brilliant. Frasier tells Roz exactly how angry and depressed he is, and why, in full earshot of the hiding staff members. He asks Roz if there is anything that can possibly make his life any worse. 'Surprise!' scream the staff of KACL.

3.21

'Where There's Smoke There's Fired'

Written by Joe Keenan
Directed by Philip Charles MacKenzie
First UK Transmission: 29.11.96

Skyline: A helicopter rises up from the skyline and departs.

Synopsis: KACL has a new owner, a Texan millionaire called Wilford S. Boone – better known as Big Willy. Frasier immediately starts to research him: he has heard that he gives national syndication contracts to the presenters he's particularly fond of. But, before Frasier can find some way to suck up to the new boss, Big Willy offers him the perfect solution himself. Willy is about to marry his young mistress, but won't do so until she gives up smoking. If Frasier can make her kick the habit in just three days, then the marriage can go ahead. Frasier, of course, agrees to try but doesn't realise exactly how tough the job will be until he meets the blushing bride-to-be. It's Bebe Glazer, his maniacal agent.

Bebe spends the weekend trapped in the Frasier apartment as he forces her to try to kick the habit. Over dinner, it comes to light that both Martin and Daphne are ex-smokers. They both try to reassure her, but it's no good: Bebe launches into a long, inspiring speech about the delights of the cigarette, and Martin and Daphne's resolve begins to crack.

Late that night, everyone is bed. Daphne sneaks out on to the balcony for a sneaky cigarette but, as she lights the match, Bebe awakes and tries to cajole a cigarette out of her. Daphne refuses, so Bebe locks her outside. All the commotion wakes Frasier, who also discovers his father taking a quick smoke in the bathroom. Soon, fights break out as Bebe's craving gets the better of her. Finally, Frasier – pointing out that she might lose her inheritance when the ageing Willy dies – persuades Bebe to give up smoking.

Three weeks later, the happy day arrives . . .

Guest Cast: Big Willy (Richard Hamilton).

Where Everybody Knows Their Name: Bebe (Harriet Sansom Harris) is back and, of course, so are the ill-natured barbs about her. When Niles says that she is a barracuda, Frasier points out that 'a barracuda's what you want from an agent'. At the opening of the episode, Frasier is worried because he's not sure where Bebe's got to. Niles assumed that, to get hold of her, you 'just drew a pentagram on the floor and chanted, "I summon thee!" three times'.

At the station, Gil Chesterton (Edward Hibbert) is eager to impress the new owner too. But Bulldog (Dan Butler) has told him that he's a Greek, so Gil has tailored his show all around that: he recommends the delights of feta cheese – 'It's not just for shepherds any more!'

Subtitles: Waiting To Inhale; Three Smoke-Free Weeks Later.

Strange Bedfellows: After the events of the wedding, the things Roz announces that she will miss most about not getting the syndication deal are 'the beach house' and 'the pool boys'.

Bebe touches on the depraved things Big Willy made her do in bed. 'Ever worn a saddle?' she asks Roz. Roz just looks up and says, 'Do I have to answer that?'

Full-on Moon: Daphne has smoked for years, but she has never become addicted. On hearing this, Bebe says, 'You know, there's a word for people who can do that . . . What is it? Oh, yes . . . Bitch!'

Out Of Sight: Niles knows all about addiction, thanks to Maris's 'Cough Syrup Years'.

Frasier Has Left The Building: Gil Chesterton sits in his studio, wearing a ten-gallon hat and chewing on a rib. A fellow worker slips him a note and so, with a sigh of relief, he puts down the rib and takes off the hat.

On The Couch: A dazzling episode that is more about addiction than it is about its guest star. Bebe is manic enough at the best of times but take her away from her crutch and see her scrabbling for comfort, and she becomes truly terrifying. The scene between her and Daphne in the dead of night is pure brilliance: impeccably scripted and wonderfully acted. The highlight, though, has to be Bebe's monologue on the sensuality of smoking a cigarette: reaffirming for smokers, maddening for ex-smokers, and indescribably tempting for nonsmokers.

Bebe's relationship with Big Willy also has to be seen to be believed. This shark among women, this powerful woman who will always get her own way, cowed before a diminutive little man she calls 'puddin'' and 'daddy'. The swings Harriet Sansom Harris manages between the Bebe that we know and the one that Big Willy knows are breathtaking.

From beginning to end, classic, riotous *Frasier*.

3.22

'Frasier Loves Roz'

Written by Suzanne Martin
Directed by Philip Charles MacKenzie
First UK Transmission: 06.12.96

Skyline: Fireworks explode over the skyline.

Synopsis: Roz is sick of always being the bridesmaid. Her friends back in Wisconsin all seem to be settling down, and she isn't. Frasier recommends a change in the type of man she's looking for and Roz agrees that the next man she sees that she'd normally dismiss, she'll try out (bar Bulldog, of course . . .).

Trouble is, two weeks on, she's going out with a man called Ben, whom Niles has been treating. He's a compulsive womaniser who calls his 'victims' 'sunshine' and dumps them at the first sign of commitment. Frasier wants to warn Roz, but Niles won't let him as it would be a breach of patient confidentiality. But, Frasier wails, someone like Ben is 'the last man that Roz should be with'. Niles smirks back, however, 'Don't worry. Knowing Roz, he won't be!'

While Martin steadfastly refuses to make a video for Frederick about his life, Daphne tells Roz that she thinks Frasier's antagonistic behaviour every time she talks about Ben is maybe because he's in love with Roz himself.

Roz thinks about this and suddenly things begin to fall into place . . .

Which is a shame, because Niles and Frasier are hatching a plan to get around their medical ethics by declaring Roz mentally incompetent . . .

Guest Cast: Ben Collins (Michael Mitz).

Where Everybody Knows Their Name: There are passing references to Frasier's failed marriages, and the video he wants of Martin is for Frederick. Bulldog (Dan Butler) is the owner of the camera, and wants it back to video himself and his new girlfriend. Frasier suggests getting a police sketch artist instead, which appeals to Bulldog's devious (or is that deviant?) mind.

Who's On The Line?: Tom (David Duchovny), who is having great regular sex with his girlfriend, even after six years, although he's not sure if he's actually in love with her for the right reasons.

Subtitles: No One Said Anything Particularly Amusing For Two Weeks, And Then . . .; Another Curiously Humorless Week Passed Until . . .; Bridesmaid Revisited.

Culture Vultures: Frasier has to talk Niles through his plane trip to Switzerland, not because he's afraid of flying, but because it's his first time going coach. Oh, and Frasier's manipulation of Niles into helping him with the Ben problem is neat – by using Freud against his Jungian little brother.

Strange Bedfellows: Well ... the whole episode revolves around this theme ...

Out Of Sight: Maris is in Switzerland having her annual goats'-placenta treatments and, when being pursued across the mountain by Niles, leaves no footprints.

Eddie Takes The Biscuit: For the second day in a row, rather than bits of wood or dead animals, Eddie has bought a bunch of flowers back from his walk. Yesterday it was roses, today it's daffodils.

Frasier Has Left The Building: One of the best ever – Roz is finally chucking out her hideous bridesmaid's dresses, much to the delight of the collection man, whom Roz later sees in full wig and make-up strolling through Seattle in her green outfit.

On The Couch: A brilliant episode, hovering between good *Frasier* and good farce, as every move, every sentence Frasier makes, convinces Roz that he's in love with her. The pace never slackens, the subtitles are excellent, the two plots are witty ... Everything just comes together in this classic episode. But highest kudos goes to the sixty-four-year-old Martin, finally doing his video memoirs – and dying just as he's telling the secret combination for the laundered millions ...

3.23

'The Focus Group'

Written by Rob Greenberg
Directed by Philip Charles MacKenzie
First UK Transmission: 13.12.96

Skyline: A shooting star passes overhead.

Synopsis: Daphne is a bit tetchy because Joe has chosen to celebrate their six-month anniversary by heading off to Las

Vegas with his friends – although Martin knows a few good
clubs he could go to. Niles, meanwhile, is also a bit tetchy
because he's being hounded for $4,000 to repair a painting he
accidentally damaged. Their moods cause a friction which
leads to a slanging match. While Daphne is horrified by the
outburst, Niles is very turned on by it and sets out to instigate
rows at every available moment.

Frasier is equally tetchy, because only eleven of a twelve-
strong focus group set up by KACL adore his show. Typically
unable to appreciate that, he becomes obsessed with finding
out why just one man didn't like him but couldn't offer up an
actual reason.

On their way to dinner, Frasier spots the man in his
news-vendor shack, much to the distress of a hungry Martin
and a terrified Niles, who believes their car will be attacked –
either by the postal service workers or the schoolgirls playing
in the rain. Frasier sends Martin to ask the vendor, Manu, why
he didn't like Frasier's show. Martin returns to the car with
the knowledge Manu finds Frasier annoying. But this isn't
enough for Frasier, who confronts Manu to find out exactly
how he is annoying. He soon gets his answer . . .

Guest Cast: Manu (Tony Shalhoub), Data Collector (Cameron
Watson), Leader (Henry Woronicz), Amanda (Marita Geraghty),
Cathy (Heather Macrae), Gary (Pat Skipper), Chuck (David
Breitbarth), Anne (Lin Shaye), Paul (Abdul Salaam El Razzac).

Where Everybody Knows Their Name: Bulldog (Dan
Butler) is also undergoing a focus-group session which
proves, to him, that all the men love him while 'the chicks
pretend not to . . .' Oh, there's another brief reference to
Daphne's ongoing romance with Joe.

Who's On The Line?: Billy, who is showering his reticent
girlfriend with presents she doesn't want.

Subtitles: Looks Like He Had A Side Of Sausage Too; Liar,
Liar, Pants On Fire.

Culture Vultures: An outraged Niles, being pursued by a belligerent gallery owner, wonders 'how he could notice a fleck of foie gras on a Jackson Pollock'.

Strange Bedfellows: Roz is immediately attracted to the eager young data collector who admires her throaty laugh. She subsequently gives him a lot more demonstrations . . .

Eddie Takes The Biscuit: Eddie was responsible for introducing Frasier to his good art restorer after the little dog licked his Liechtenstein.

Frasier Has Left The Building: Bulldog watches from behind the two-way mirror as Roz and the young data collector make out rather aggressively on the table.

On The Couch: A thoroughly unpleasant episode which, instead of giving us our usual paranoid, egotistical Frasier, provides us with an alien duplicate who has no morals or manners. Having destroyed Manu's entire livelihood, and at the same time, had a satisfactory answer to his question, Frasier just wanders off, admittedly offering to pay, but with no concern for Manu's loss. Compare this with the similar speech Martin gives about his chair (see 1.19, 'Give Him The Chair!') and the effect that sentimental attachment to inanimate objects has on Frasier and this underlines how out of character our man is in this show.

There are a couple of nice moments – Martin's refusal to play along with Frasier's insistence that he tell Manu he's a businessman from Cleveland, and Niles's growing hysteria about being parked 'between Heaven and Hell' (i.e. the Ritz and the docks), but beyond that, this is rather insipid and one of the dullest episodes ever. Even the Niles/Daphne sequences lack any real sparkle, and just reinforce the general misery of the show.

Luckily for Channel 4 viewers, eager to see out the third season with a bang, the station ran this episode and immediately followed it with the season finale, perhaps aware that people would remember that one and not this . . .

3.24
'You Can go Home Again'

Written by Linda Moore and Vic Rauseo
Directed by David Lee
First UK Transmission: 13.12.96

Skyline: A hot-air balloon rises from behind the skyline.

Synopsis: It is 21 May 1996, three years to the day that Frasier launched his show on KACL 780 FM. He and Roz trade anniversary gifts – he gives her earrings, she presents him with a tape of that first show.

Arriving home, Frasier finds Daphne talking to her mother, trying to get out of spending her week's holiday in Manchester – she'd rather go to Acapulco, but she'll feel too guilty if she does. As she goes off to study brochures and make her mind up, Frasier puts the tape on and settles down, Eddie on his lap. 'Fasten your seat belt,' he tells the dog, 'it's going to be a bumpy ride . . .'

The broadcast starts off Frasier's daydream as he remembers the actual day of that first broadcast. After finding his way around the studio, he meets Roz Doyle, his new producer, who thinks psychiatry is bull and would rather do a gardening programme. Frasier's previous producer, Dave, has quit after doing the demos, unable to cope with Frasier's demands, and Roz imagines she too will go. After the disastrous opening to the show, she compiles a list of at least twenty-five points of improvement.

At Café Nervosa, he accidentally bumps into Niles, who takes him to see their father in his apartment. Martin is none too keen on Frasier and, after Niles has left them alone, they try to find some common ground . . .

Guest Cast: Waiter (John Rajeski).

Where Everybody Knows Their Name: Hester Crane receives a couple of mentions, both in moments of bitterness.

First from Niles, who points out that, since she died, he has had to look after Martin, and later Martin himself observes how Frasier stopped visiting Seattle once Hester died. And Boston gets quite a few namechecks (Frasier was there for fifteen years), although the Cheers bar is curiously absent from his reminiscences.

Who's On The Line?: Angela (Sherry Lansing), whose husband is dead, was Frasier's first ever caller and later we hear of someone who apparently called in to congratulate him on his third anniversary.

Subtitles: May 21, 1993 1:57 PM; May 21, 1993 5:13 PM.

Culture Vultures: On Frasier's first ever visit to Café Nervosa, he witnesses a prime example of Niles's snobbery as he orders his coffee. 'A double decaff, non-fat latte, medium foam, dusted with just the faintest whisper of cinnamon.' When there is too much cinnamon on it, Niles berates the waiter and Frasier hopes he never becomes as fussy about his coffee (probably a swipe at his actions most discernibly demonstrated in 1.24, 'My Coffee With Niles'). Watching Niles heap foam and cinnamon on to his napkin, Frasier remarks that he has 'forgotten what a weird little person you are', to his brother.

Full-on Moon: Daphne dreads heading home because she and her mother get all their news out of the way on the journey home from the airport and there's precious little else to do all week except listen to her father retell the story of how he 'shared a cigar with Winston Churchill during the blackout'.

Out Of Sight: 'Like the arctic puffin,' to which Niles likens his relationship with Maris, 'we've mated for life.' Frasier's look says it all.

The Buddy Show: Rather than talk to his newly returned son, Martin opts to head down to Duke's with the guys for a drink.

Eddie Takes The Biscuit: In both time frames, Eddie spends a lot of his time doing his traditional staring at Frasier. The spell is broken when Frasier surprises the little terrier by suddenly giving him an enormous kiss.

Frasier Has Left The Building: The now traditional (but incomplete) thanks-for-calling listing: Brooke Adams (Marilyn in 3.05, 'Kisses Sweeter Than Wine'), Joan Allen (Lydia from 3.17, 'High Crane Drifter'), Billy Barty (Chris from 3.17, 'High Crane Drifter'), Matthew Broderick (Mark in 3.01, 'She's the Boss'), Blair Brown (Jill from 3.02, 'Shrink Rap'), Cyd Charisse (Polly in 3.07, 'The Adventures of Bad Boy and Dirty Girl'), Billy Crystal (Jack in 3.04, 'Leapin' Lizards'), Laura Dern (June from 3.06, 'Sleeping with the Enemy'), David Duchovny (Tom in 3.22, 'Frasier Loves Roz'), Carrie Fisher (Phyllis in 3.01, 'She's the Boss'), Jodie Foster (Marlene in 3.13, 'Moon Dance'), Teri Garr (Nancy in 3.01, 'She's the Boss'), Eric Idle (Chuck from 3.17, 'High Crane Drifter'), Sherry Lansing (Angela in 3.24, 'You Can Go Home Again'), Ray Liotta (Bob in 3.09, 'Frasier Grinch'), Mary Elizabeth Mastrantonio (Eileen in 3.03, 'Martin Does It His Way'), Armistead Maupin (Gerard in 3.11, 'The Friend'), Paul Mazursky (Vinnie in 3.08, 'The Last Time I Saw Maris'), Jerry Orbach (Mitch from 3.17, 'High Crane Drifter') and Faith Prince (Brandy in 3.15, 'A Word to the Wiseguy').

On The Couch: After three years, there are plenty of regular set pieces and subtle in-jokes to pack this flashback episode to the brim with quality. With everything – from the start of Eddie's fascination with Frasier (previously it was Niles but, as the younger Crane triumphantly proclaims 'the torch has been passed'), Frasier's dislike of call-screening to Martin's Sinatra fascination (look at the records on the sideboard) – they're all there. With Roz and Niles colliding, and even a familiar young Englishwoman (in a very frightful hat) asking for the sugar, everyone has their moment from the past.

But again, the show belongs to Frasier and Martin as they try to find some common ground upon which to walk.

Foreshadowing so much of the antagonism that played out during the early episodes, this is great because, although you know it cannot go right in this flashback, knowing it will eventually makes it much sweeter. Add to this a tremendously different, less skittish and almost malevolent performance from David Hyde Pierce as the put-upon Niles, and you have one of the best *Frasier* episodes so far, and a marvellous way to sew up the third, crest-riding season.

Season Four

4.01

'The Two Mrs Cranes'

Written by Joe Keenan
Directed by David Lee
First UK Transmission: 11.07.97

Skyline: Fireworks explode over the skyline.

Synopsis: Niles is still living with Frasier, although driving his brother mad by continually picking out and discarding the currants and nuts from his nut-and-currant breakfast muffins. Daphne has received a telephone call from Clive, her ex-fiancé, while Martin is preparing for his trip to Rattlesnake Ridge for an old army reunion, as soon as he can twist one of his boys' arms into driving him there.

Preparing for Clive's forthcoming visit, which she is dreading because the last thing she wants is a lovesick Clive all over her again, she looks as dowdy as possible. When Clive turns up, he again proposes to Daphne. Without thinking, she hurriedly introduces Clive to her husband, Dr Niles Crane, whom she married six months previously. Delighted by his sudden promotion, Niles easily plays the adoring husband and bundles her into the kitchen. Briefly alone, Clive then meets Frasier and they talk about Dr Crane's wife. Assuming he means Maris, Frasier is subsequently appalled to realise the scam that is going on, especially when Niles points out that Frasier is staying there, in *his* apartment, while he gets over his 'spat with his wife, Maris'! Frasier takes Daphne into the kitchen and says this has to stop, but before anything else can happen, Niles – delighted to have every excuse to keep kissing Daphne – asks Clive to stay to dinner. Frasier agrees to keep the story going only if Daphne takes Martin to Rattlesnake Ridge.

Martin then returns and is quickly let into the charade, and he delights in trying to upset the applecart. Frasier says he should leave but Martin refuses and begins charming Clive with tales of when he was a leading astronaut – claiming he gave Buzz Aldrin his nickname (he was apparently scared of bees!).

When Roz arrives, she becomes 'Maris' but takes an instant shine to Clive, who then reveals he's now quite a rich entrepreneur. Daphne is suddenly interested and so the two Mrs Cranes begin flirting outrageously, stabbing each other in the back and generally out-bitching each other for Clive's affections . . .

Guest Cast: Clive (Scott Atkinson).

Where Everybody Knows Their Name: Gil Chesterton (Edward Hibbert) is at the station, and the man-eating Bonnie Weems gets a mention but no appearance.

Who's On The Line?: Keith, a narcoleptic who, it transpires, wants to work in air-traffic control, rang in earlier.

Subtitles: Next In The Repertory 'Cosi Fan Tushy'.

Strange Bedfellows: Roz borrowed Frasier's opera glasses when a man moved into the apartment opposite hers. He was a bodybuilder, and Roz copied his name down from his mailbox, looked him up in the phone book and then called him whenever he was in the shower. This meant he had to cross the room, naked, to answer the phone and Roz would then watch through Frasier's glasses. Devious or what?

Full-on Moon: Clive is Daphne's ex-fiancé from England (though you'd never know it from his curious Dick Van Dyke-esque 'Gawd bless yer, Murry Poppins' accent). They were engaged for years but Daphne couldn't see a future with him as he had no drive and no ambition, and just wanted to mess around with car engines. When she dumped him, she added that if they were both still free in five years, she'd reconsider. And here he is!

The Buddy Show: Martin has received a message from one 'Bud' Farrell, an old army pal. His platoon are having a reunion at Rattlesnake Ridge. Among the other ex-soldiers going are Stinky (who wants a lift), Wolf-Man, Boom-Boom and Jim – whose real name is not Jim but he gets his nickname because of the copious amounts of a certain brand of whisky. For that matter, Bud's real name is Hank, but he's called Bud because he drinks an equally famous brand of American beer.

Eddie Takes The Biscuit: Although he actually has nothing to do, it is worth noting that the only thing that everyone can agree on in this episode is to tell Clive that the dog is actually named Eddie . . .

Frasier Has Left The Building: Frasier, Daphne and Niles are on the sofa, with the younger Crane picking bits out of his cookies.

On The Couch: 'I'll never understand how two men like you could have been spawned by that sweet, courageous old astronaut!' Poor Clive, swept along with this spur-of-the-moment charade and having to try to keep up with who has married whom, who has argued with whom, who is pregnant by whom and who is infertile. Frasier magnificently stays aloof from it all, taking every jibe and insult (but undoubtedly storing them up) and, with Niles's 'love toll' every time Daphne passes by and Martin's fantastic adventures as Commander Crane, Astronaut, this episode opens the fourth season with a bang.

Among the best bits are Roz and Daphne, getting more and more evil towards each other, with Niles stirring things up every so often and Roz's initial reaction to being Maris!

The only letdown to the whole thing is Scott Atkinson's dreadfully cod English accent – the poor man has clearly seen *Mary Poppins* once too often and he really needed to burst into 'Chim-Chim Cheree' to alleviate the awfulness of the whole thing. But ultimately, who cares? Because this really is *Frasier* at its best – although any new viewers would probably miss most of the jokes because it does rather depend on your knowing the entire life history of the characters.

4.02

'Love Bites Dog'

Written by Suzanne Martin
Directed by Jeff Melman
First UK Transmission: 18.07.97

Skyline: A crescent moon rises from behind the skyline.

Synopsis: While Bulldog is on the telephone, breaking up with a girl whose name he can't even get right, Roz is trying to set Frasier up on a blind date with a sporty girlfriend of hers (Frasier's love life having been somewhat drought-ridden for the last year).

Daphne is aghast when an angry Martin returns to the apartment having walked Eddie – the terrier has ruined Martin's favourite shoes by making him walk through puddles. Daphne chucks the shoes into the microwave to try to dry them, but they go up in flames.

At Café Nervosa, Niles confides in Frasier that he has been so successful in sorting out the patients at his practice, he's running out of paying customers. As a result, he is placing an ad in *Seattle Style*. Frasier is appalled – Niles is selling out. Niles tartly points out that Frasier has been doing that for the last few years, via his radio show. Frasier reads the advert: ' "Doctor Niles Crane. Jung specialist. Servicing individuals, couples, groups. Satisfaction guaranteed. 'Tell me where it hurts'." Well, that's excellent, Niles. All you're missing is a very tasteful cartoon of you smiling brightly and holding a shrunken head.' Niles shrugs. 'Sorry, I didn't hear you – I was too distracted by your face going by on the side of a bus.'

Niles leaves when Roz arrives, having set Frasier up with her friend Sharon. Frasier and Sharon begin to talk animatedly, and so Roz leaves them to it. But when Bulldog arrives and knows Sharon from her golfing, the two strike up a rapport, and then go off together, leaving Frasier alone again.

The next day, Bulldog arrives at KACL, glowing. He's completely smitten with Sharon and in love. 'On the way to work,' he says dreamily, 'all the songs on the radio made sense to me. Have you ever listened to the words of "Time in a Bottle"?' He also stresses that he didn't have sex with Sharon – 'we made love'. As he goes away to prepare for his show, Niles turns up, distraught that the *Seattle Style* magazine has misprinted his advert, and Frasier rereads it, but with the new word 'Hung' in place of 'Jung'.

Outside, in the corridor, Bulldog is calling Sharon but she dumps him. Distraught, Bulldog tries to get on with his show, but feels his life crumbling. He flees the studio, leaving Roz to try to talk to him and Niles to analyse him, while Frasier becomes the guest presenter of Bulldog's show . . .

Guest Cast: Sharon Payton (Jen Campbell), Wino (Kay E. Kuter).

Where Everybody Knows Their Name: Bulldog's producer, Pete (Michael Whaley), makes a brief, decidedly laconic, return while Hester Crane comes up in the conversations about Martin's favourite shoes (Martin once bought her a pair).

Who's On The Line?: Absolutely no one on Frasier's own show, but, as soon as he takes over on *The Gonzo Sports Show*, he has to deal with Mike ('Dr J' Erving), who wants to know about the Yankees, and Jake (Bob Costas) who enquires about the strategy of the Sonics. Bulldog's collapse is begun by Jerry (Marv Albert), who asks about the possible departure of the Seahawks from Seattle.

Subtitles: It's Hammer Time; Who Are You And What Have You Done With Bulldog?

Culture Vultures: Niles's concept of poverty means his being forced to wear Spanish leather. If that wasn't bad enough, Roz delights in doing so and compares belts with him!

Eddie Takes The Biscuit: Poor Eddie. He looks so miserable when Martin is angry at the mutt for getting his favourite shoes wet. Ahhh, and he tries so hard to make amends by bringing his master his slippers.

Frasier Has Left The Building: Niles and Frasier are miming to violinists, while Eddie hides his head in shame.

On The Couch: Dan Butler gets a chance to shine in this show, but sadly the story doesn't make the most of him. Instead, it seems to be telling too many different stories, none of them in enough depth. The subplot of Daphne and Martin searching for the shoes (with a delightful cameo by Kay E. Kuter as the gay wino) is simply irrelevant as, frankly, is Niles's ad, which is just a build-up for one, admittedly very funny, joke about the misprint.

'Please stop being a shrink and be, well, like a guy . . .' pleads Bulldog to Frasier at the end, and for one very funny moment, Frasier complies until Niles literally knocks sense into him. But if the whole episode has been a build-up to that one moment, it ain't worth it . . .

4.03

'The Impossible Dream'

Written by Rob Greenberg
Directed by David Lee
First UK Transmission: 25.07.97

Skyline: Lights go on in various buildings.

Synopsis: Frasier wakes up in a seedy motel room, with the word 'Chesty' tattooed on his forearm. Stepping out of the shower, ready and eager is Gil . . . Frasier wakes up – it was a dream!

At the studio, Frasier asks Roz about his dream, without revealing who his partner for the night was. She starts trying to guess, but when Gil comes in with a pastry for Frasier to try, his embarrassment immediately tells Roz the truth and she tells everyone else (except Bulldog, whom Frasier actually tells himself).

At Café Nervosa, Frasier tells Niles about his dream – he wants a Jungian interpretation rather than his own Freudian one. When Niles learns that Gil is the cause of his brother's fears, he is amused. Niles approaches it from a free-association angle. Frasier remembers a crescent-shaped lamp in the motel room. Niles nods: 'Run with that. Crescent. Moon. Daphne Moon. French Maid. Brass Bed. Satin Ropes ...' Frasier interrupts, 'This is my dream,' he says. Niles agrees: 'I was just showing you the process.' But Frasier remains unconvinced: 'You were three words from a cigarette!'

But the word association takes Frasier to croissant, and he realises that maybe his subconscious is telling him to stop dieting. And as Gil is a food critic, perhaps he is symbolic of the food he has been denying himself.

However, that night the dream recurs and, despite the presence of a beautiful girl in the shower, Gil is now in bed with him.

A comment about their mother from Martin makes Niles wonder if Chesty is actually Hesty, possibly a nickname for their mother. But if it is just a simple case of confusing Gil with their mother ('Food. Criticism. Mother!') why doesn't the dream go away?

Guest Cast: Doctor Sigmund Freud (Byrne Piven), Dream Girl (Lisa Melilli).

Where Everybody Knows Their Name: Rebecca, a waitress at Café Nervosa (Pauly P) makes her first appearance, while Elizabeth (Betty Rae) makes a welcome reappearance. Hester Crane is mentioned briefly, but the episode is stolen by Gil Chesterton (Edward Hibbert) at his campest and bestest. If anyone had any lingering doubts about the sexuality of this likeable but stereotypical queen, this show puts them to ... er ... bed once and for all.

Who's On The Line?: Jimmy (Kieran Culkin) is a fourteen-year-old who thinks his parents are stupid. 'Well, hang on, Jimmy. Your parents are going to be stupid for another seven years.' Frasier at least manages to avoid Rudy (Christopher Durang), the compulsive weeper. Or so he thinks . . .

Subtitles: Why Gil? Why Now?; Psychiatrist . . . Crane . . . Frasier . . . Niles . . . Idiots; Thank God He Was Wrong About That 'Mother' Thing.

Frasier Has Left The Building: Eddie is dreaming about finding muffins laid out for him in the kitchen, but permanently just out of reach . . . This is a clever remake of the closing scene from 1.22, 'Author, Author', except there, Eddie did get the muffins!

On The Couch: A thoroughly bizarre episode in which Frasier ends up questioning his sexuality at the age of forty-three, Martin gets embarrassed and Gil simply delights in telling everyone in Café Nervosa that Frasier has had an erotic, albeit somewhat tacky, dream about the two of them. The lack of real resolution is unusual, but then, what isn't in this episode? It is certainly very funny and quite a brave thing for an American sitcom to dabble in gay storylines, especially as the characterisation of Gil is a throwback to that very seventies ideal of a gay man: camp, prissy and suggestive.

While the parts work, the whole is a bit uneven, although there are a few genuinely funny bits. And, without a doubt, they are Daphne's fish-association pieces of deduction: 'Who was in the shower? Gil. What is a shower? Running water. Who needs water? Fish. What do fish have? Gills! D'you see where I'm going?' Frasier nods. 'Insane' – although Jungians may feel put out at their pet theories being dismissed so easily. But, funny as they are, these moments don't mark the episode as one of the best. Most curious of all is the off-the-wall appearance by Sigmund Freud. Frasier's hero or not, it is superfluous, mistimed and at odds with the rest of the episode. Why is it there?

But we love Gil and think that, in a parallel dimension, he and Frasier would be very good for each other . . .

4.04

'A Crane's Critique'

Written by Dan Cohen and F. J. Pratt
Directed by Jeff Melman
First UK Transmission: 01.08.97

Skyline: The elevator goes up the Space Needle.

Synopsis: The Crane boys are taking their father on a shopping trip to buy him some clothes. Martin, needless to say, is dreading this. They are resting at Café Nervosa with Roz when the two psychiatrists spot the reclusive author T. H. Houghton leaving a shop opposite. As the author of just one highly praised novel, *Time Flies Tomorrow*, he is chased after by Niles and Frasier, who drag Martin with them.

Having lost track of him, they go into a bar, where Martin opts to stay and watch the Mariners game, while his sons continue their search. Houghton comes out of the toilets and begins talking to Martin about the appalling baseball on the television.

Later, the Crane boys return for their father, only to find him talking animatedly to Houghton about some family known as the Cartwrights. Houghton brusquely departs, putting down an eager fan as he does so. The Crane boys are so upset to have missed their chance to discuss Houghton's seminal book with him.

Some days later, Frasier is told by Daphne that Houghton is on his way over, and Martin explains that they're going out together before the writer delivers the manuscript for his new book, *The Chameleon Song*, to a publisher. A new Ted Houghton novel! The boys are astonished and delighted. Ted indeed arrives but, after he and Martin have gone, Frasier and

Niles realise he's left his manuscript behind. As they sit down to read it, they fail to hear the author returning . . .

Guest Cast: T. H. Houghton (Robert Prosky), Bar Patron (Steven Rotblatt).

Subtitles: In Another Part Of The Forest; Question: How Did Babe Ruth Change Musical Theater History?

Culture Vultures: In an effort to get rid of Niles, Frasier sends him off to get a crate of a particular '82 vintage wine. At the last minute not only does Niles remember that there was no '82, owing to a drought, but this particular wine comes in bottles and never crates. Curses, foiled again!

Eddie Takes The Biscuit: Eddie has a special alarm system for Daphne when she's relaxing rather than working. As the elevator outside stops, he barks. This works for Daphne but when he tries to do the same trick for Niles and Frasier, they tell him to shut up. More fool them, as it turns out . . .

Frasier Has Left The Building: Eddie is rubbing himself all over Frasier's beloved brown suede sofa until Daphne alerts him to the sound of the elevator.

On The Couch: One of those shows where you just know that everything is going to go wrong for Frasier and Niles, but despite a good start, this season is slipping slowly into predictability, and thus losing its edge. You know that Houghton is going to be uninterested in their adulation; you know they're going to find his new manuscript; you know they'll get caught and the book will be ruined . . . The only surprise is that T. H. Houghton is such a deeply unpleasant character it stretches belief that Martin would spend time with him, let alone that the Crane boys' hero worship would remain untarnished.

This is a meandering episode and, once the opening scene with Roz is over, it lacks many laughs at all. The *Bonanza* joke is fun, if obvious, as is Daphne's blackmail, but throughout this episode Frasier and Niles are portrayed as rather spoilt and selfish (OK, they always are, but usually you love them for it; here you just get bored with them), and you neither worry nor care about the entirely obvious outcome.

Dull, dull, dull – luckily a rarity in *Frasier*, but that just means our expectations are higher than they would be with any other series.

4.05
'Head Game'

Written by Rob Greenberg
Directed by David Lee
First UK Transmission: 08.08.97

Skyline: The light atop the Space Needle glows.

Synopsis: Frasier is going to a works' convention in the mountains, he tells Niles at Café Nervosa. Niles is amused by this. 'Just think, hundreds of radio psychiatrists all in the same location. One well-timed avalanche and the dignity of the entire psychiatric profession could be restored.' His amusement fades when Frasier asks him to stand in for him at KACL for a week – otherwise, his slot will be taken by Helen Grogan's gardening show, *Ma Nature* (see 2.22, 'Agents in America, Part Three').

At the end of Niles's first afternoon, Bulldog enters, preparing for his show. One of his guests is Sonics star Reggie Maclemore, who has been going through a bad patch recently. This is costing the basketball team badly and the player asks Niles for some help. Niles does his best but isn't much good, he believes. He is also unable to replicate the sportsman's handshake Reggie and Bulldog gave each other, so Reggie just ruffles Niles's hair.

That night, Reggie leads the team to victory, and, live on television, he thanks Niles for his help. After sixteen years of practice, Niles has finally done something his father can be proud of, and the next day everyone at KACL treats Niles like a hero. He begins to enjoy the accolades – 'Suddenly I'm being revered as a god by the same troglodytes who at junior high school tried to pack me into my own briefcase. It's glorious.' A grateful Reggie provides Niles with season tickets to the game and he takes Daphne and Martin with him.

At the match, things do not go well for Reggie despite Niles's counsel, until Reggie touches his hair again, and goes on to win. Niles soon realises it is not his psychiatry that is helping Reggie at all, but simply the fact that, by touching Niles's hair, Reggie boosts his confidence. Niles heads down to the Sonics to have a last talk with Reggie . . .

Guest Cast: Reggie Maclemore (Lorenzo Newton), Sportscaster (Stu Lantz), Guard (Ken Magee), Fan (Loren Lazerine), Cheerleader (Lisa Dergan), Lenny (Christopher M. Brown), Hank (Geoff Callan), Game Announcer (Jim Graci).

Where Everybody Knows Their Name: Daphne's boyfriend Joe gets a mention as they're off to the movies together.

Who's On The Line?: Linda (Wendy Wasserstein), who feels that no one listens to her, least of all her cat, who won't eat.

Subtitles: Stranger In A Strange Land; Hoopla; Ay, There's The Rub.

Out Of Sight: When Niles refuses to do Frasier's show, his older brother reminds him of a deal they made some years back. Frasier agreed to go out with Maris's sister, Bree, who smuggled an incontinent Chihuahua into the opera. Bree also licked Frasier's ear and had a cold, which was not pleasant for a woman with only one nostril! We wonder, is Bree the sister who resides in Chicago? (See 1.14, 'The Show Where Lilith Comes Back'/1.15, 'Can't Buy Me Love'.)

Frasier Has Left The Building: Daphne and Martin are playing cards, and Martin rubs Niles's hair for luck.

On The Couch: Well, it has moments, but even this Niles-heavy episode lacks something. As with the last couple of shows, everyone is going through their paces and, despite the odd great one-liners, the characters still seem to be turning into caricatures. Bulldog always has been, but Daphne and Martin here come off very badly, the latter especially. His sulk because Niles refuses to go to the game is particularly dumb. No matter how disappointed he is, Martin Crane doesn't normally act like this.

On the plus side, there is one brilliant set of exchanges between Martin, Daphne and Niles as they get to the game, and Niles cannot understand what his father is talking about. 'Right on the hardwood!' says a jubilant Martin. 'Five feet from the baseline.' At Niles's confusion, Daphne just whispers, 'Front row orchestra, stage right,' and Niles gets the message. There are a couple more of these and they are wonderfully observed moments, both about Niles's inability to comprehend sport and Daphne's ability to balance the father and the sons by having a foot in both camps. Excellent.

4.06

'Mixed Doubles'

Written by Christopher Lloyd
Directed by Jeff Melman
First UK Transmission: 15.08.97

Skyline: A streak of lightning crosses the sky.

Synopsis: Daphne has broken up with her long-term boy-friend Joe. Niles immediately sees an opportunity to move in but Frasier cautions him to wait. At least an honourable twenty-four hours. 'Niles,' he says slowly, ' before you do something this rash, perhaps you should consider it from all angles.' Niles is desperate. 'I've spent three years considering Daphne from all angles.'

This, unfortunately, gives Roz enough time to take Daphne to a singles bar where she meets Rodney. As a result, Niles goes there the following evening and meets Adelle. Nice as Adelle is, she can never be exactly what Niles wants – whereas Rodney seems to be perfect for Daphne. After all, he's identical to Niles.

As Niles tries to cope with this terrible fact, another cloud beckons. It seems that Adelle goes for a certain type as well . . .

Guest Cast: Rodney Banks (Kevin Farrell), Adelle Childs (Allison Mackie).

Where Everybody Knows Their Name: Although not seen, Joe plays an important part in this episode.

Subtitles: Where Everybody Knows Her Name; Staremaster.

Culture Vultures: In a clever opening moment which proves we should all know better, it looks as if the brothers Crane are doing a Peeping Tom act on a neighbour via Frasier's telescope. In fact they're admiring a Brancusi armchair, much to Martin's disappointment.

Later, when Martin tries to get his elder son to watch a ball game, Frasier explains that he prefers listening to Pavarotti's Poliarchi.

Frasier's antiques dealer has finally succeeded in providing our hero with an Anne of Cleves antique coffee-cup set depicting the six wives of Henry VIII. Catherine of Aragon, sadly, fails to survive beyond the moment Niles hears Rodney sniffing Daphne's hair. Adding his penn'orth, Martin points out to Adelle that he's still searching for a Wilma to complete his Flintstones juice-glass set.

Strange Bedfellows: Roz gets off remarkably lightly in this episode, although the singles bar she frequents at Granvilles is known as the Sure Thing. 'How flattering,' remarks Frasier. 'They've named a bar after her.'

Full-on Moon: Daphne's build-up to her revelation regarding her separation from Joe is pure . . . well, Daphne really. Lots of detail about potatoes, causing Frasier to urge her towards the 'post-potato portion of the dialogue'.

The Buddy Show: After meeting Rodney for the first time and realising he and Niles are frighteningly similar, Martin receives a phone call from Duke, but says he'll call back because 'I'm in the Twilight Zone'.

Eddie Takes The Biscuit: Frasier and Eddie are trying to outstare each other. Eddie, naturally, wins.

Frasier Has Left The Building: The continuation of the staring match between Eddie and Frasier. Frasier, of course, hasn't a hope.

On The Couch: At last the series is back on form, and to prove it, this one is nothing short of a classic, not just of *Frasier* but of any sitcom. Niles steals the show and among his best moments are his constant attempts to comfort Daphne at the start of the show, and then, later, his arrival at Granvilles to meet Roz. 'Well, I'm here. I forgot to gargle, I'm wearing mismatched socks and I'm so nervous I could wet myself.' Roz tries to be helpful and she is, after all, an experienced guide. Which is useful when you are as verbose as Niles Crane. 'If you're going to use words like milieu,' she says looking around the singles bar, 'you might as well show up here with a sore on your lip and a couple of kids.'

The final scene between Daphne and Niles, back in the singles bar as she informs him of her future plans, is fantastic, with Niles taking each knockdown in his stride. The episode closes on one of the most tear-jerking exchanges ever as Daphne realises how good a friend Niles can be. 'Oh, I love you, Dr Crane,' she says, platonically tapping his hand. Niles just smiles. 'I love you too, Daphne.' After three and a half years of watching Niles desperately trying to get his desire, and coming so close once again (see 3.13, 'Moon Dance'), you cannot help but feel sorry for him.

4.07

'A Lilith Thanksgiving'

Written by Chuck Ranberg and Anne Flett-Giordano
Directed by Jeff Melman
First UK Transmission: 22.08.97

Skyline: A streak of lightning crosses the sky.

Synopsis: It's Thanksgiving and the Crane men and Lilith (whose broom apparently touches down at 11) are taking Frederick to Niles's cabin in the Rockies. That is, until Lilith rings from Boston to say that their son has successfully passed his qualifying exam to enter Mulberry Academy, the most exclusive private school in Boston, open only to children of alumni or generous benefactors. All that is left now is for his parents to meet with Dr Campbell, the head-master, who will decide whether or not Frederick gets in. Plans for Thanksgiving, therefore, have to be altered, and the celebrations have to be held at the other side of the country.

Frasier and Lilith head for the academy, leaving Martin to look after Frederick. A series of mishaps ensue as Frederick gets black eyes, nosebleeds and so forth from failing to catch a football ('Dad, when are you going to learn the only thing Crane boys are skilled at catching are sarcastic nuance and the occasional virus?'). Meanwhile, Niles attempts to cook the turkey. 'I'm nearly done defrosting,' explains Lilith, placing it on the table. The look from Niles says it all, but even he cannot resist, 'And the turkey?' With a withering look, Lilith retorts, 'Might I suggest you stuff it?'

Dr Campbell, however, is clearly not a man to be impressed by bonhomie and flattery. He explains that there is only one place, and it becomes evident that his dislike of the two doctors will stop Frederick joining the academy. They realise they must join forces and convince Campbell that they are sincere. ('This may be the most important thing we ever do to ensure his happiness,' says Lilith of Frederick's dreams for Mulberry. 'Not counting our divorce,' offers Frasier.) So they return to the school and finally disrupt Dr Campbell's Thanksgiving dinner, despite bringing their own turkey.

Guest Cast: Dr Colin Campbell (Paxton Whitehead), Pamela (Lisa Banes), Preston (John Prosky), Cynthia (Jane Lynch), Elliot (Richard Gilbert Hall). No credit given to the actors portraying the poor unfortunate children of the dreadfully snobbish parents listed above, but their names are Reagan and Wesley. Wesley ended up at Berkeley.

Where Everybody Knows Their Name: A superb performance, as always, from Bebe Neuwirth as everyone's favourite ice queen, Lilith Sternin, and a return appearance by the ever-precocious Frederick Crane, now played by Trevor Einhorn. Mention is also made of Brian, Lilith's husband (see 2.10, 'Adventures In Paradise', Part 2), who will not be joining them for Thanksgiving. He's in New Zealand studying a volcano. According to Niles, Lilith cannot be with him because 'if she accidentally fell in the shock wave from the hottest thing in nature meeting the coldest would actually crack the Earth in two'. Frasier merely says, 'As if a smile from Maris couldn't freeze Mercury.' Martin caustically observes that 'no one's gonna win this one'.

Subtitles: Stop Saying 'Doctor'; Beware Geeks Bearing Gifts.

Culture Vultures: Niles, sorting out the cabin over his mobile with Buck, lets slip that he has ordered a case of Montrachet and wants mints on the pillows. Frederick, rapidly becoming as bad as his father and uncle, possessing a science award, a medical bracelet and 'pills for everything' (but clearly not his allergy to anchovies), points out that he believes playing with balls is for the 'slow children' and that bikes have pretty much the same appeal. We hold his mother to blame for this. After all, she is the one who explains that rather than joining the kids in the street Frederick prefers to just study their play patterns. He apparently also enjoys watching *Pocahontas* and then writing a satirical essay about the historical inaccuracies. Best of all, though, is the joke Frasier shares with his son about some bears and a rabbit, which has the punchline, 'No, no I said Oedipal not edible!'

Strange Bedfellows: Roz is left looking after Frasier's plants and apartment while they are away, so the only hint we get of her shenanigans is Frasier pointing out that he frowns upon overnight guests. Slick as ever, Roz suggests that this explains why the doctor has very little luck with the ladies.

Full-on Moon: Daphne is off to have a traditional Thanksgiving with her transvestite uncle, Jackie (see 1.12, 'Miracle On 3rd Or 4th Street'), who doesn't dress like a woman all the time because his congregation would never stand for it. As she shows Roz where everything in the kitchen lives, they begin discussing Frasier and how each of them deals with his eccentricities.

Out Of Sight: Maris has never been one for Thanksgiving as the sight of pudding reduces her to tears. Indeed, this is Niles's first Thanksgiving without her since they were married. Niles also mentions that the best way of breaking bad news to Maris is to crush a tranquilliser into her Slim Fast.

Frasier Has Left The Building: Dr Campbell discovers the destruction wreaked upon his bird-decorated cushion.

On The Couch: A marvellous show, really, as is anything involving Lilith. There are times when you wish she were part of the regular team, but then she would quickly become stale, no doubt. Like a good wine, Lilith is best left to be sipped lightly now and again. The snobbery of the storyline is unusual for *Frasier* – instead of being worthy of a few one-liners, the entire narrative is about who can be the best snob. Lilith and Frasier try to impress Dr Campbell with tales of Golda Meir and her son Oscar (a rare moment where Frasier is so totally wrong even he knows he's blown it). Then we see Dr Campbell himself pointing out that the Mulberry sixth-form talent show spawned a cast album, saying he once refused the son of a senator, claiming that in twenty-two years he's never accepted a bribe, and trying not to put down Berkeley School – and failing.

There are some marvellous moments, however, back at the house, mostly revolving around Niles's (surprisingly) successful attempts at cooking his first Thanksgiving turkey – until Lilith nicks it. Classic farce as he opens every door of the oven looking for it. Some great lines too, our favourite coming when Niles is trying to explain Frederick's injuries to his unobservant parents. Lilith cautiously tells Frasier that if he will 'overanalyse every detail, you will rob us of the joy of the moment. It will be our wedding night all over again'. To which Niles turns, smiling, and says, 'Speaking of unexplained bruises . . .'

4.08

'Our Father Whose Art Ain't Heaven'

Written by Michael B. Kaplan
Directed by Jeff Melman
First UK Transmission: 29.08.97

Skyline: A helicopter rises up from the skyline and departs.

Synopsis: The Crane men have been out for an evening, to see a Jean-Claude van Damme movie, much to Frasier's astonishment. Apart from learning that bullets are useless against a man who can kick 'really high', an argument has broken out concerning the fact that Frasier always pays. Martin insists that he get the bill for their next outing.

The opportunity rises when Daphne tells them she's going to cook sheep's-head soup and they dash off to a swanky French restaurant run by one of Frasier's friends, Francoise. The restaurant is displaying some very gaudy Spanish artwork, which Frasier and Niles compliment Francoise on in order to get a good table. Martin mistakenly believes Frasier

genuinely adores it and buys one for his son to hang over the
fireplace. Frasier agrees the fireplace is the perfect area for it.

The next day Frasier tries to get advice from Roz about
how best to tell Martin he positively hates the painting and
Roz explains that every year her grandmother sends her a new
ceramic hippopotamus because she wasn't honest about how
awful the very first one was. 'Thank God for that earthquake,'
she says.

Returning home, Frasier brings up the topic of an old silk
smoking jacket he once bought Martin and found his father
had subsequently thrown out, using this as an analogy about
why people should be more honest about dealing with gifts
they don't like. After Niles is honest about a wine rack Martin
has bought him from Price Busters to use at his forthcoming
party, Frasier bites the bullet and tells Martin he hates the
painting. To his horror, Martin begins to cry because he can
never seem to do anything to please his son. Frasier also starts
to cry, as does Niles, although that's more because 'no one
wants to come to my party'.

Guest Cast: Francoise (Nicholas Walker).

Who's On The Line?: Greg (John Cusack), who is a first-
year psychology student suffering from the symptoms he has
been studying. Frasier suggests avoiding the study of male
sexual disorders until after the spring break.

Subtitles: Sometimes Le Cigare Is Just Le Cigare; Our Father
Whose Art Ain't Heaven; Family Ties.

Culture Vultures: Not much in the way of culture this time
around, although the snobbery of the restaurateur is marvellous, especially as he finds a table for Frasier's party and
cancels a booking by a Dr Durban because he always brings
his own wine. Niles doesn't invite Frasier to his party for his
Country Club friends, but does want to borrow his brother's
Waterford punch bowl.

Full-on Moon: Daphne's statement about cooking Grammie
Moon's sheep's-head soup (and that her shopping bag

contains said animal's freshly decapitated head) is merely a ruse to get the men out of the apartment so that she can have a quiet night with her new beau, Marshall. She does the same trick the next night, this time claiming she's going to cook haggis.

Out Of Sight: Niles is having a party on the same night as Maris. After leaving twenty messages before finally getting a call back, he learns that his estranged wife is circulating a rumour that Niles is having a karaoke machine, which begins to whittle his guest list down. Even Winchette Cooke claims to have fallen mysteriously ill at the last moment. Niles decides Maris has pushed him around too much. Metaphorically of course, because in reality she can hardly push at all – especially after getting trapped in the revolving door at Bergdorf's. Unfortunately, the karaoke threat has worked and, when he's down to just three guests, Niles angrily phones Maris to have it out with her and ends up accepting an invitation to her party. Frasier sighs. 'Thank God for the starch in that shirt or there'd be nothing holding you upright.' Maris is also flying an ice sculptor in from Sweden to make a statue of her. 'Ah,' says Frasier, 'the perfect marriage of subject and medium.'

The Buddy Show: Although not directly involving any of his buddies, it is worth noting that neither Frasier nor Martin cried when the latter was shot.

Frasier Has Left The Building: Roz unwraps a huge box containing a number of ceramic hippos.

On The Couch: A bit of a lacklustre affair this time around. Daphne's plot to rid herself of everyone else is superb, and the sequence at the radio studio with Roz is fun, but otherwise the episode is an overdose of schmaltz and atypical sentiment. It does, however, bring up the question we've all been asking ourselves: Martin says his friends have been asking him for forty years just how Frasier and Niles could be his sons – a nice twist on the series' concept – in other words, how he could be their father. The episode produces few laughs and the climax, which involves Martin's police badge, is very predictable.

4.09

'Dad Loves Sherry, The Boys Just Whine'

Written by Joe Keenan
Directed by James Burrows
First UK Transmission: 05.09.97

Skyline: A hot-air balloon rises from behind the skyline.

Synopsis: At Café Nervosa, Niles and Roz are discussing her latest foot ailment while Frasier and Maureen Cutler (see 3.20, 'Police Story') are deep in discussion. When she has left, Niles announces to Frasier that he has won the Marriot Fassbinder Award for Distinguished Contribution to the Literature of Psychology. However, as the award ceremony is a huge banquet with his peers, Niles is nervous about inviting Martin. Not to do so will upset him, but can he be trusted to behave himself? Frasier adds to Niles's fears by pointing out that it is their father's birthday the coming weekend and Maureen has just told him she's going to end their relationship. Martin will need cheering up.

Frasier tells Daphne back at his apartment what is likely to happen, and, despite her pretence otherwise, Daphne's own problems surface – she has learnt that Joe (see 4.06, 'Mixed Doubles') is getting married and Frasier packs her off to bed with her tears and a not-too-expensive bottle of wine.

Martin and Maureen return to the apartment but Maureen heads off, clearly with something on her mind. Bemused Martin, who has eaten a curry and has an upset stomach as a result, is further surprised when Frasier is trying to be comforting and goes into a spiel about how it's better that Martin and Maureen have split up – then Frasier realises Maureen hasn't said anything about this at all. But Martin is overjoyed

– he has wanted to end the relationship anyway as he's met someone else. Maureen suddenly returns and blurts everything out and Martin pretends to be surprised and upset. When she has gone, Martin calls Sherry, his new lady friend.

It is Martin's birthday and he is eagerly awaiting the arrival of Sherry, hoping the boys and Daphne will like her. When she arrives, all bright clothes, lots of make-up, very cheap champagne and loud, brassy and lewd, the boys are devastated. Nevertheless, they pretend to like her.

A few days later, Niles is profusely apologising to Frasier for a missed dinner engagement the previous night, but Frasier is not stupid. He knows that Niles is avoiding having to spend time with Sherry – and he cannot really blame him, since at least Niles has been spared a night of Sherry's limericks about a well-travelled man called Horatio. Then both are aghast when she and Martin arrive, shattering the sanctity of the café. 'Quick, Niles, pull up the ladder. She's found our clubhouse!' Too late – and Martin says that, because Daphne has a cold, Sherry is coming to the awards banquet. 'What fun,' grins a delighted Frasier.

Later at the apartment, Frasier assumes that Niles has told Martin that he doesn't want Sherry at the ceremony and so begins apologising for the fact that neither of them can stand Sherry. But Niles has chickened out . . .

Where Everybody Knows Their Name: Lilith, Nanette and Diane get veiled mentions when Frasier discusses his relationships; and later, when he's baiting Martin with a threatened visit from Lilith, Frederick gets a mention. Amid the same arguments, Hester Crane is referred to, and making a reappearance after a bit of an absence is Maureen Cutler (Jane Kaczmarek). But the episode undoubtedly belongs to the new recurring character, Sherry Dempsey (Marsha Mason) as Martin's new love interest, and arch-foe of the Crane boys' sensibilities. We discover that she is a divorced, banjo-playing bartender at McGinty's who lives on the fourth floor of her building and trod the boards in Las Vegas – as a dancer rather than actress, we suspect.

Who's On The Line?: At some point in the past Frasier dealt with a friend of Sherry's called Donna. It transpires that Donna's marriage was on the rocks and Frasier's advice did little to help.

Subtitles: Fasten Your Seatbelts; No Girls Allowed.

Culture Vultures: Niles has been successful in the awards with his entry about a narcissistic opera singer called 'Mememememe!'

Out Of Sight: Maris is referred to by Martin as Frosty the Snow Wife amid various insults about each other's partners hurled around with gay abandon in this episode.

The Buddy Show: We'll slip Maureen Cutler in here because we like her – she's on the force and is a buddy of Martin's. And she's unlikely to get another crack of the whip.

Frasier Has Left The Building: Frasier and Niles are forced by Martin to endure Sherry's banjo playing. Eddie, quite rightly, is hiding his head.

On The Couch: A tour de force of comedy as hardly a second goes by once Sherry has made her first appearance without some of the series' best one-liners queuing up to be used. The best has to be after Frasier realises Niles has not spoken to Martin about Sherry and his younger brother looks shocked and cannot believe Frasier is being unkind about that 'sweet woman'. Frasier just gives him one of those looks and snarls, 'Oh, knock it off. I see you're still waiting on that spine donor.'

The episode offers us a rare moment of Frasier genuinely angry with Martin when he realises his father is being a hypocrite, having never hidden his own distaste concerning either Frasier's or Niles's choice of wife. But the subsequent eulogy about Hester and what Martin sees in both her and Sherry is a remarkably sobering sequence, with a nice bit of pathos for the older man.

Other great moments include the repeated joke of Frasier blundering in assuming people have told Martin their tales of

229

woe; the oft-used cries of 'gotcha' from Sherry when she manages to get one over on the Crane boys (and Frasier's delightful use of it on Niles); and Martin crushing Sherry's hand as he tries to look happy at the prospect of a visit from his ex-daughter-in-law.

A tremendously good show, that introduces a new character (which any good comedy show needs now and again to keep it fresh), played wonderfully by Marsha Mason.

4.10
'Liar! Liar!'

Written by Chuck Ranberg and Anne Flett-Giordano
Directed by James Burrows
First UK Transmission: 12.09.97

Skyline: Party balloons float up from behind the skyline.

Synopsis: It is the night of the annual SeeBee awards and Bulldog has won. The group have retired to Frasier's place (along with a waiter that no one knows) and a drunken Bulldog tries to get everyone motivated. The subject of lies – good, bad and white – comes up. Martin is horrified to learn after all these years that Niles and Frasier lied about a school prank that resulted in the person blamed getting expelled. It had been the brothers who let off the school sprinkler system and Martin had defended them. Angrily, Martin goes to bed and the party breaks up.

Frasier, struck by guilt and against Niles's advice, tries to track John Rajeski down. Rajeski had been the school bully (Niles being his usual victim – he once put Niles on a tray and into the dishwasher just for sitting on his favourite chair and another time hung him from a flagpole), and so they are unsurprised to learn he is now in jail. Frasier opts to visit him and see if the time is right to confess his guilt, whereas Niles wants nothing to do with it – indeed, he tells Frasier to say he's living in Italy.

Frasier goes to visit John in prison and learns he is having marital problems. It becomes clear that John is still a bully and telling the truth might not be such a good idea. Instead, Frasier decides to visit his wife and see if he can try to help their marriage. Then John is released and comes home . . .

Guest Cast: John Rajeski (Saul Stern), Susan Rajeski (Carlene Watkins), Prisoner (Rosey Brown).

Where Everybody Knows Their Name: Frederick gets a mention when we learn that he has taken to telling his schoolfriends that Lilith is an alien with eyes in the back of her head (cue the usual and obvious gags from everyone else). Luck Hari's waitress makes a welcome return to the show.

Who's On The Line?: No one as such, although yesterday Frasier reconciled a divorcing couple and today he helped Molly overcome her addiction to sweets (and not Swedes, as Daphne thought).

Subtitles: Dead Man Talking; A Jar Of Liniment, Some Chunky Monkey And Thou.

Culture Vultures: A bizarre moment where both brothers arrive at Café Nervosa to discover they are wearing identical clothes, right down to the shoes. 'Why didn't you take my strong chin and swimmer's build?' says an aghast Niles. Frasier's clothes were bought by his personal shopper, Renaldo. Apart from the fact that their clothes are presumably very expensive, this is a quite irrelevant and surreal moment.

Strange Bedfellows: Not so much a successful romp through her bed, but the inebriated Bulldog believes Roz when she flirts with him and gets him out of Frasier's flat, telling him to call the elevator. She then slams the door on him. 'No good lies, my ass,' she says triumphantly. She also reveals that she lies to her grandmother every year about winning. She does this very convincingly, by the way, as we witness. 'She's old and it makes her happy,' she justifies. 'She smiled for a week when I won the Miss Seattle Pageant.'

Full-on Moon: Daphne, slightly tipsy by now, reveals that when she was at school she used to tell her friends that she had an embryonic sister attached to her hip. Niles sensibly removes the wine from her hand at this point. She later falls for Niles's obvious attempts to get a massage by saying he has injured himself playing squash and doing a movement that mixed 'a pirouette with a scissor kick'. Martin knows better and suggests he got the injury adjusting the seat in his Mercedes. Niles later regrets this, as Daphne's massages are more painful than the sprain.

Out Of Sight: Maris once, unsuccessfully, took to wearing Spandex and, in an effort to make her feel better, Niles lied to her, saying it was 'supposed to blouse'.

Frasier Has Left The Building: Daphne is attempting her own form of physiotherapy again on Niles, who pretends he's petting Eddie.

On The Couch: A strange episode, rather humourless and with a terrible dénouement in the Rajeskis' apartment that suggests the writers ran out of both time and good ideas. There are a couple of gems, however, particularly as we learn more about Niles's, Frasier's and John's schooldays. The best line comes during the prison sequence when John asks after Niles. Remembering his brother's instructions, Frasier explains, 'Niles is abroad now.' Without missing a beat, John winces. 'Oh, that must have hurt.' Brilliant.

4.11
'Three Days of the Condo'

Written by Michael B. Kaplan
Directed by David Lee
First UK Transmission: 19.09.97

Skyline: A shooting star passes overhead.

Synopsis: Martin and Sherry are trying to have a few moments alone when everyone from Daphne to Eddie seems intent on interrupting them. Frasier returns home with a new Japanese door knocker, to which Sherry guffaws that she hasn't seen decent Oriental knockers since a Shanghai revue. 'She's as funny as she is classy,' laughs Martin to Niles. 'No argument there,' comes the reply.

After putting the knocker up, Frasier receives a 'no-no' note from Ms Langer, president of the Condo Board, telling him to remove it. Frasier goes to a board meeting with the other residents to plead his case, but loses. In anger, he turns on Langer, describing her schoolmarmish attitude as being akin to that of a tyrant.

Although incurring Langer's enmity, Frasier is contacted by Dr William Dorfman, who leads a sort of resistance movement to Langer's domination and pleads with Frasier to stand against the woman as president in the forthcoming elections.

A series of 'no-no' notes against Daphne (for parking her car where she always parks it) and Martin (for taking Eddie up in the main elevator rather than the freight elevator) finally persuades Frasier to go for it. When Daphne finds another 'no-no' note for Martin, Frasier decides enough is enough and begins defending his father at the meeting, trying to get the sympathy of the others, although they seem strangely reluctant. Which is not surprising, as the last 'no-no' note was for bathing naked in the public hot tub, and nothing to do with Eddie at all . . .

Guest Cast: Ms Langer (Dana Ivey), Dr Dorfman (Austin Pendleton), Molly (Christopher Templeton).

Where Everybody Knows Their Name: Sherry (Marsha Mason) makes her second appearance, seemingly continuing her quest to appal the Crane boys in their father's choice of companion. As always, Niles cannot get far enough away from her, whereas Frasier tends to be more hospitable, albeit through gritted teeth. Seeing that Frasier collects antiques, she offers to give him a novelty lamp she has featuring two passion-entwined frogs. When switched on, the lamp glows in their hearts. When asking for a good time to drop it off, Niles smiles and says, 'Preferably when I'm here.' Frasier just aims an electric drill at him. And with Niles no longer with Maris, Nguy is referred to as Niles's ex-houseman.

Subtitles: Deep Ear, Nose And Throat; What We Have Here Is A Failure To Communicate.

Culture Vultures: Although Frasier needs prompting to use a screwdriver to attach the Japanese door knocker, and directions where to find the tool drawer, he is horrified to have his Bea-Ella Roushan samovar described as 'the tea-chest thing'. Frasier's obsessive behaviour about how his *objet d'art* should be arranged is beginning to wear on Daphne, especially as he has now provided her with a diagram. Niles, offering Martin and Sherry his bachelor pad for them to get some peace and quiet, reminds them, 'Just remember – always use coasters, no snacking in the carpeted areas and always close the art books after viewing so you don't crease the spines.' Niles heads off to see a production of *La Traviata*, which is quite appalling. The sight that greets him on his return home, however, is far worse. His father and Sherry are having sex.

Full-on Moon: Daphne arranges it so that, when Frasier returns home, she has her feet up while Eddie is running from one end of the coffee table to the other with a duster. Daphne suggests she has been training Eddie to do this – Frasier comments that he could guess as much from the quality of the dusting. Upset by the 'no-no' note for parking, she imagines caving the back of Langer's head in with a tyre iron, much to the consternation of everyone else not familiar with Daphne's more homicidal tendencies.

Out Of Sight: When Niles is trying to explain how he cannot face his father after discovering him and Sherry together, Frasier is reminded of the time he encountered Maris in the shower when they were all away for a weekend in the cabin.

Months of awkwardness and avoidance followed. 'You get a vision of Maris,' moans Niles. 'I get an eyeful of Dad.' Ever sympathetic, Frasier merely suggests that they have 'hit about the same level on the "yikes" meter'.

Eddie Takes The Biscuit: Eddie delightfully licks Sherry's and Martin's faces to stop their canoodling. When Frasier later gives Sherry a brief peck on the cheek, he immediately susses that Eddie's tongue has been there recently.

Frasier Has Left The Building: Ms Langer gets into the elevator unaware that Daphne, standing behind her, is brandishing a breadstick rather like a tyre iron.

On The Couch: A very odd one this, not very funny except for the farcical moments at the end where Frasier talks about Martin's little friend Eddie to the board. *We* know he means the dog – *they* think it's something completely different. The double entendres (not normally a staple of the series' wit) are tremendously successful. And the *X-Files*-style car park meeting with the incompetent Dr Dorfman (who hides his identity despite driving a car with vanity plates, and sending messages on headed notepaper) is an amusing idea that goes on too long. Not one of the best by any means.

4.12
'Death and the Dog'

Written by Suzanne Martin
Directed by James Burrows
First UK Transmission: 26.09.97

Skyline: Nothing happens.

Synopsis: It's a dull day at KACL, probably due to the good weather, and Frasier is short on calls. He encourages anyone to phone in. 'How about all the agoraphobics? I know you're not outside.' A depressed caller does so and, to lighten her mood, he tells a story from three days ago.

Eddie is depressed and nothing seems to cheer him up. 'Do you suppose a dog psychiatrist is the answer?' offers Daphne, to which Frasier waspishly retorts, 'Only if the question is what is the most asinine thing we could possibly do.' Martin tries to convince Frasier that Eddie needs a new companion, another dog for instance. 'Oh come on. What could be more fun than to have a little brother or sister around the house to play with?' 'I fell for that trick once, Dad,' replies Frasier.

After a series of new toys, including Mr Carrot and a squeaky hamburger, fail to impress Eddie, a dog psychiatrist is summoned, in the form of Dr Arnold Shaw. While he tries to understand Eddie, the Frasier boys take the mickey out of him mercilessly. After preparing a 'What if Eddie were a human?' list of likes and dislikes, Dr Shaw decides Eddie is depressed because those around him are depressed.

As a result, they all try to discuss why they are depressed, which sinks further into a heavy talk about living and dying and why we are alive . . .

Guest Cast: Dr Arnold Shaw (Zelijko Ivanek), Dr Stephen Kagen (Tom Lagleder).

Where Everybody Knows Their Name: Niles reintroduces us to his pet dog (see 3.18, 'Chess Pains'), the rather insipid-looking whippet that appears to be known only as 'girl'. Martin likens it to Maris. 'It acts like Maris, it barks like Maris. Aside from the fact that it eats now and again, they could be dead ringers.' When discussing their depressions at the end, Hester Crane gets a mention.

Who's On The Line?: Alice (Patty Duke) is depressed for no reason she can put her finger on but cheers up after Frasier's story. She's particularly interested in Roz's story as well . . .

Subtitles: Happy Talk.

Culture Vultures: Among those quoted from by Frasier and Niles as they discuss death are the (very dead) writers Plato and T. S. Eliot.

Strange Bedfellows: Roz is introduced to Dr Kagen, a friend of Frasier's who is staying in Seattle. He asks Roz if she can show him the local hot spots. 'Oh, I think that can be arranged,' says Frasier. However, on learning that Kagen is a gynaecologist, Roz begins to lose interest, especially when she learns he collects antique gynaecological instruments. However, Frasier tells all this to Alice and the other listeners, eventually causing an embarrassed Roz to tip a glass of water over him to shut him up.

Full-on Moon: Daphne, like Roz, shares a dislike of gynaecologists. And dentists. And after seeing Eddie going through his physical, she's not too keen on dating vets any time soon, either. To try to cheer Eddie up, she makes some of Grammie Moon's sugar biscuits. When answering the questions about 'human Eddie', Daphne answers each one with a wistful 'I don't know why'. Even when Dr Arnold has finished, Daphne hasn't, likening Eddie to George Harrison. Frasier finds it difficult to believe that Daphne has yet to be committed. Daphne also mentions that a psychic she visited told her she would go insane and murder everyone in the house with a kitchen knife before killing herself. 'She was right about me moving to Seattle, though,' causes a few looks of concern among the others.

Out Of Sight: Apart from the likening to the whippet, Maris is remarkably untouched upon in this episode, except as a cause of Niles's sadness.

Eddie Takes The Biscuit: Well, it's his show, after all. And his Barbie doll made its first appearance way back in 2.08, 'Burying A Grudge'.

Frasier Has Left The Building: Dr Kagen meets a girl in Café Nervosa and goes to buy her a coffee. Roz slips by and whispers something to her and she hurries away, leaving Kagen to return to an empty table.

On The Couch: A weird episode that purports to be about Eddie but ends up being a rather depressing look at what makes our cast tick. Or not, as the case may be. While Martin's moroseness is due to his wife's death, Niles's due to his separation and Daphne's because she and Joe have split and no one noticed she had her hair cut off months ago, it is Roz who steals the moment. Pointing out that she doesn't live there, so Eddie can't have got it off her, she suggests that 'maybe Frasier picked up something through contact with me'. 'He wouldn't be the first one who –' Niles starts, but then shrugs. 'Oh, I'm too depressed.' Frasier's own misery stems, according to his father, from his lack of success in dating. 'Not to mention two failed marriages.' 'And yet you did,' his son tartly replies. We learn lots of other things. For instance, Roz, whose great-grandma was ninety-two when she died, wants to die on her hundredth birthday, and her husband to be so upset he drops out of college. And Niles thinks that even in heaven all the dead people will be too cool to hang out with him. 'Mozart will tell me he's busy but then later I'll see him out with Shakespeare and Lincoln.'

4.13

'Four for the Seesaw'

Written by David Lloyd
Directed by Jeff Melman
First UK Transmission: 03.10.97

Skyline: Lights go on in various buildings.

Synopsis: It is the flu season in Seattle and Frasier is having his shots live on the air (and is terrified, although he no longer recites Puccini's operas – see 1.11, 'Death Becomes Him'). Martin and Daphne have come for their shots, but scare stories frighten Martin off, resulting in neither of them getting the vaccine. Roz, meanwhile, has designs on the young doctor administering the preventive medicine.

Niles and Frasier meet up with two young kitchen designers in Café Nervosa and strike up a rapport. Before long, they are planning a weekend away together in the mountain cabin, because Martin and Sherry cannot go.

However, Niles is nervous – this is his first serious date since separating from Maris and neither he nor Frasier is entirely sure what their two friends are expecting. That is, until the two women make it clear that the Crane boys are exactly what they want. The only trouble is, Niles has to contact Maris on his mobile and clarify the exact nature of their separation . . .

Guest Cast: Laura Paris (Lisa Darr), Beth Armstrong (Megan Mullally), Dr Morris Claman (Andrew Heckler).

Where Everybody Knows Their Name: Sherry is mentioned by Martin and, by allusion, Lilith is mentioned by Frasier, for, when Niles and Frasier first see Laura and Beth, Niles whines, 'We can't sit with strange women.' Frasier's only comeback is, naturally, 'Why not? We married strange women.'

Subtitles: Designs; Let's Vuitton With It.

Culture Vultures: Frasier, showing Laura and Beth around his apartment, is flattered by Laura's comments about his antiques collection. 'Oh, just an *objet* here, an antique there . . .' It is the pretentious use of the French '*objet*' (as in *objet d'art*) that earns the quote its place here.

Strange Bedfellows: Roz clearly intends (and indeed gets) Dr Claman, despite Niles's suggestion that it'll be 'another "till dawn do us part" relationship'.

Full-on Moon: Daphne has flu thanks to Martin's fear of the injections. As penance, Martin must follow the trend set by Grammie Moon and read Daphne a story to send her to sleep. The steamy nature of her historical romance, *The Rose and the Rapier* by a former Elliot Bay Towers resident, Dierdre

Sauvage (see 3.07, 'The Adventures of Bad Boy and Dirty Girl'), makes Martin decidedly uncomfortable.

Out Of Sight: Maris has more input into this episode than many others simply by changing her mind at the last moment about whether or not Niles can sleep with Beth. 'I know we're allowed to see other people,' he says to her. 'The question is, how much of them are we allowed to see?'

The Buddy Show: Martin is off to see Duke again at McGinty's and he's already late, meaning Duke will have got stroppy and eaten all the free brazil nuts just to annoy Martin.

Frasier Has Left The Building: In the cabin, Frasier and Niles sleep in front of a dead fire, minus their women. Frasier wakes and takes a murderous lunge at Niles with the pillow . . .

On The Couch: A marvellously farcical show, in which Frasier's resentment towards Niles and Maris finally makes him reveal his innermost thoughts about Beth and Laura. Trouble is, they're listening and the viewer is left cringing – almost shouting at Frasier to shut up before he spoils it all. This is a perfect example of what makes *Frasier* so good – fast comedy, good one-liners, all the characters and some great odd moments. Our favourite? Has to be Laura telling Martin that she and the others have been to see *The Man Who Came to Dinner*, and explaining that it's about a family with whom an invalid comes to live, miserable and aggressive, resulting in the family wanting to kill him. 'Comedy?' asks Martin, apparently innocently. 'I used to think so,' Frasier mutters darkly. *Très magnifique!*

4.14

'To Kill a Talking Bird'

Written by Jeffrey Richman
Directed by David Lee
First UK Transmission: 10.10.97

Skyline: The elevator goes up the Space Needle.

Synopsis: While Roz is setting Frasier up on a blind date, Niles is moving into a swanky new apartment in the highly sought-after Montana building. Unable, however, to keep his whippet, he exchanges it for a white cockatoo named Baby. But Baby is highly nervous and tends to dig in with her talons when alarmed, especially by the door buzzer or fire.

Niles decides to have a dinner party for some of the other residents and Frasier invites a neighbour of Niles's called Stephanie. However, shortly before everyone arrives, Baby attaches herself to Niles's head and will not come off. So, while Frasier tries to entertain his guests, Niles must try to remove a cockatoo that not only has very sharp talons but also a very good ability to mimic everything it hears. And repeat it at inconvenient moments . . .

Guest Cast: Stephanie Garrick (Patricia Wettig), Christine (Lisa Akey), Elaine Hensley (Nancy Linari), Carol Larkin (Rosemary Murphy), Alfred Larkin (Jack Sydow), Wella (Brandi Burkett), Peter Soutendeck (Wayne Alexander).

Where Everybody Knows Their Name: A final appearance for Niles's whippet before it goes to live somewhere else. Niles, of course, refuses to accept that he has the dog as a Maris substitute (see 4.12, 'Death and the Dog') until Frasier throws what Niles calls 'psychobabble' at him. 'She is highly strung, cold to the touch and ignores you,' Frasier explodes. 'My God, stand her upright, take ten pounds off her and put her in a Chanel suit, what have you got?' Niles still refuses to accept this until Frasier reminds him of Maris's pillbox hat. He upturns an ashtray and puts it at a jaunty angle on the dog's head. With a gasp, realisation hits Niles and he faints!

This episode also marks the introduction of Baby the cockatoo. Martin, however, still sees this as a Maris substitute. 'She's very exotic,' Niles explains, 'only eats every other day and so white she's almost blue.' Martin looks satisfyingly shocked. 'That's what he said just before he introduced us to Maris.'

Subtitles: Just Call Me Stinky; Get A Grip.

Culture Vultures: Niles, showing his father and Daphne around his new home, is heard to mention as they descend the stairs that something is inlaid with Philippine mahogany. When Frasier arrives, he sarcastically points out that the Montana cannot be as exclusive as Niles thought: 'Your doorman waved me right through.' Niles concedes, 'That's because he knows who you are.' Frasier smiles knowingly. 'Ah. Fan of my show?' And, with a voice oozing with one-upmanship, Niles says, 'No. He lives in *your* building.'

Strange Bedfellows: Roz doesn't get a man herself this episode but is very keen on giving Frasier advice, having set him up with her friend Rita for what turns out to be a disastrous blind date. When Roz explains that women can smell fake men trying too hard, Frasier decides he must resemble 'a dead squirrel in a heating duct'.

Out Of Sight: Apart from the analogous fauna littering the episode, it transpires that one of the dinner guests, Elaine, is Maris's very best friend, and Niles suspects she has been dispatched to see how badly his dinner party is going.

Frasier Has Left The Building: After the dinner party is over, Niles is on the phone to the vet, apparently explaining Baby's preponderance for gripping people's scalps, and we see that Frasier is the bird's latest perch.

On The Couch: A very clever episode, of which the star is undoubtedly the bird whose inappropriate mimicry supplies what in other shows would be tedious and predictable comments, but they are used so sparingly here as to make it genuinely funny. With Niles now permanently settled into the Montana, the show takes another move forward and supplies us with a new regular setting. Although the sight of Niles and his pathetically slender whippet was always a joy, his relationship with Baby looks set to provide new scope for him, which should lessen the need to rely on a few cracks about Maris to keep the character fresh and amusing. His attempts to relax the bird once it is stuck on his head (placing a tea towel over it, for instance, to try to make it think it's night-time) reveal that Niles is about as suited to owning pets as he is to dating women, but there is no doubt that the image is an enduring one.

Oh, and the award for best line of the episode goes to Martin, right at the beginning, when Frasier is anticipating his date with Rita. 'She's thirty-two, has a terrific body and thinks I'm God's gift to broadcasting.' Without missing a beat, Martin mutters, 'Well, at least you have one thing in common.' A classic.

4.15
'Roz's Krantz and Guildenstern Are Dead'

Written by William Lucas Walker
Directed by Jeff Melman
First UK Transmission: 17.10.97

Skyline: The light atop the Space Needle glows.

Synopsis: Returning from a squash game, Niles and Frasier spy a highly embarrassed Roz working amid a party of roadside litter cleaners. Roz confesses she is doing community service in response to a speeding fine.

She explains that her only other option was to work in an old folk's home. 'Walking the streets, picking up trash,' says Niles, 'you can see how Roz would go with the familiar.' Her reasons for not working with the elderly have more to do with the reminders it provides of her own ageing process and mortality, but Frasier persuades her to go to the home anyway. Within days, she is nicknamed the Angel of Death as first Mr Krantz then Mr Guildenstern die in her care.

Frasier, meanwhile, is feeling very down, believing that his career as a radio psychiatrist does not give him the feedback he requires. After a disastrous attempt to get past callers to phone in, he goes with Roz to the home, where he meets Norman, a blind man who loves Frasier's show. Norman keeps a cast of the face of his late wife Helen beside his bed, which Frasier inadvertently breaks.

Roz, meanwhile, is enjoying a cigarette and reminiscences with an elderly but very energetic old lady.

Guest Cast: Norman (James Earl Jones), Moira (Lois Smith).

Who's On The Line?: Chet (Eric Roberts), who previously suffered low self-esteem until Frasier got to work on him. Now he's an arrogant jerk. Not the result Frasier had hoped for, no doubt.

Subtitles: Roz's Krantz and Guildenstern Are Dead; Noses Off.

Culture Vultures: Not much culture (bar Niles losing his Tiffany cufflinks), but a great deal of snobbery. Niles automatically places newspaper on the back seat of Frasier's car so that the dishevelled Roz can sit, but when she demands they escape before her supervisor returns, Frasier, pious as ever, refuses. Thus Roz threatens to spear Niles with her litter stick. This has no effect on Frasier, but once she threatens the upholstery, well, off he drives . . .

Strange Bedfellows: Unusually, Roz doesn't actually get to sleep with any of the men she meets in this episode – instead, they just die on her. There are some great moments when first Bulldog and later Niles believe she is talking about men being unable to have sex with her. Oh, and she had a cat but it died.

Full-on Moon: Daphne's reassuring comments to Roz terrify poor Martin. 'Oh, I've lost more patients than I like to count,' she tells the distraught radio producer. 'I used to keep a tally in me diary, but it made me a bit sad.' Fabulous stuff.

Out Of Sight: Maris, we learn, has a phobia about both cruises and buffets. 'The legendary smorgasphobia,' ridicules Frasier. Niles, by the way, is a guest at a pagan wedding between two of his 'Fear of Commitment' group. Maris goes, too, but refuses to hug a tree, pointing out that the only tree she will embrace is her family tree. Disaster strikes when a group hug starts and Maris is last seen apparently 'racing toward her Mercedes emitting a high-pitched shriek that caused the wedding doves to attack one another'. One rather feels that even Niles is beginning to tire of his wife's ... eccentricities now.

Eddie Takes The Biscuit: Eddie eats Frasier's Truffle foie gras and does a mean polka.

Frasier Has Left The Building: Roz reads to Moira until Eduardo arrives to give the old lady her bed bath.

On The Couch: A tremendously funny but poignant episode, outlining both the need to care for the elderly and not take life too seriously. Roz, arriving for the third time at the home, is horrified to see old people running from her, believing she is the Angel of Death. With Krantz and Guildenstern dead, who's next? 'They always die in threes,' she wails. 'Oh that's just celebrities,' snaps Frasier.

The show is undoubtedly stolen by the two guest stars. First, Lois Smith as Moira, who just lives for each day as it comes and to hell with being cautious or overly optimistic. When Roz arrives, Moira asks her for her cigarettes. 'These come with a warning,' admonishes Roz. Moira just shrugs. 'So do you, darlin'. And I let you in.'

Moira's take on life is amazing, and her sense of fun, such as hacking into the computer and arranging Eduardo's shifts so it is only he who ever gives her a sponge bath, is inspiring to anyone thinking old age means your mind goes.

Equally inspiring is James Earl Jones's characterisation of Norman. Despite his wife's death and his blindness, he remains incredibly cheerful and makes Frasier realise how even on the radio, he can bring pleasure to so many people he doesn't actually know.

4.16

'The Unnatural'

Written by Michael B. Kaplan
Directed by Pamela Fryman
First UK Transmission: 24.10.97

Skyline: A crescent moon rises from behind the skyline.

Synopsis: Frederick Crane is coming for the weekend to stay with his father and has made just one request – to visit the Microsoft complex in Seattle. Frasier, of course, tells Frederick that he has arranged it but in fact has singularly failed to do so.

While at the station, Bulldog is talking about their softball team and comments that one of the team has let them down for Saturday's game. Frederick innocently suggests his father, and Bulldog decides to bolster Frasier's reputation (he cannot play softball to save his life!) and say he's too good for them. Frederick asks to cancel his Microsoft trip so that Frasier can ensure the team's victory.

While Martin tries to instil some baseball skills into his son, Frasier begins to realise this is the moment every father fears – when the son will discover that his father is not perfect.

Guest Cast: Bobby Sherman.

Where Everybody Knows Their Name: Frederick (Trevor Einhorn) makes another guest appearance, and Lilith is mentioned a few times, most notably when cooking is discussed.

Subtitles: Who Delivered The Gettysburg Address?; The Unnatural; 15% . . . 20% If The Service Is Exceptional.

Culture Vultures: We discover that the Crane boys were bullied on boy-scout camping trips because, rather than camping bags, they took monogrammed train cases. Also, when attending a fancy-dress party, they wore rubber swimming pools shaped like pigs around their middles, intending to represent the Bay of Pigs. When nobody got it, they changed it to Swine Lake. Needless to say, no one got that either. Frasier spends much of his time quoting from *A Streetcar Named Desire* while Niles's only concession to ball-game attire is to wear a tie with a 'subtle diamond pattern' in it.

Strange Bedfellows: Roz used to go out with Scott Blancman, an executive at Microsoft, who became obsessive and pestered her for ages. She finally got rid off him but now Frasier wants her to ring him and arrange a visit for Frederick. When she refuses, Frasier reminds her of a story she once told him about how upset she was as a little girl when her mother would not take her to meet the singer Bobby Sherman, upon whom she had a crush. 'I hate you,' says Roz as she gives in and calls. Scott, however, has left Microsoft. Roz is currently dating a man with a seminary, while she feels that Gary, the KACL team's shortstop has 'a butt you just want to . . .'

Full-on Moon: Daphne has very little weirdness, but is the focus of Frederick's desires. He has a massive crush on her and she plays up to this, much to Niles's displeasure. In fact, he becomes positively jealous . . .

The Buddy Show: Martin has just bought an outrageous Viking helmet and reckons that the guys at McGinty's will love it.

Frasier Has Left The Building: Roz is delighted when Frasier introduces her to Bobby Sherman and she begins acting like a lovesick teenybopper – much to Sherman's terror!

On The Couch: A marvellous episode, with lots of little moments. Frederick asking Bulldog why he's called Bulldog; Frasier telling Martin when he realised he wasn't perfect (it was when he realised Martin couldn't do maths in his head – cue lots of jokes about figures for the rest of the show); the sequence where Martin attempts, gallantly but fruitlessly, to teach Frasier to play ball and they discuss his childhood; but best of all is Frederick outdoing Niles in the Daphne stakes. Everyone says it's innocent, but Niles thinks differently. 'Frasier, do you really think it's healthy for a little boy to be so obsessive with a woman he can't possibly have?' Completing this charming picture is the fact that Frederick not only knows exactly what he's doing, but that Uncle Niles is so green with envy . . .

4.17
'Roz's Turn'

Written by Joe Keenan
Directed by Joyce Gitlin
First UK Transmission: 31.10.97

Skyline: Fireworks explode over the skyline.

Synopsis: Martin is refusing to do his exercises, much to Daphne's annoyance. He thinks he's in tip-top health, but Daphne is unconvinced, fearing that his activities with Sherry will cause him problems – 'two hips and no hooray', she delicately puts it.

Roz arrives at Frasier's announcing that Gertie, host of a cookery programme on KACL, has a million-dollar TV deal and is leaving the station. 'Good news for Gertie,' says Frasier through gritted teeth. 'And for the many atheists who will welcome this new proof of their theory.' Roz has decided to put in for her slot, doing a show called *Love Matters*, in which she will use her experience to help out people with disastrous affairs of the heart. Although sad that he might lose Roz, Frasier and everyone else help her out with the audition tape.

At KACL Roz has a very positive interview but Frasier mentions to his agent, Bebe – who is there with a shambolic set of potential new recruits – how sad he'd be to lose Roz.

The news comes from Bulldog that Roz hasn't got the job – because Bebe has told the station boss that, without Roz, Frasier would quit. Horrified at Bebe's interference, Frasier talks to Roz, who innocently thanks him for his help with the audition tape. 'It was because of you I was second choice,' she says bravely. 'I can't argue with that,' agrees Frasier, and then confesses to Roz about Bebe's role in everything. Roz angrily demands he resign from Bebe's agency, saying that Bebe is misrepresenting everything he says. 'If you said you liked my eyes,' she explodes, 'they'd be on your desk tomorrow in a Tiffany box!'

The two of them go to Bebe's office and have it out with her, and, despite her attempts to manipulate their emotions, Frasier stands firm: his contract with her is finished. But Bebe has an ace up her sleeve, as always . . .

Guest Cast: Vera (Kathryn Joosten), Professor Pete (Doug Carfrae).

Where Everybody Knows Their Name: A magnificent return for, and indeed an episode-stealing performance from, Bebe Glazer (Harriet Sansom Harris), and a mention or ten for Sherry – best of which comes when Martin says, 'There isn't a woman alive with her fashion sense,' and Niles can only agree, pausing to comment, 'Carmen Miranda having passed on.' And Bebe is very pleased to see Bulldog (Dan Butler) at the station during the auditions.

Who's On The Line?: Although we don't hear from her, we know that Frasier has been talking to Carla, who believes she hails from the planet Krypton.

Subtitles: Any Port Manteau In A Storm; Across The River Styx.

Culture Vultures: Niles is busy trying to sell highly expensive tickets on behalf of one of his Country Club chums – one Esmee Bing, 'the Walnut queen', who is trying to raise cash for the Esmeralda Bing International Doll Museum. Frasier refuses to help, claiming he's a patron of 'the arts, Niles, not the crafts'.

Full-on Moon: Daphne is asked by Roz, during the audition tape recording, to 'pretend to be a woman who doesn't believe in sex without love but just feels so horny sometimes she wants to jump anything in pants'. Daphne agrees to this, saying, 'I'll try. And while I'm at it, I'll see if I can fake a British accent.'

Frasier Has Left The Building: Another of Bebe's angry clients is getting the pill-popping tales of woe from his agent, but gives up before she can get on to the car crash/orphaned niece part of her charade.

On The Couch: A delightful tour de farce, with Bebe, Roz and Frasier's final confrontation throwing out classic one-liners one after another. These range from a fairly mild 'Your tongue could open a wine bottle' to 'We're going to need a shovel to get out of here' after Bebe has tried every kind of ruse to make them think she adores them. Finally, Roz begins to relent, saying to Frasier of Bebe, 'It's not like she worships the devil.' 'She doesn't have to,' retorts Frasier quick as ever, 'He worships her!'

It seems bizarre that Bebe can have her two favourite clients at KACL (Bulldog and Frasier) and then also represent a bunch of no-hopers such as Professor Pete, the human encyclopedia (who, frankly, isn't), and the delightful couple Hank and Hannah Finch, reportedly guaranteed to provoke lively debates. He's a right-wing Baptist preacher, she's a fun-loving bisexual.

This is the high point of the season so far, a perfect example of what makes each of these characters work so beautifully. Frasier, caring but a little selfish, Martin, genuine and down to earth, Daphne, devoted but a bit touchy, Niles, driven but ultimately weak and Roz, hard-working and strong, but always seeing an opportunity. Even Bulldog is his usual self – one second terribly disappointed for Roz, the next flirting with Barbara, the successful candidate, from the newsroom.

4.18

'Ham Radio'

Written by David Lloyd
Directed by David Lee
First UK Transmission: 07.11.97

Skyline: A cloud passes above the skyline, and it rains.

Synopsis: It is anniversary time at KACL and so it has been decided to recreate *Nightmare Inn*, the station's very first live drama broadcast. Frasier will direct it, and is very excited. Martin is as cynical as ever, while Niles is alarmed. He reminds Frasier that, as a director, he can develop what he terms an 'Orson Welles complex. By the end of the week you'll not only be directing, you'll have rewritten the script and played the lead.' Frasier pooh-poohs this, but Martin observes that the script already reads 'Frasier Crane's *Nightmare Inn*'.

Frasier sets about preparing the show at very little notice and, having assembled much of his cast, and, of course, opted to play the lead himself, retires to his apartment with them to do a timing rehearsal. The English actor Mel White is playing a majority of the parts. The cast also features Bulldog as the sinister silk merchant Mr Wang. Bulldog cannot cope with the name without laughing childishly, so becomes Mr Wing. As soon as he puts on a corny stereotyped Chinese accent, Roz is appalled. 'No,' she says. 'Chinese Embassy on line one!' Gil Chesterton originally thought he might play Bull Cragen, the brutish gamekeeper, but Frasier instead casts him as Nigel Fairservice, drummed out of the Royal Air Service under mysterious circumstances. 'With him playing it, they may not seem so mysterious,' fears Roz. Roz herself is the owner of the inn, Carlotta Thorndyke.

With Daphne timing the rehearsals, Frasier's 'Orson Welles complex' takes over and Mel White walks out after Frasier criticises his Hans the butler for not being more Austrian (rather than German), his Prudence McAllister (White's playing both sisters) for not being spinsterish enough, his Bull Cragen for being too cultured, his O'Toole the handyman for being more Protestant than Catholic and his Peppo the dwarf for being 'too tall'.

Come the night of the broadcast, Frasier drags a reluctant Niles in to play the various parts, but doesn't tell him about the different accents. Roz arrives having been to the dentist and barely able to talk; Gil throws a strop because all the lines about his boyhood in Surrey 'romping with my schoolchums' have been cut; Bulldog goes mute with fear; and his latest girlfriend Maxine, playing the maid, is dyslexic. As the play descends into chaos, Niles bravely tries to carry on until Frasier makes the mistake of trying to direct him personally, live on air . . .

Guest Cast: Ian (Jack Betts), Mel White (Richard Easton), Maxine (Hope Allen).

Where Everybody Knows Their Name: KACL regulars Gil Chesterton (Edward Hibbert) and Noel Shempsky (Patrick Kerr) make welcome reappearances – it's been a very long time for Noel.

Who's On The Line?: A woman with paranoia had phoned in earlier, and Roz feels that Frasier's trail for *Nightmare Inn* might not have helped her mood very much.

Subtitles: Ham Radio.

Culture Vultures: At prep school, Frasier tried to direct *Richard III* but offended everyone, resulting in his being abused by the actor playing Richard, who attacked him with his hump.

Frasier Has Left The Building: Noel, having been relegated to sound effects, now has the studio to himself. He begins acting to the microphone until Roz surprises him.

On The Couch: A quite astonishing episode with so much good stuff crammed in, yet it still feels a bit flat. The second half, with Niles using helium to give him a squeaky voice for Peppo the dwarf, and Maxine's hopelessly politically incorrect but clever 'Look out he's got a nug', all builds towards the final dénouement where Gil refuses to die and Niles becomes a mass murderer, leaving a shell-shocked Frasier completely deflated. You can see he doesn't understand why everyone has turned against him, but a common fault with later shows is that the ending just happens because the programme either ran out of time or the writers out of jokes. As a result, despite some brilliant moments of mayhem, this episode fails because it ends up going nowhere.

4.19/4.20

'Three Dates and a Breakup'

Written by Rob Greenberg
Directed by Jeff Melman
First UK Transmission: 14.11.97 and 21.11.97

Skyline: Party balloons float up from behind the skyline.

Synopsis: While enjoying a coffee at Café Nervosa, Niles and Frasier are interrupted by a dishevelled, sweating Roz, who has been jogging. Anxious for her to leave, they suggest she have a wash – 'Flattered, as we are, that you have chosen our company over that of a shower . . .' After she has gone, Martin and Sherry arrive, and Frasier presents them with tickets for Nashville on Ice – the all-skating country jamboree. ('You try skating and blowing into a jug,' Frasier tells a bemused waitress, 'while your heart's breaking.') This is in an effort to clear them out of the apartment, as he is hosting a benefit party for the Seattle Theater Ensemble. After Martin and Sherry slip away, Roz, still looking dreadful, bumps into an old schoolfriend, John, who is going to their friend Marcy's wedding, sending Roz into despair about her appearance.

At the theatre benefit, Niles is trying unsuccessfully to get a date – specially with Natalie Spence. 'Her lips said "No" but her eyes said "Read my lips",' he says resignedly. Frasier, however, manages to get three, one for each night of the approaching holiday weekend. 'I'm a babe magnet,' he proudly boasts to his brother. 'I'm catnip!' Niles just shrugs. 'I think I feel a furball coming up.' To add to his discomfort, most people who know Niles call him Miles (a joke begun back in 2.13, 'Retirement Is Murder', by Bulldog), while Daphne complains she found a man in her room trying on her shoes. When Frasier asks who, she points out one Matthew Pinnick. Seeing a delightful opportunity for blackmail, Frasier points out that Pinnick is one of the benefactors and that 'something tells me the theatre's going to get that new sound system'.

Frasier's first date is with Kimberly Egan, a Catholic, animal-loving vegetarian. The early return of Sherry and Martin, who bring Frasier a piece of veal and discover Eddie locked whimpering in Martin's room, swiftly ends that date.

The next morning, Frasier and Daphne arrive back after shopping to find Sherry and Martin in a row – which ends with their relationship over and a distraught Sherry leaving. Although Frasier and (especially) Niles are overjoyed ('I feel like a seafront village after the Vikings have left'), Daphne feels Martin is burying his disappointment.

The following night, Frasier's date is Adair Peck, but Sherry turns up to collect some things and, thinking Adair is Kimberly, says they met the previous night. When Adair finds out yesterday's date was Kimberly, who broke up Adair's first marriage, that date is over.

The following day, Sherry talks to Niles and Frasier, revealing that she told Martin she loved him the night they broke up – Martin's response was the same, but hesitant. Much against Niles's wishes, Frasier agrees to talk to Martin.

That evening, Leslie Wellman is Frasier's date, but again Sherry turns up, horrified to see Martin. Apologising to Leslie, Frasier has to leave her on the sofa while he talks to

Martin. The elder Crane is feeling guilty about being in love with Sherry because of Hester. Frasier must now try to get his father to overcome his guilt, get back with Sherry and enjoy his final date of the weekend. But will Sherry again say something inappropriate and scupper the whole thing?

Guest Cast: Leslie Wellman (Maria del Mar), Adair Peck (Donna Bullock), Kimberly Egan (Rebecca Bush), John Coughlin (Jeffrey Corbett).

Where Everybody Knows Their Name: Again there is a reference to Frasier's first wife Nanette during the all-important conversation with Martin about Hester Crane, to whom he was married for thirty-five years (although there is a suggestion in 4.08, 'Our Father Whose Art Ain't Heaven', that it was over forty years). It is worth noting that Hester did her damnedest to stop Diane Chambers marrying Frasier back in *Cheers*, which certainly implies she kept a strong eye out for her boys. Sadly, she had presumably passed away prior to Frasier marrying Lilith or Niles marrying Maris, neither of whom she would probably have approved of. Rebecca, the waitress (Pauly P) returns. Sherry (Marsha Mason) features heavily and is at her outrageous best in the early half – she even finally gets to touch Niles. 'What's that on your cheek?' she asks and then, before he can react, she kisses him. 'My lips!' she cries triumphantly. Niles looks like he's going to be sick and then leaves hurriedly because he has to get to his therapy group where 'the compulsive gamblers were betting the passive aggressors they couldn't make the overeaters cry!'. We also see, for the first time, the more realistic, positive side of Sherry as she is bewildered by Martin's dismissal of their relationship and goes to Frasier and Niles, who she clearly adores, for help.

Who's On The Line?: The night after the benefit, a date-giddy Frasier has, according to Roz, spent most of his time comparing dating to unemployment, claustrophobia and bed-wetting. The latest recipient of advice was Doug (David Benoit), going through a dry spell without work.

Subtitles: Hat Trick; A Fly In The Ointment; He Couldn't Have Waited Until He Got In The House?

Culture Vultures: Frasier woos his women with good food and by playing Vivaldi, not too loud. He discusses Brecht with Adair, and quotes from Alexander Pope (at great length) during his speech at the benefit. Whenever Frasier introduces Sherry to people, his description changes. At the start of the episode, she is Martin's 'inamorata' then 'companion', 'ex-girlfriend' and finally 'lady friend' – her status restored. There's a lovely moment, too, when Niles arrives at Frasier's house triumphantly on hearing of Sherry's departure. As Frasier opens the door to his brother he says he would offer him a sherry but he's 'fresh out!'

Strange Bedfellows: When Frasier is glowing about his three dates over three days, Roz points out that she once had 'three dates on a Saturday and still had time to defrost my fridge and rotate my tyres'. Roz spends much of the episode trying to glam herself up because she feels she's looking bad. Sherry helps little when, on being introduced at Café Nervosa when Roz is looking her worst, says 'we all have our bad days once we pass forty'. On seeing Roz towards the end of the episode, looking glam, she says she thinks she's met her older sister.

Full-on Moon: Daphne has decided that she is victimised for her English accent and so begins practising her American, usually at odd moments, even terrifying Niles out of his wits. She also reveals that the elevator to the apartment has a hidden spy camera in it, through which she talks to the porter, Mr Hicks (is this perhaps Tony from 1.13, 'Guess Who's Coming To Breakfast'?).

Eddie Takes The Biscuit: At the end of each date, Eddie gets to devour Frasier's uneaten food, but at least has the decency to wait to be given permission first.

Frasier Has Left The Building: Niles finally has a date in Café Nervosa, so Frasier sends Sherry over to spoil it by introducing herself.

On The Couch: Possibly the best episode of the fourth season, a full hour of great jokes, a marvellously witty script and a series of events that, in true farcical pattern, keep repeating themselves but become more and more frenzied each time – especially Frasier's identical dating scenes which he almost repeats with Sherry. The only thing to fault this episode on is actually nothing to do with the programme directly. No, it's Channel 4's fault. They opted to split it over two weeks, rather than give it the hour-long slot it needs. This therefore kills nearly every visual joke because you need to see each date in succession to understand the irony of it. Similarly, if you hadn't seen the first episode, Frasier's stuff in the elevator with his umbrella and trousers makes no sense because you don't know Mr Hicks is watching. Oh, there are so many reasons why they made this a one-hour special rather than a two-parter and … aaargghhhh! An hour-long *Frasier* is unique and it seems sad to think that Channel 4 probably did not actually watch it and thus realise it needed to be shown in one go.

Of course, there is a very serious side to the episode – Martin's inability to let himself fall in love with Sherry because he feels he is betraying his deceased wife, Hester. Frasier handles this brilliantly and the final moments between his father and Sherry are wonderful. Overall, a fifty-minute masterpiece.

4.21
'Daphne Hates Sherry'

Written by Chuck Ranberg and Anne Flett-Giordano
Directed by Kelsey Grammer
First UK Transmission: 28.11.97

Skyline: A shooting star passes overhead.

Synopsis: Frasier is suffering a bad summer cold and his mood is not helped by the fact that the constant presence of

Sherry in the apartment has begun to get to Daphne. Martin is eating all the wrong things now, not doing his exercises and getting very out of shape. Daphne's concern for Martin is clashing with Sherry's overwhelming self-confidence and their arguments get worse and worse. Martin is oblivious to this, believing that people love Sherry for her ability to raise any mood, leaving people happier than before. 'You wanna see them smile when Sherry leaves the room,' he says proudly. 'I can imagine,' Daphne says through gritted teeth.

After returning from work, Frasier discovers the situation has worsened. Sherry thinks Daphne is too thin and needs to get a man – she believes Daphne's lack of a sex life is making her irritable. Daphne's already testy mood is not lightened when a strange man called Jack phones, saying that Sherry told him to ask her out. Sherry is appalled at Daphne's rudeness to Jack, and hopes that when the next one, Kenny (who has a boat), rings, she'll be more polite. That is the last straw for Daphne. She realises that all Sherry ever thinks about is sex. 'It's like you're part rabbit. People ought to rub your feet for luck!' After Frasier refuses to become involved because he is feeling ill, Daphne storms out.

She takes refuge at Niles's apartment, where the heat is unbearable. As time goes on, and the double entendres get heavier, it looks as if Daphne is coming round to Sherry's way of thinking, feeling she's been on the shelf too long. 'I'm feeling a little like the best china,' she says sadly. Niles nods, adding, 'Something should be eaten off you every day.' Gradually, he and Daphne are drawn together, culminating in her suggesting they share a room for the night, ostensibly to share a fan, but the undercurrent of something else is there.

Then she remembers that her thyroid pills are back at Frasier's and Niles gallantly offers to go and get them, saving Daphne the trouble of bumping into Sherry again . . .

Guest Cast: Coughing Man (Roger Keller).

Where Everybody Knows Their Name: Bulldog (Dan Butler) spends much of his time arguing with Roz while Sherry (Marsha Mason) of course upsets everyone. Baby the cockatoo, who still has a phobia about Niles's door buzzer, makes a guest reappearance.

Who's On The Line?: Mark, whose wife is keeping a pumpkin in a bassinet.

Subtitles: Tennessee, Anyone?; Cat Fight On A Hot Tin Roof; Suddenly This Summer; The Night Of The I Wanna; The Bath Menagerie.

Culture Vultures: Frasier is using one of his analogies to try to shut Bulldog and Roz up, but fails due to his cold. 'You see how weak I am?' he cries. 'I can't even finish a Visigoth metaphor!' Also, when trying to finally create a peace between the two women in his bathroom, he initially likens them to two animals marking out their territory (i.e. Martin). When he objects to that, Frasier tries again, suggesting his father is the Roman emperor Tiberius, with the women as Livia, his mother, and Vipsania, his wife. No one but Niles can, of course, see the significance of this – he no doubt would see Sherry as Livia. Oh, and best of all is Frasier's snobbish refusal to leave his bath to sort the women out because 'unless blood has been spilled – and on a carpeted area – I don't care!'.

Full-on Moon: Although this is very much Daphne's episode, apart from her lack of sex life since separating from Joe (4.06, 'Mixed Doubles') and the fact that clearly Marshall went nowhere (4.08, 'Our Father Whose Art Ain't Heaven'), we learn very little new about her, except that she has a slightly overactive thyroid, for which she has prescription pills.

Out Of Sight: Maris, we discover, rarely holds hands as she has 'a slight webbing that made her self-conscious'.

Eddie Takes The Biscuit: The poor dog spends much of his time hiding under cushions to avoid the atmosphere in the apartment.

Frasier Has Left The Building: Having finally got everyone out of his bathroom so that he can resume his long soak,

Frasier is again interrupted, this time by Eddie, who wants to join him in the water.

On The Couch: A fabulous second half clearly makes this a superior episode as Niles and Daphne's relationship takes an unexpected twist. And is resolved by a further twist even poor Niles could not foresee (although when he does, his reaction is wonderful). The first half of the episode is taken up by lots of good bitchy moments, but it seems unlike Martin not to take a stand and try to put a stop to it himself – although admittedly, by the time he does (describing Sherry and Daphne as old fishwives), he knows it's too late.

The only slightly odd thing about this is that, with Daphne and Niles having got so close to actually becoming intimate, it's all forgotten by the next show, which is a shame. This revelation of their, however fleeting in Daphne's case, mutual attraction could have underscored a few more episodes.

Take note, by the way, of the Freudian imagery regarding the food, the champagne and the CD tray. Beautifully done!

4.22

'Are You Being Served?'

Written by William Lucas Walker
Directed by Gordon Hunt
First UK Transmission: 05.12.97

Skyline: A streak of lightning crosses the sky.

Synopsis: Leo Pascalé is leaving KACL and everyone except Frasier is going to his farewell bash. Frasier is repulsed by the modern need to hug everyone – he's not a tactile person.

Later he meets up with Niles at Café Nervosa. Niles has just had a meting with Maris, where he suggested they get counselling or consider their marriage over. Proud of Niles's stand, they both receive a shock when a messenger delivers a package from Maris – she has filed for divorce!

Martin returns from walking Eddie to find Daphne having a clearout of his old things, including his Steamaster 2000 clothing steamer and a Hot 'n' Foamy shaver set. He's none too pleased to find his treasure trove of useless items being ditched.

Niles and Frasier are later rummaging through it when they discover an old notebook of their mother's. Frasier skims it while Niles, who confesses he has sent Maris's divorce papers back with a note begging her to take him back, listens. They read Hester Crane's opinions on Niles and Frasier, realising that Frasier has a bit of a touch phobia and Niles is spineless and easily dominated by both his older brother and particularly women. This leads Niles to decide to go through with the divorce and they head to his old house to retrieve his letter before Maris returns.

However, they find themselves trapped inside the house by her new Doberman guard dogs and, having escaped them, Frasier learns even more frightening things from their mother's notebook while Niles has a close encounter with his father's Hot 'n' Foamy . . .

Guest Cast: Leo Pascalé (Alan Wilder), Tom (Gerry Gibson), Messenger (Michael McFall).

Where Everybody Knows Their Name: Yoshi, Maris's gardener, is briefly referred to, and the familiar waitress (Luck Hari) turns up again.

Subtitles: Ties That Blind; Thank God Tuesday Isn't Soup Day.

Culture Vultures: Frasier dreads Leo's leaving party because, apart from the prerequisite hugging, it'll have 'twist-top wine'. Niles has bought lots of apology presents for Maris over the years including a Dresden China shepherdess and a Louis XIV candelabra.

Strange Bedfellows: Roz, on trying to get Frasier to hug Leo, points out that, according to the experts, 'if you have physical contact on a regular basis, it can extend your life'. Frasier tartly observes, 'Well, in that case, you should outlive styrofoam!'

Out Of Sight: Maris has been married to Niles for twelve years, so they must have got married very shortly after Lilith and Frasier. Lilith was at their wedding, which was seven years before Lilith's arrival in Seattle, five years previously (see 1.14, 'The Show Where Lilith Comes Back'). Maris had a painting commissioned of her and Niles in their garden for their third anniversary. Subsequently, she has had Niles painted over with a tree, and placed a skunk in the bushes with Niles's face on it. He is wearing a tie, made from her 'fat' pants in celebration of her surviving a winter where she had an obesity scare. Frasier remembers well 'her struggle to lose that holiday pound'. As a result of this, Maris had Yoshi burn a topiary shaped like a hippopotamus because she felt it taunted her. On seeing Maris that afternoon, Niles observes that 'I saw a twinkle in her eye I haven't seen since the neighbourhood children discovered our new electric fence.' While looking for some way to dispose of Maris's new Dobermans (both wearing diamanté collars by the look of it – and they are replacements for her previous duo, Gerhardt and Gestalt), Niles suggests breaking some of Maris's green tranquillisers into some food. 'What if Maris is out of pills?' warns Frasier but Niles just laughs hysterically, and Frasier realises what a foolish question that is!

The Buddy Show: Duke and two guys from the precinct see Martin walking Eddie – both suffering the indignity of wearing a vile hat and, in Eddie's case, matching jacket knitted by the well-meaning but clearly colour-blind Mrs Foster – and ask if Martin has taken up knitting dog jackets. Martin also tells the story of a man who killed his wife because she was obsessively clearing his things away – but Daphne is unrepentant and is still determined to see Martin's things go.

Frasier Has Left The Building: Mrs Foster delivers a new outfit for Eddie, but Martin chucks it into the rubbish box. Eddie retrieves it and begins to destroy it as quickly as possible.

On The Couch: From the opening shots of Frasier belittling Leo's leaving party (despite the fact there are countless episodes where Frasier has been more than happy to hug friends) to the final foam-laden hug between the two Crane brothers, this is a roller coaster of an episode as we see Niles's reaction to his impending divorce changing minute by minute. Between the laughs is a very serious study of how dependent Niles is on other people telling him what to do – even his mother can control his actions from the grave!

There are moments of pure frenetic madness, especially Frasier trying to cope with Niles's hysteria after the final revelation about their mother's notebook and the subsequent Hot 'n' Foamy moment, but also some nice moments as Niles signs away twelve years of his life with the very sad realisation that his marriage is over for good.

And a very nice episode, with a resolution that easily lends itself to creating some forthcoming long-needed progression in the Niles/Maris situation.

4.23

'Ask Me No Questions'

Written by Dan Cohen and F. J. Pratt
Directed by Jeff Melman
First UK Transmission: 12.12.97

Skyline: A helicopter rises up from the skyline and departs.

Synopsis: It is exactly a month since Maris served divorce papers and then agreed to see a counsellor with Niles – a Dr Deutsch, apparently, who requires them not to see each other outside their therapy sessions. This is having the effect that when they talk on the phone, they become sickly sweet, Niles constantly referring to his estranged wife as 'Pumpkin' or 'Bunny'. Niles casually asks Frasier, 'Do you think Maris and I are meant to be together?' Frasier goes to great lengths to avoid answering this, as it clearly needs some thought. He does not want to see Niles hurt, either by loneliness or by Maris, and cannot make his mind up.

Daphne and Martin meanwhile are having problems when Daphne gives Martin a cardigan she has knitted. He returns the favour by buying her a very expensive basket of toiletries and the two soon begin arguing over whether or not one gift automatically requires the giving of another. 'It's like Christmas morning in the Gambino household,' Frasier cries and then tries to explain that gifts are best enjoyed when spontaneous. 'Didn't you ever give Mom anything without warning?' 'Yes,' replies Martin. 'You.'

Niles persists in asking Frasier for his opinion about his marriage and so Frasier asks Roz's opinion on the best way to answer. She says that people aren't looking for honesty but reassurance, citing that the pants she is wearing might make her look fat. No matter what Frasier says subsequently, it is the wrong answer!

When Frasier begins to realise that Niles considers his opinions so important, it begins to dominate his every action, so he asks Marta for her opinion but this goes nowhere and his thoughts eventually cost him a date with the delicious Elise (who is clearly besotted with him). Eventually he takes a walk through downtown Seattle and solves his problem. He heads to Niles's Montana apartment in the early hours and awakens his younger brother, who is strangely anxious for Frasier to leave . . .

Guest Cast: Elise (Cindy Katz).

Where Everybody Knows Their Name: Lilith gets a brief mention when Frasier is discussing Niles and Maris's relationship with Elise. A return appearance for Luck Hari's Café Nervosa waitress and long-time-no-see for Irene Olga Lopez as Maris's housemaid Marta, who has undergone a bizarre transformation. She has been learning English Maris-style and was very excited when 'Missy Crane' gave her a Chanel Basket for her recent birthday, although Marta suspects it to be a 'knock-off'. Oh, and a brief mention for Hester Crane, by allusion.

Subtitles: The Question; The Answer Is 'Yes'; So The Answer Is '~~Yes~~' '~~No~~' '~~Yes~~' 'No'?

Eddie Takes The Biscuit: A wonderful moment where Frasier becomes the patient and Eddie watches and listens like a psychiatrist. He also falls for the old 'bathtime' routine to avoid Frasier having to take him for a walk. Silly dog, he should know that one by now!

Frasier Has Left The Building: Niles is taking a breakfast tray to a figure hidden behind a newspaper . . . but it's Marta.

On The Couch: A strange coda to the previous episode and one that spends too long getting to the point, but offers some marvellous ancillary comedy moments in the meantime. Best of these are two recurring motifs. One is Frasier gabbling away, thinking people are listening, but they're not. They've left the room or gone on a walkabout, beautifully timing their return to answer him. The other is the joke on seeing Maris. Frasier waves at a woman in Café Nervosa dressed exactly as you'd expect Maris to be, but she goes past him and he's actually waving to Marta. There's a similar moment over the end credits where you think Niles is giving the breakfast tray to Maris but it is, of course, Marta again. There are other good moments such as Frasier twice interrupting Niles and Maris on the cellphone by calling in from across the room and, later, Frasier's comment that he doesn't want to 'play God'. Apart from Niles's marvellous double take, he then asks Frasier what he would do. 'For a start,' Frasier concedes, looking at Eddie, 'I'd issue a recall on some of my lesser species.'

But great jokes do not make a *Frasier* episode alone, and unfortunately this is a bit weak – Frasier's night-time walk goes on too long and the dénouement at Niles's place is both obvious and rather unfunny. Nice to see Marta, though, whose new grasp of English thanks to Maris's coaching is a delight, especially her farewell to Frasier.

4.24
'Odd Man Out'

Written by Suzanne Martin
Directed by Jeff Melman
First UK Transmission: 19.12.97

Skyline: Lights go on in various buildings.

Synopsis: It is Roz's birthday and Frasier has booked them a table at an Italian restaurant, but Roz has a date. She suggests he do something spontaneous and go and find a date, but spontaneity isn't really Frasier's 'thing'. He goes home to discover that Niles appears to be attached to Daphne – literally. His tie is caught in the zip on her dress. He tries to get both of them and Martin to dine with him, but they all have plans (Martin is going to Sherry's, Daphne is out with Greg and Niles and Maris are recreating their first ever date). On the answerphone is a message from Laura, saying she's arriving at the airport tonight – sadly it's a wrong number.

Frasier heads to the restaurant by himself – 'Just because I'm alone doesn't mean I'm lonely' – but, surrounded by engaged couples, expectant parents and inquisitive children, he feels lonelier than ever. When you think his evening couldn't get worse, he gets red wine all over his shirt and ends up eating with a family he's never met before.

Returning home, Frasier is as low as he can get about his lack of social life – 'Not since Quasimodo strolled the streets of medieval Paris have so many people uttered the phrase "that poor man",' he explains. He checks his messages again – Laura has called again, hoping someone called Molly will collect her from the airport.

After much gentle persuasion, Frasier decides to go to the airport and meet the apparently lonely Laura, but there is one thing her messages failed to impart . . .

Guest Cast: Laura (Linda Hamilton), Maître d' (Carl Reggiardo), Waiter (Tom Astor), Johnny (Mile Marsico), Woman with Chair (Dulcy Rogers), Ethan (Joshua Greene), Amanda (Kris Edlund), Husband (Laque Beamer).

Where Everybody Knows Their Name: Sherry is making Martin dinner, and he later returns with a sample of her 'mock' apple pie, made from crackers instead of fruit. Hester and Martin Crane, we are reminded, met over the chalk outline of a murder victim (see 2.09, 'Adventures In Paradise', (Part 1). In subsequent years, they regularly made gingerbread men for their kids but with bent legs and crooked necks. Niles is aghast, having grown up believing they were meant to be dancers! Martin also reveals that, had Frasier been a girl, he'd have been named Laura, which is better than Hester's preference, Priscilla. Marta gets a swift mention. The Woman at the Airport (Lisa Coles) appears briefly at the end of the episode.

Subtitles: On The Plus Side She Did Lose Two Pounds; Love Among The Ruins.

Culture Vultures: Frasier is attracted to Laura because she plays the cello, speaks French, is neat and tidy, drinks sherry (and expect the airport bar sherry to be ghastly) and thus is, as she describes herself, 'the perfect snob'. She, unfortunately, means it disparagingly – Frasier doesn't. Rather than pin-ups of David Cassidy, Laura grew up with posters of Pablo Casals on her wall as a girl. Frasier confesses his pin-up was Sigmund Freud. Niles displays a wonderful moment of pretension on spying Frasier's wine-stained shirt. He looks at the colour, then sniffs at it, declaring it to be a Merlot whereas it is, as Frasier points out, a Cabernet.

Strange Bedfellows: Roz has a date with a waiter she and Frasier saw at lunchtime the day before. Roz's date is a result of the fact that she didn't have enough for a tip!

Full-on Moon: When Daphne was eighteen, she met a man at Stonehenge who claimed to be a direct descendant of the druids. She is currently dating Greg, a man even Martin acknowledges is gorgeous. 'Of course, he doesn't have a thought in that pretty little head of his,' sighs a wistful Daphne. 'This could be the one . . .'

Out Of Sight: Maris and Niles's first date was at a restaurant. To get there, they borrowed Martin's 1982 Impala. 'I'll never forget her look of wonder on touching vinyl for the first time,' recalls Niles cheerfully. 'She said it made her feel cheap and dirty. She liked it! I was her first "bad boy"!' Frasier nods sagely. 'Yes, I remember the way you used to carry her inhaler around, rolled up in the sleeve of your T-shirt.' On returning to Maris's home after that first date, Niles was apparently shot at by her father (now deceased by the way) with a blunderbuss. This very evening, their recreation of that day is topped off by Marta, drunk, standing atop Maris's house, shooting meatballs at them from a similar gun!

Frasier Has Left The Building: As it's the end of the season, the now customary 'Thanks For Calling' caption precedes a selection of photos of callers to Frasier's show. These are Marv Albert (Jeff from 4.02, 'Love Bites Dog'), David Benoit (Doug in 4.19, 'Three Dates and a Breakup'), Bob Costas (Jerry from 4.02, 'Love Bites Dog'), Kieran Culkin (Jimmy, who was in 4.03, 'The Impossible Dream'), John Cusack (Greg from 4.08, 'Our Father Whose Art Ain't Heaven'), Patty Duke (Alice from 4.12, 'Death and the Dog'), Christopher Durang (Rudy from 4.03, 'The Impossible Dream'), Julius Erving (Mark in 4.02, 'Love Bites Dog'), Eric Roberts (Chet, 4.15, 'Roz's Krantz and Guildenstern Are Dead') and Wendy Wesserstein (Linda in 4.05, 'Head Game').

On The Couch: 'She's called me twice today. That's already the best relationship I've had this year!' Thus Frasier sums up his mood after hearing from the mysterious Laura again – and it's just one delicious moment from this superb episode.

Centred on Frasier's loneliness and his initial unwilling-ness to do anything impulsive, such as jump on a plane to Acapulco as Roz once did, the episode is a tour de force for Kelsey Grammer's marvellous physical comedy, as every look, every twist of his head or gesture, says far more than dialogue ever could. His transformation from depressed divorcee – 'I'm forty-three and alone' – to childlike, eager-to-impress suitor when he meets Laura is fantastic.

The others each have their moment as well (bar Eddie, who is absent from the entire episode, despite how much of it occurs in the apartment), but only Niles really gets good lines – especially when discussing the effect voices can have on perceptions of people they've not actually seen in person. 'I was once told – imagine the impertinence – I sounded uptight!'

As the conclusion to the season, this is a perfect ending to a good set of stories and, to cap it all, it leaves you wondering just what Frasier will do on his impulsive holiday to Acapulco . . .

Season Five

5.01

'Frasier's Imaginary Friend'

Written by Rob Greenberg
Directed by David Lee
First UK Transmission: 09.01.98

Skyline: Fireworks explode over the skyline.

Synopsis: Frasier has boarded his plane to Acapulco, planning to take his unexpected holiday. He tries to find some female company and, after an abortive start or two, finds romance with a supermodel, Kelly Easterbrook, who is currently studying for a Ph.D in zoology at the University of Washington. She wants their relationship to continue back in Seattle, but asks Frasier not to tell anyone because she is in the midst of a messy break-up with her boyfriend, a footballer for the Seahawks.

On his return home, his family, already concerned over Frasier's sudden, out-of-character vacation, are further worried when he tells them he is dating a very high-profile supermodel which requires discretion. 'Ah yes,' says Niles, 'that pesky Club Bed oath of silence.' Frasier relents and tells them what is going on. 'Before I identify her for you, I have to ask you not to ever repeat this to anyone,' he says. 'I'd urge you to do the same,' replies Niles. To reinforce his claims, Frasier shows them a photograph of Kelly, but it is just one torn from *Sophisticate* magazine and thus his family think he has totally flipped.

At Café Nervosa, Frasier receives a call from Kelly and they meet at a restaurant – with Martin, Niles and Daphne sneaking behind him, hoping to catch him out. At the table, Kelly explains that she has to return to her lab as her iguana eggs need careful attention and she leaves. Seconds later, Martin and the others arrive, seeing a happy Frasier eating alone.

That night, Kelly turns up at Frasier's apartment, explaining she is going away, to the Galapagos Islands for two months to study the reptiles there. They decide to have one last night of passion and later, when Kelly is asleep, Frasier attempts to take a photograph of the two of them in bed together, to finally prove to the others that he is telling the truth . . .

Guest Cast: Kelly Easterbrook (Sela Ward), Felicity Stafford (Kim Oja), Stewardess (Leslie Ishii), Waiter (Andrew Philpot).

Where Everybody Knows Their Name: The woman at the airport (Lisa Coles) reappears – she is the one from the closing moments of the previous episode (4.24, 'Odd Man Out'), who persuades Frasier to go to Acapulco. She now has a name, Joanna.

Subtitles: Strangers On A Plane; Shadow Of A Doubt; The Lady Vanishes; Psycho.

Culture Vultures: An excellent moment ensues in the midst of a conversation in Café Nervosa where Niles and Martin disagree over the pronunciation of 'charade' (Niles is correct, by the way). And we learn that when Frasier was at school, in an effort to impress his family and peers, he began forging letters from Leonard Bernstein 'and told everyone they were penpals'. The game was up, of course, when one of the letters revealed that Bernstein's Broadway debut was *Candide* when, as Niles smugly points out, everyone knows it was really *On The Town*. Martin says the childish writing also gave the game away somewhat. And, while nothing to do with the Cranes, the repartee between Bulldog and Roz gets a good deal of exposure here. 'Don't you have better things to do than discuss my sex life?' wails Frasier. Bulldog just laughs. 'Frasier Crane's sex life. Hey, there's a word for that – it's a

... oxy ... oxy ...' 'Moron!' finishes Roz, but Bulldog is unrepentant. 'Hey, whoa, easy,' he argues. 'I'll get it ...'

Frasier Has Left The Building: Frasier is woken up alone, of course, in bed by Eddie licking his face. Frasier shrugs and goes back to sleep, hugging the dog.

On The Couch: 'I did not come back empty-handed! I came back with two huge handfuls!' And so begins the fifth season of *Frasier*, with this testosterone-packed episode of sexual farce. From the opening moments aboard the aeroplane to Frasier's final line to his astonished 'family', this terrific premiere not only sees Frasier exhibiting all the signs of creating a fantasy, but everyone else's reaction is completely spot on. 'We love you, Frasier,' says Martin, in a rare display of affection for what he thinks is his delusional eldest boy. Frasier understandably finally loses his cool – 'I am dating a supermodel zoologist whom I stole away from a professional football player and she is off to the Galapagos Islands to artificially inseminate iguanas! Is that so hard to believe?' Says it all, really.

Oh, and to cap the whole thing off, we have a superb guest appearance by Sela Ward, making you ache for the relationship to work because adding her to the mixture would have been marvellous. With Daphne and Roz forever searching for nuptial happiness, Niles still separated from Maris and Martin settling down with Sherry, it is so nice to see Frasier successfully getting the woman of his dreams.

5.02
'The Gift Horse'

Written by Ron Darian
Directed by Pamela Fryman
First UK Transmission: 16.01.98

Skyline: The light atop the Space Needle glows.

Synopsis: It is Martin's sixty-fifth birthday and, while Sherry and Daphne battle to organise a party, Frasier and Niles embark on their annual contest to outdo each other and buy a better, more expensive present for their father. Despite agreeing a price limit, Niles immediately goes overboard and a series of purchases, refunds and bigger purchases ensues.

As they talk about Martin's party, Sherry produces photographs of Martin's past life as a cop (including him with a seventies perm) to decorate the walls with. One shows Martin riding his police horse, Agides (see 2.05, 'Duke's, We Hardly Knew Ye'), and he recalls how much he loved his old four-legged friend.

Frasier gives in and buys what he knows his father has always wanted – a wall-sized TV system with massive mounted speakers that dominates the entire apartment. Once it is set up, Frasier sadly gazes at this barnacle on his home. 'Dear God,' he says, standing amid the speakers. 'It's Stonehenge!' While he and Daphne try to make the best of it by placing plants and *objets d'art* around it, Niles reveals that he has located Agides, bought him and put him into Briarwood Stables.

They take Martin to see his old friend but are surprised when Martin becomes melancholy.

After the party Sherry returns home without Martin, assuming he left with the already returned brothers. They head off to find him while Sherry tries to find the Nashville Channel.

Sure enough, he's with Agides at the stables and, although he loves the horse, the two sons know something is wrong . . .

Where Everybody Knows Their Name: Sherry (Marsha Mason) makes her return this episode, arranging Martin's party – but in fact she does very little except assume Daphne will do the donkey work. As the episode progresses, Daphne's murderous looks grow from a quick knife between the shoulder blades to full hanging, drawing and quartering. At one delightful moment, Daphne tells her everything she has done, to which Sherry sighs, 'This party is just going to wear me out.' Whatever words go through Daphne's mind right then are, thankfully, hidden from the viewer but her look says it all.

Subtitles: Come Again When You Can't Stay So Long; Sure, But Can He Do Long Division?

Culture Vultures: Frasier, desperately trying to convince Niles that the wall-sized TV is perfect for all the family, explains that it will 'enhance the majesty of the Metropolitan Opera, or the thrilling artists of the Bolshoi!' Niles just looks daggers at him. 'You're quite a Bolshoi artist yourself!'

Strange Bedfellows: Roz is trying to avoid Stan, a stock-broker she recently had a tryst with, who was unable to pronounce Frasier's name correctly, constantly calling him 'Fraser'. She opts to snog Frasier in front of him, but this is witnessed instead by a bemused Niles, who comments that the 'Haven't-Kissed-Roz Club of Seattle' now consists of just him and the archbishop. It instantly loses another fifty per cent of membership when Roz snogs Niles and then walks out. All Niles can say is, 'Everyone kisses better than Maris!'

The Buddy Show: Martin Crane shared mounted patrol with Mickey Dougan (see 2.05, 'Duke's, We Hardly Knew Ye'). One April Fools' Day, they dressed their horses in brassieres – Mickey using one of his wife May's oversized pairs. The night before his birthday, Martin was taken out to dinner by Duke, and Ed Flanagan bought everyone in the bar a drink in Martin's honour. Trouble is, Martin has no idea who Ed Flanagan is!

Eddie Takes The Biscuit: In one of the very best pieces of Eddieness, Frasier refuses to acknowledge the dog while he reads his newspaper. He raises the paper, so he can no longer see the poor animal, so Eddie begins making vertical jumps into the air, springing even above the top of Frasier's paper. Ahh, ain't he adorable . . .?

Frasier Has Left The Building: Frasier and Niles lead a blindfolded Martin through the apartment to a birthday cake, while around them, workmen remove the TV system.

On The Couch: A variable episode that relies too heavily on one-liners and reactions (Frasier's realisation that Niles has purchased Agides is tremendous) and tries to be serious amid it all by having Martin depressed by his ageing. No matter how good the jokes, one cannot help but feel that by putting them where they do, the writers are almost apologising for writing a quite serious episode about the passing of the years. As a result, 'The Gift Horse' is a bit unsatisfying.

For the record: Frasier buys a wallet and matching keycase, followed by binoculars – 'something just about perfect' (but we don't know what, except that it's portable and inside a green carrier bag) – and finally the TV system.

And Niles purchases membership of a beer club that delivers a case from a different brewery every month, followed by football season tickets for the Seahawks, and finally, of course, Agides and his allotted stable space. What exactly comes between the tickets and the horse we don't know.

5.03

'Halloween'

Written by Suzanne Martin
Directed by Pamela Fryman
First UK Transmission: 23.01.98

Skyline: Party balloons float up from behind the skyline.

Synopsis: Niles is preparing to host a costume party for the Library Association at Halloween to which everyone has to come as a literary figure. Then, at Frasier's apartment, Niles learns that Martin was unable to join Daphne and Frasier on their trip to the brewery because Eddie had had an encounter with a poison oak. Niles is aghast to learn that not only did his

brother and Daphne have a great time but they stayed overnight in a motel. Jealousy rears its ugly head.

At KACL, Roz's attention is not on her job and she
confesses to Frasier that she believes she might be pregnant.
She's waiting to hear from her doctor and declines going to
Niles's party. Frasier asks her to reconsider, suggesting it's
just the sort of thing to take her mind off her problem. 'For
me,' he pleads. 'You know you want to.' Roz nods. 'That's
exactly the kind of talk that got me into this!' Roz swears
Frasier to secrecy over this.

Nevertheless, they do all attend the party, where Roz keeps
using Niles's phone to check her answerphone messages. Roz
and Daphne have a conversation during which Roz suggests
she's had a little accident. Daphne thinks she's talking about a
shunt in her car and talks to Frasier who, thinking Roz has
told her the truth, mentions the pregnancy, and thus Daphne
becomes privy to the secret.

Daphne and Frasier retire to the kitchen, where Daphne is
having problems with her false eyelashes and they discuss
Roz's pregnancy. A decidedly tipsy Niles overhears, believing that it is Daphne who is pregnant and Frasier is the father,
and becomes indignant at Frasier's callous attitude. This is
heightened further when Frasier flirts with a guest dressed as
Eve and Daphne wants to go home because her eyelashes are
making her cry. As Niles becomes more drunk, he tells
Martin about the pregnancy. But Martin knows, although he
is aware it is Roz, and is amazed when Niles says he's going
to do the honourable thing and marry the poor single mother.
'I didn't even know you liked her,' Martin says. Still thinking
he means Daphne, Niles drunkenly replies, 'Yes, I wore that
mask well!'

Finally he summons the courage to propose to a bewildered Daphne and challenges his dishonourable brother to a
duel . . .

Guest Cast: Eve (Camille Donatacci Grammer), Man at
Party (Jonathan Fraser), Dr Krovitz (Mark Monuz), Dracula
(Joey Zimmerman).

Where Everybody Knows Their Name: Sherry is mentioned, but she is not going to Niles's party as she's off visiting her mom in prison. Maris's housemaid Marta gets a brief mention and we learn she is an arachnophobe (obviously something Niles cannot cure her of). And Gil Chesterton (Edward Hibbert) makes his first appearance this season (and one of the campiest ever), dressed as Chingachgook who, as he explains to Martin, was the Last of the Mohicans. 'Oh,' says Martin quietly. 'Another mystery solved.' And Baby is of course still resident in Niles's apartment.

Who's On The Line?: Well, Ted, who is feeling a little disconnected, was on the line, as was Bill, going through a difficult transition. But the only person Frasier actually gets to talk to on air is Roz's manicurist, Dorothy (Cindy Crawford).

Subtitles: Whimsy; Panache.

Culture Vultures: Well, it's a potpourri of literary references at Niles's party. Niles of course is Edmond Rostand's Cyrano de Bergerac while Frasier and Daphne are the Narrator and the Wife of Bath from Geoffrey Chaucer's *The Canterbury Tales*. Martin is Conan Doyle's famous detective Sherlock Holmes and Gil is Chingachgook from James Fenimore Cooper's *The Last of the Mohicans*. Roz comes as O from *The Story of O* by Pauline Réage. On learning of her mishap at the hairdresser's, Niles suggests Maris come as the Bald Soprano, from Eugéne Ionesco's play – in Britain, we'd of course say the Bald Prima Donna! At the beginning of the episode, Niles attempts to get Martin to dress as Lord Peter Wimsey from Dorothy L. Sayers's novels, and among the other party guests are Eve from the Bible ('Now I know why they call it the Good Book,' smarms Frasier), along with a devil, presumably from the same source. We can also spot a Rhett Butler from Margaret Mitchell's *Gone With the Wind*, Victor Hugo's Quasimodo, Edgar Rice Burroughs's Tarzan, Harrison Ainsworth's Dick Turpin, plus a host of other historical and fantasy figures from all eras and nations, including a couple of Robin Hoods, a Paul Bunyan and a Merlin. The kid that comes to the door is dressed as Bram Stoker's Dracula, and the latecomer Dr Krovitz is the monster from Mary Shelley's *Frankenstein*. Oh, and Bulldog comes as Waldo from those *Where's Waldo* picture books (known as *Where's Wally* to us Brits, of course!). See, we can be culture vultures too!

Strange Bedfellows: Well, this is it – the start of the pregnancy storyline as Roz discovers she may well be expecting. 'Even the best protection is only effective ninety-nine times out of one hundred,' she explains to Frasier. 'I can't beat those odds.' 'Yes,' agrees Frasier. 'I suppose you've been dodging that bullet for a long time.' But as to who the father is . . . ? That's a mystery for the next episode to solve.

Full-on Moon: Daphne, thinking Roz is talking about car accidents, informs Frasier she has been rear-ended 'at least a dozen times'. Frasier thinks she means something quite different, naturally.

Out Of Sight: Maris has to take water pills after hearing Niles utter the phrase 'my juicy wench' over the telephone, and we later learn that she has a wig vault, containing thirty-seven hairpieces.

Frasier Has Left The Building: One of Niles's hostesses is seeing the last party guests out of his Montana apartment (Eve, by the way, is going home with the devil), while an unconscious Niles is on the fainting couch with Baby.

On The Couch: Possibly the best episode in the lifetime of the series so far, this is a nonstop comedy of errors, as each party guest is fed a titbit of erroneous information about who is pregnant, who the father is, who is going to propose to whom and so on. The conversations between Daphne and Frasier, who are blissfully ignorant of the effect it is having on Niles, are so beautifully laden with double entendres you cannot help but wince. And, when Niles finally decides enough is enough, you want to scream at him to stop before it all goes horribly wrong.

At the centre of this, of course, is the distraught Roz, who awaits her doctor's report to discover if she really is expecting a baby, and that brings us right up to the TO BE CONTINUED . . . caption at the end.

A superbly written and paced episode, each actor infusing their character with a progression of hysteria as it goes on. Only Martin remains fairly cool (his brief moment with Gil concerning Chingachgook is sublime), but even he gets slightly manic when he thinks Frasier is the father. An absolute classic . . .

5.04
'The Kid'

Written by Jeffrey Richman and Suzanne Martin
Directed by Jeff Melman
First UK Transmission: 30.01.98

Skyline: A crescent moon rises from behind the skyline.

Synopsis: It is the morning after Roz 'and a large portion of Seattle' found out she was pregnant. After almost convincing Bulldog he's the father (a joke which he eventually sees through when Roz refers to his lovemaking as 'tender and caring'), Roz tells Frasier that the father is an architect, currently in Cairo.

Later, at Frasier's home, she tells the others that he is an archaeologist in Cairo she met in a bar, which Frasier spots. Eventually he wheedles out of her that she has not revealed the real father at all.

The following morning, Roz bumps into Frasier at Café Nervosa and he twigs that their waiter, Rick, is the father. He is a college junior, whose twentieth birthday was just three weeks ago. And, as Roz later finds to her horror, Rick's mom is thirty-seven – indeed, Rick comments that Roz even looks a bit like his mom!

Back at her apartment, Roz awaits Frasier, who is taking her to dinner, when Rick arrives, saying he's dropping out of college and not going to study in Paris, but will marry Roz. She gently lets him down, saying that it would not be practical and that she's going to raise their child on her own. He leaves, taking with him the first sonogram of his baby.

When Frasier arrives, however, Roz begins to wonder if she's ready for motherhood . . .

Guest Cast: Rick (Todd Babcock).

Where Everybody Knows Their Name: Sherry is referred to as buying 'foundation garments' (i.e. bras and knickers) with her sister. When Roz is becoming distraught at the fact that she knows nothing about motherhood, Frasier tries to cheer her up, commenting that one of his fondest memories was bringing Frederick home from the hospital. Roz's depression is sparked off by the fact she's forgotten to buy fresh milk, feeling that if she cannot do that, how can she bring up a baby. 'You can know about the milk,' she cries to Frasier. 'Lilith can know about the bootees and Snuggles.' Frasier shrugs: 'You never met Lilith, did you!'

Subtitles: Let's See Alec Guinness Blow Up One Of Those.

Strange Bedfellows: Hard as it is to believe, this is apparently the first time anyone has actually proposed marriage to Roz. And what a delightful proposal it is, too. We think she should have said yes – guys like Rick don't come along very often, girl! By the way, could Rick be the waiter Roz went out with on her birthday (see 4.24, 'Odd Man Out' – the fact she and Frasier met that particular waiter one lunchtime may suggest Café Nervosa as their eatery rather than a restaurant)?

Out Of Sight: Explaining how he'd love to have children, Niles explains that Maris is 'a tad older' than he is and that her biological clock is winding down. 'Luckily she flies to Zürich twice a year to have it reset.'

Frasier Has Left The Building: Roz is stuffing pillows up her sweater to see how she will cope when the baby begins to show.

On The Couch: As with 'The Gift Horse', this episode mixes comedy with serious issues. This time it's all about motherhood. Unlike 'The Gift Horse', this works because the humour is where it is needed, but the serious stuff, notably the final sequence in Roz's condo, is just amazingly well written, acted and delivered. Roz's discussion with Rick and then her breakdown before Frasier is wonderful. Rarely have we had the opportunity to see beyond the flirtatious, wise-cracking Roz, and this episode demonstrates both the character's depth and the underrated acting talents of Peri Gilpin. A very clever mix here – the comedy is sublime (Niles, Daphne and Martin eavesdropping on Frasier and Roz at Frasier's place, and later Martin's realisation that the person correcting the grammar and spelling in the Café Nervosa toilet graffiti is, naturally, Niles) while the drama is touching. As the pregnancy develops and Roz's situation changes, this will add a whole new dimension and a much-needed character progression to the whole series.

5.05
'The 1,000th Show'

Written by Christopher Lloyd and Joe Keenan
Directed by David Lee
First UK Transmission: 06.02.98

Skyline: Fireworks explode over the skyline.

Synopsis: It is Frasier's 1,000th broadcast and he has piously told Roz that he doesn't want any kind of celebration of this, claiming 'the work is its own reward'. Obligingly, Roz tells KACL's station manager Greg this and so Frasier is faced with nothing to celebrate, unlike rivals Bob and Nipsey over at KTLK. Of course, what he really wants is 'a small, tasteful, low-key pubic rally' and after dropping hints to Roz again, this is what he gets, at the foot of the Seattle Space Needle.

The Mayor declares it to be Frasier Crane Day and organises a rally to give him the key to the city. Although Niles receives his own 'gift from the self-esteem fairy' (an acknowledgment amid numerous other eminent psychologists in a medical journal's letters page), he is incredibly jealous of Frasier, who unfortunately is caught up in his own self-publicity and wallows in the attention. They opt to walk to the Space Needle, Frasier cheerily waving to people, calling out 'I'm listening' when they smile at him, although Niles points out, 'The ones with cameras are tourists. They have no idea who you are, much less why you're "listening".'

Passing through the market, Niles spills coffee on Frasier's shoes and they head for a shop to buy a new pair. By the time they are finished, they are running late and Roz has to begin the rally by introducing Martin, who gives a dreadful speech, written, of course, by Frasier himself.

Taking a shortcut, the Crane brothers are mugged and, now penniless, steal a quarter from a blind musician. Their crime is seen by a load of schoolgirls, who give chase, and eventually the pair escape on to the monorail. Just as they finally get to the Needle, the train breaks down and it looks as if Frasier will never make it to his own celebration . . .

Guest Cast: John (Mark Blum), Male Fan (Allen Galli), Female Fan (Melora Marshall), Conductor (Demane E. Hall), Schoolgirl (Charlee Baugh), and Norman B. Rice, Mayor of Seattle.

Where Everybody Knows Their Name: This is the first appearance for a new semiregular Waiter (Tom W. Chick) whose running gag appears to be never remembering what Niles wants to drink.

Subtitles: One Of The World's Foremost Experts On Hair Pulling; It's The Most Wonderful Time Of Year.

Culture Vultures: Aghast at the damage to his shoes, Frasier bemoans their value, stating that they are Joan and David. Unusually ignorant (or maybe playing Devil's Advocate, although that seems unlikely bearing in mind the mood of the Crane brothers), Niles retorts, 'You named them?'

Strange Bedfellows: Still suffering from her wild mood swings, Roz is overjoyed to find a gift from Bulldog, because he thinks she'll make a fabulous mother. They hug – but for too long. Bulldog claims he just wants to feel the baby kick, but gets kicked himself because Roz screams, 'You just wanted to hug me because my breasts are getting bigger!'

Full-on Moon: Well, where to start here? Despite this being about Frasier Crane Day, the best moments of the episode are Daphne's. Her friend Xena (a Greek, resident in the US) wants to travel out of the country with Daphne to meet Xena's mother, who is arriving by ship from Greece. Daphne's passport has run out and she is having trouble getting it renewed. Her heated phone conversation with the passport agency ends when she yells that she is a resident alien from England. 'You know, the country that used to own you people!' Martin, listening, just shrugs and reads his paper. 'You'll go right to the head of the line now.' But without a doubt, the best piece of Daphne Moon insanity occurs at the rally, where she wanders over to the Mayor's enclosure and introduces herself to Norman Rice. 'I can't say I care for the way you treat us poor aliens,' she starts, and it's downhill from then on. 'My friend Xena and I – she's an alien too – were trying to get down to rendezvous with her mother's ship . . .' Clearly thinking he's got an *X-Files* nutter on his hands, he has her 'looked after' by two aides. 'You two work for the Mayor?' she asks. 'Well, I suppose I should know that already. You see, I'm a bit psychic . . .' And off she is led, never to be seen again this episode.

Eddie Takes The Biscuit: The only bit of Eddie business is at the rally, where, like the rest of us, he yawns at poor Martin's Frasier-written speech about his son.

Frasier Has Left The Building: Nothing to do with the story here – this is footage of Kelsey Grammer on stage at the real Frasier Crane Day, 11 September 1997, singing 'Tossed Salad and Scrambled Eggs' to the Seattle audience.

On The Couch: Frankly, for the real 100th episode, this is a very poor piece of *Frasier*. The second half is all on location around Seattle, which is visually pleasant but somehow the show ceases to be *Frasier* simply by getting away from the familiar confines of a studio. The script is certainly inspired – the repartee between Niles and Frasier provides some of the bitchiest but cleverest lines ever. Watch out for Niles's comment, for example, after Frasier has pointlessly waved at yet another person on the street. 'He was hailing a cab,' explains the younger Crane, 'to get away from the scary "listening man".' But the actual joke of Frasier failing to get to his own party simply falls flat. The mugging, the schoolgirl chase and the monorail sequences are frighteningly predictable, while the climax (with Niles abruptly discarded because his role in the story is over) is too much, too late. It might be a sort of atonement for Frasier's ego-driven plans for his day, but it is too late by then. For the first time in 100 episodes, we actually don't care what happens.

5.06
'Voyage of the Damned'

Written by Jeffrey Richman
Directed by Pamela Fryman
First UK Transmission: 13.02.98

Skyline: A cloud passes above the skyline, and it rains.

Synopsis: The 14th of the month is Maris and Niles's wedding anniversary and, although they are in counselling still, Maris has chosen not to celebrate it with her estranged husband, but by flying to the Swiss Alps for an experimental rejuvenation treatment. 'Only one man performs the procedure,' explains Niles, 'and she wants to see him before he's extradited.'

Frasier meanwhile has been persuaded to join Roz on a freebie cruise to Alaska in return for his delivering a talk, and suggests that Niles and his father join him. Talking with Martin, Frasier suggests talking to Maris but Martin warns him off interfering and Frasier agrees. Daphne, who has forgotten to collect Martin earlier and caused both him and Eddie to get soaked in the Seattle rain, does not join them.

Martin is an experienced cruiser, and tries to get Niles to eat as much as possible. Frasier is far more interested in the fact that everyone has a bigger and better cabin than he has. He is further alarmed when he discovers that Gore Vidal is not sharing the top billing with him, but instead it is the seventies Latin singing sensation Carlos 'the Barracuda' Del Gato, Lance Gould – a magician – and the comedy stylings of Giggles O'Shea. 'You've booked me on a floating *Gong Show*,' Frasier explodes at Roz. She points out he has top billing. 'Of course I've got top billing. I'm the only one up there I've ever heard of.' His mood is later reduced further when he realises the crowd will be somewhat smaller than he expected.

Niles meanwhile has been spotted by a fellow Country Club regular, Mimi Cosgrove, who flirts outrageously with him. Niles's discomfort is further enhanced when a waiter arrives with a drink sent by another passenger, and then throws it in Niles's face. With horror, Niles sees Maris is there and clearly thinks he is having an affair with Mimi.

To make matters worse, Frasier confesses that it was he who invited Maris, hoping it would help the couple reconcile. Martin similarly contacted his daughter-in-law, but the situation goes from bad to worse when it becomes clear that Maris is out for revenge by bedding 'the Barracuda' . . .

Guest Cast: Mimi Cosgrove (Stephanie Faracy), Carlos 'the Barracuda' Del Gato (Miguel Perez), Waiter (Joe Reynolds), Maid (Beecey Carlton).

Who's On The Line?: Karl, who must either have his tattoo removed or embark on a round-the-world journey, hoping to find another girlfriend named Fredwina.

Subtitles: Ship of Fools.

Culture Vultures: Frasier in finally persuaded to take the freebie trip because (apart from the massaging of his ego) the cruise liner has 'mahogany wainscoting'. The fact that Gore Vidal might also be present is but a further incentive. Back at his apartment, Frasier goes through a series of bizarre rituals to ensure that Martin, Niles and Eddie don't drip rain over his freshly waxed wooden flooring (and fails). Best of all, when Del Gato asks Roz to speak to him in the 'universal language' (i.e. luuurve), Frasier icily suggests Roz 'say something amusing in Esperanto!'.

Full-on Moon: We learn a lot about Daphne's bizarre mother here (and, by default, a great deal about Daphne). For instance, when discussing rain – something Manchester and Seattle share copious amounts of, it seems – 'my mum would always say, "Enjoy it while you can. There'll be no water in hell." Of course that was her answer to everything. "Eat your veggies. There'll be no Brussels sprouts in hell." "Have a lie down. There'll be no naps in hell."' This routine returns later, when Frasier in annoyed by Eddie shaking rain all over the previously noted waxed floor. 'There'll be no dogs in hell,' offers a conciliatory Daphne. 'I sincerely doubt that,' returns Frasier.

Out Of Sight: We learn a frightening amount about Maris in this episode – hardly surprising as we actually get to see her! Well, her silhouette, at least, as she gargles – an act Niles knows means she's preparing for romance. Having no pigmentation, Maris can wear only black and a veil on the cruise because otherwise she'd fry. She's a big fan of Carlos 'the Barracuda' Del Gato from the seventies. This was because the Barracuda was a dance she could do. 'The Hustle was too strenuous. She had no "booty" to shake, but her fetching little underbite was just perfect for the Barracuda.' The Hustle, by the way, was a dance made popular by the American singer Van McCoy in his hit single 'Do the Hustle', which reached number three in the UK pop charts back in 1975. For those who really want to know, the Hustle was then given a new lease of life in 1988 by Funky Worm with 'Hustle! (To The Music)', but that reached only number thirteen. You really did want to know that, didn't you?

The Buddy Show: We have a reference not just to Duke this episode, but also to his sadly departed bar (see 2.05, 'Duke's, We Hardly Knew Ye'), where Martin remembers getting the best hot toddies to drink.

Frasier Has Left The Building: As the others watch, 'the Barracuda' finds his victim for the night – Mimi Cosgrove.

On The Couch: A peculiar episode that veers from the sidesplittingly funny to the downright banal. Martin and Frasier's agreement not to interfere (a nice back-reference to newly discovered vocabulary for Martin in 4.23, 'Ask Me No Questions') is beautifully parodied later when each chastises the other for doing exactly that. Frasier learning everyone else has a better cabin than he has is inspired because it really plays on Frasier's predilection for finery and here he is cut off from it and the running gag of the waiter chucking drinks at Niles every so often is curtailed at exactly the right moment. But beyond that, 'the Barracuda' is a stereotyped character that belongs in an eighties bad sitcom; the cruise scenario is pointless (it could so easily have been a party, a meal in a restaurant or even a shopping trip); and the whole Mimi/Niles/Maris situation is a ridiculous plot contrivance that seems wholly out of place. The farcical final scenes in Maris's cabin and loo are great fun though – especially as we (just about) see Maris for the first time. 'In all these years, I've never seen her face,' says Roz. Frasier just nods. 'Well, I haven't seen her most recent one, so this must be a new experience for both of us.' As a result of this, Roz gets to start the best joke of the sequence: 'I can see her coat on a hat rack,' she explains, peering through the toilet keyhole. 'Look closer . . .' warns Frasier. Roz does and then realises she's seeing Maris! Her reaction is spot on. In actual fact, this idea of Roz and Maris not having met seems a little bizarre, since they shared a dinner table once (see 2.06, 'The Botched Language of Cranes').

Ultimately, Niles sums up the plot best. 'It says a lot about our marriage. No trust on either side.' Sadly, it's not really a strong enough plot upon which to hang the entire episode.

5.07
'My Fair Frasier'

Written by Jay Kogen
Directed by Jeff Melman
First UK Transmission: 20.02.98

Skyline: A crescent moon rises from behind the skyline.

Synopsis: Frasier buys Roz a gift to thank her for her hard work on some recent trailers which have seen off the rival programme by Doctor Frank on KTLA. Roz bursts into tears, not just because she hates the gift, a black sequinned purse, but because her moods and emotions are all over the place due to her pregnancy.

Frasier returns to the store where Jill, the salesperson, refuses to exchange it because it was a sale item. Frasier is then helped by the lawyer Samantha Pearce, who talks Jill into letting Frasier exchange the purse, and the two agree on a dinner date.

That evening, before his date, a positively glowing Frasier settles down with Martin, trying to show an interest in the Seahawks ball game, and Daphne twigs he's got a date. She spies his silver tie pin, which he wears only on such occasions. 'Good work getting the tarnish off,' she says, answering the door to Niles. Niles has arrived with the tickets for the boat show – and is aghast when Frasier explains he cannot go as they have an agreement to support each other when taking Martin somewhere they hate. 'I gave up *La Traviata* tickets to support you at Tractor Pull,' he moans. Frasier softens the blow by giving his ticket to Daphne – 'Very crafty,' mutters a mollified Niles.

At the date, Frasier and Sam find conversation difficult, so she suggests they simply go to bed and have sex, which they do at Frasier's. Afterwards, she is introduced to Daphne, Niles and Martin.

Sometime later, Frasier is cooking for Sam when she is called away to a meeting, returning briefly to give Frasier flowers by way of an apology. The others begin to suggest that Frasier is taking on the 'traditional' female role in their relationship. This is confirmed when, three weeks since they started dating, Sam takes Frasier to a lawyers' ball, where he meets lots of lawyers' wives who sympathise with his feelings of insecurity. Frasier begins to explain they'll have more time soon, but the women chorus knowingly: 'As soon as the trial is over.' They've been hearing this for years. 'Oh, there's always another trial,' explains the oldest wife, Jennifer.

Frasier decides it's time to talk to Sam about their roles in this relationship . . .

Guest Cast: Daniel Gill (Steve Arden), Jennifer (Beverley Leech), Cindy (Yasemin Maytok), Vanessa (Cyndi Pass), Saleswoman (Shirley Prestia) and Larry King.

Where Everybody Knows Their Name: Hester gets a brief mention, at Niles's expense, and the episode introduces us to Samantha Pearce (Lindsay Frost) who manages to return Frasier's unwanted purse. 'You should see me return something hard, like a house or a kidney!' Sam's a very high-profile 'noted attorney', defending a murderer in Seattle. During an interview with Larry King, we learn she's (reportedly) had flings with the likes of Brad Pitt and Kevin Costner. 'Maybe,' says Daphne with delightful tactlessness to Frasier, 'she's had her fill of attractive men and is ready for a change.'

Subtitles: And I'll Have You Know I'm A Size 11; He Once Nailed A Borderlaise At 20 Yards.

Culture Vultures: Frasier is very proud of his new Cartier watch and delightfully displays it to the lawyers' wives' club!

Strange Bedfellows: Roz, going through tremendously emotional mood swings due to her pregnancy, is upset because she has been trying to date a wicker-furniture salesman. She hoped her 'radiant glow would do the talking for me', but apparently it didn't, because, when she said she was pregnant, he fled.

Full-on Moon: Daphne relays the tale of a man she once dated. He 'went through' several top UK thespians and then met Daphne. 'Of course, after he'd got through slumming it, he dumped me and went back to actresses.' All she got out of it was an autographed photo of Helena Bonham Carter riding a pony!

Out Of Sight: Maris is brought up by Martin when he's trying to make a point about men in the Crane family not letting women dominate their lives. Niles just nods. 'Poor Uncle Frank,' he says ignorantly.

Frasier Has Left The Building: Roz, sitting in her studio, is rapidly going through a variety of different emotions.

On The Couch: A superb piece of role-reversal comedy as Frasier, no matter how hard he fights it, gets swept up in the role of wife – with Kelsey Grammer noticeably camping it up outrageously. The pinnacle of this is his and Sam's final conversation on the balcony, where each of them begins to spout platitudes you've heard a million times before in any kitchen-sink drama. But they are amusing here because of who actually says them. The fact that Frasier is so easily bribed by the Cartier watch is excellent, as is his showing it off to the other wives.

The rest of the regular cast get very little to do – except react to Frasier's situation, which is unusual. This is especially so of Roz, whose mood swings one suspects are going to be an ongoing plotline.

Best sequence of all, however, is at the beginning in the shop, when Jill refuses to take the purse back. Having established it was not a gift for either Frasier's wife or girlfriend, she begins to suspect something else, and talks about Frasier as if he's got a male lover. 'I would thank you, when you say the word "friend", not to italicise it,' he blusters, but it's too late. Everyone in the store, including Sam at that point, suspects there's more to this than meets the eye.

5.08

'Desperately Seeking Closure'

Written by Rob Henning
Directed by Pamela Fryman
First UK Transmission: 27.02.98

Skyline: A crescent moon rises from behind the skyline.

Synopsis: A week after the last episode, Frasier returns after a ski weekend away with Sam in the mountains. Niles, trying to drink a double-short, low-fat, no-foam latte, finds his stomach lining being inflamed not just by the unwanted nutmeg on his beverage but by Frasier's insistence on telling him about all the famous people he has met. 'Can I get you anything else?' asks the coffee-delivering waitress. 'Just a dustpan to sweep up some of these names,' says Niles tartly.

Later, Frasier and Sam are having their one-month 'anniversary' dinner when Sam drops the bombshell. It's not working and she wants to call it off, assuring Frasier he is not at fault.

The next morning, Frasier tells them that Sam dumped him, but remains unconvinced it wasn't his fault. 'It was a mutual decision. Well, a little more mutual on her part than mine.' There has to be something wrong with him, he decides.

Later that evening, while Martin cannot find the TV remote and Niles waits anxiously to go to dinner with his brother, Frasier becomes more and more paranoid. Roz arrives, going to the movies with Daphne, but Frasier asks them to help him compile a list of his faults which, after a shaky start, soon gives everyone the opportunity to vent their feelings. A bit dazed by this, Frasier points out to Martin that he's the second person to say 'pretentious'. 'Underline it,' suggests Martin. Frasier reveals that he's left messages on Sam's answerphone and, because he has her secret code, he plays them back to everyone, who agrees he sounds desperate. He wipes them, accidentally wiping an important one from Sam's secretary. Niles suggests that maybe Frasier was going out with Sam for the wrong reasons – he was more taken with her social connections than the woman herself. The others finally leave, trying to bolster Frasier's confidence with a list of his good points, but it's no good. Frasier heads off to find Sam at the restaurant and deliver the secretary's message.

Sam already knows, and has decided that if Frasier loves her that much, then maybe they should stay together. However, Frasier's conscience has been pricked by Niles's suggestions, so he opts to make a clean breast of it . . .

Guest Cast: Waiter # 2 (Alan Mingo), Restaurant Waiter (Matt Sullivan), Customer (Christopher Marshall), Man in Street (Nick Mize), and Lesley Stahl.

Where Everybody Knows Their Name: A second, and apparently final, appearance for Sam (Lindsay Frost) alongside brief mentions of Gil Chesterton, Bulldog (neither of whom actually appears) and even Miss Judy from the station's arts-and-crafts show, none of whom were able to explain why Sam broke up with Frasier. And Niles's ever-forgetful waiter (Tom W. Chick) turns up – getting the orders confused despite the new system of order-taking at Café Nervosa – alongside a new regular waitress (Amy Landers).

Subtitles: No, It's You; If It's Barbra I'll Kill Myself.

Culture Vultures: Among the names dropped by Frasier after his weekend away with Sam are actors Jack Nicholson and Meg Ryan, record producer and artist Puff Daddy, reporter Lesley Stahl and General Schwarzkopf, the ... er ... general. Sam later nearly persuades him to head to London simply to party with Sir Alec Guinness and Stephen Sondheim.

Strange Bedfellows: Roz apparently once believed she and someone called Steve Wilson would get married, which is why she had his name tattooed on her butt.

The Buddy Show: Unable to locate the remote, Martin gives up and heads off to watch the game with Duke.

Frasier Has Left The Building: Having built himself a new remote out of ten chopsticks and a rubber cap, Martin cannot understand why, every time he selects a channel, it changes – unaware that Daphne is right behind him with the proper remote.

On The Couch: 'No wonder you're heartbroken. You've just lost the only woman you could ever possibly sometime down the line perhaps fall in love with. I'm surprised the country-music people haven't jumped all over this one.' A bit of a damp show here, especially in the light of the previous episode. It all seems a bit sudden that Frasier is in love with Sam only because of her friends, considering he was very smitten with her last time around for just being her, and indeed, seemed daunted by her social life.

But what the heck! We do get some brilliant moments, such as when Daphne, wandering into the room when they're trying to list Frasier's good points, throws in 'conceited', to which Martin just sighs, 'Wrong list, Daph.' The other great moment in the episode also involves Daphne doing a series of foot-in-mouth comments, resulting in her quickly running away to get food to cover her embarrassment.

But overall, this is a letdown and it does seem a shame to have disposed of Sam Pearce this quickly.

Oh, by the way, we learn that Frasier's birthday is in March while Eddie's is 7 May. If only Martin could remember they were that way around . . .

5.09

'Perspectives On Christmas'

Written by Christopher Lloyd
Directed by David Lee
First UK Transmission: 06.03.98

Skyline: The Space Needle is decorated with Christmas lights.

Synopsis: Martin, Daphne, Niles and Roz are having a massage and telling the masseur how Christmas was for each of them.

Martin's Story:
Daphne returns from a walk with Eddie, unable to explain why he kept wanting to go into the local church. Frasier has noticed this as well, but Martin is dismissive. However, in the kitchen, after Frasier serves him a hot toddy with paprika instead of nutmeg, Martin reveals that he's been roped into the local Christmas pageant, playing a Wise Man, which means he must sing. He can't reach the right notes and asks Frasier to help him, and to keep it from Daphne, as he's nervous enough and knows she'll come to watch him if she finds out. Frasier assures him that he and Niles will happily help out with singing lessons.

Later, this is happening, despite the person upstairs banging on the floor each time Martin tries (and fails) to hit the high note of 'O Holy Night'.

Daphne's Story:

Daphne returns from a walk with Eddie, unable to explain why he kept wanting to go into the local church. Frasier has noticed this as well, but Martin is dismissive. As he goes into the kitchen with Frasier, Daphne confesses to Niles that she is worried – an old patient of hers kept going to church when he knew he was dying. They hear Martin suddenly coughing badly and Frasier says, unconvincingly, it's nothing to worry about. Daphne's fears are further compounded when Frasier leaves, calling back to Martin that he and Niles will do whatever they can for him.

She asks Martin how his recent physical went and he is again dismissive, then seems to look at the decorated Christmas tree, muttering about how quickly everything passes. Now convinced he's dying, a distraught Daphne later finds Martin on the phone to the local priest, asking about the right things to say when he sees Jesus. Almost hysterical, Daphne makes Martin open his Christmas present but eventually learns that all that is happening is that Martin is doing this Christmas pageant. She accuses him of leading her on about his dying, and he finds this funny. As they argue, Niles, unkempt and dazed, staggers in and collapses to the floor.

Niles's Story:

Niles is getting into the elevator at Elliot Bay Towers with three residents and a vast Christmas tree, which he fears will ooze sap on to his new silk suit. The elevator breaks down and the others force Niles into climbing on to the top of the car to open the doors manually. 'I suppose,' he whines, climbing the tree, and feeling the suit crinkle on contact with the sap, 'in times of crisis, someone must step forward and be a hero. Today that man is Niles Crane. Tomorrow it will be my dry cleaner, Mr Lee.' Niles successfully opens the door after falling in oil and the others flee, leaving him atop the elevator as it begins to ascend.

Moments later, the doors to the elevator open and Niles crawls out, disentangling himself from the tree, his suit destroyed. Then he strides purposefully into Frasier's apartment, strong and resolute.

Later he is explaining what happened to Frasier and Daphne when there is a knock on the door and it is Roz, who angrily flings a box of champagne glasses at Frasier and stomps out . . .

Roz's Story:

At Café Nervosa, Roz is nervous about the impending arrival of her mother for Christmas, and also the fact that she and Frasier have to be Mother and Father Christmas in a store that afternoon for charity. Mrs Doyle calls on Frasier's mobile and, while Roz gets a coffee, Frasier suggests that Mrs Doyle not make too many comments about Roz's current size as she's put on a few pregnancy pounds and is a bit touchy about it. Roz returns and explains that her biggest fear is explaining to her mother why she's waited three months to tell her she's pregnant. After Roz leaves, Frasier's phone rings again . . .

At the grotto, Frasier lets slip that he's already told Mrs Doyle about Roz's condition and Roz flips completely.

She later turns up at Frasier's and angrily flings a box of champagne glasses at Frasier and stomps out. Frasier persuades her to return inside and then Martin comes home, furious, from the pageant. As soon as he started singing, Eddie dived into baby Jesus's cradle and ran out of the church with the doll . . .

Guest Cast: Masseur (Albert Macklin), Albert (Conrad James), Albert's Wife (Marilyn O'Connor), Mother in Elevator (Brooks Almy), Woman in Hall (Jennifer Williams), Man in Hall (Mark Capri), Sally (Jamie Alexis), Billy (J. B. Gaynor), Big Kid (Zachary McLemore).

Subtitles: A Room With Four Views.

Eddie Takes The Biscuit: Eddie, understandably, spends much of the show with his head buried under a pillow due to Martin's frankly awful singing. We're with the person upstairs, here.

Frasier Has Left The Building: The whole gang are around the piano, singing, only to be interrupted by the person upstairs.

On The Couch: Just when you thought they couldn't top 5.03, 'Halloween', this comes along. The same story, told from four different, interconnecting points of view, with lovely little subtle changes: Niles thinks he's calm after the elevator incident, but Daphne thinks he collapses; Martin thinks Niles is being his usual self over Daphne and the mistletoe, while Daphne sees him being concerned in case it falls on her and causes an injury; Daphne sees Niles's hugs as caring but we know what they probably really looked like (this capitalising on the viewer's perceptions is an added ingredient all the way through), and so on. Best of all though is the way Daphne turns everyone else's casual conversations into death sentences for Martin. The only time this perception is broken is during Roz's story, when we hear Frasier's conversations with her mother, but who cares?

From the opening scene in the apartment to the dénouement concerning the hiring of the masseur, this is one of the funniest, most beautifully written, directed and acted shows ever. Each scene is a gem, but the best bits for snappy dialogue are in Niles's story, as Albert in the elevator peddles doom and despair and everyone who sees Niles dismisses his bizarre behaviour with a cry of, 'Oh that's Dr Crane's brother . . .'

The pinnacle has to be Frasier talking to Mrs Doyle about the pregnancy and then Roz starting to say what she's fearing most about her mother's visit. You know what's coming next but you can only squirm as you see that Frasier has nailed her coffin down rather tightly, let alone his own . . .

5.10
'Where Every Bloke Knows Your Name'

Written by Rob Hanning
Directed by Jeff Melman
First UK Transmission: 13.03.98

Skyline: Lights go on in various buildings.

Synopsis: Frasier seems to be losing interest in everything he and Niles regularly do together, causing much resentment from his sibling, and panic from Martin, who fears Frasier will join in with the poker game going on in the apartment. However, Frasier not only can't understand Duke's rules, but is totally thrown by talk of cars, garages and hardware stores, let alone Roz's ability to join in, so gives up and goes to an English pub with Daphne.

Although Daphne is confident that Frasier will go home as the date she planned to set him up with has just got engaged, Frasier feels right at home with the English ex-pats, joining in with the singing and beer drinking, and even a billiards tournament.

Daphne is livid that her only escape from the Cranes has been seized upon by Frasier, so Martin suggests she be honest and tell him. Heading down to the Fox and Whistle, she does so and he obliges, realising that as she's been coming there for years it is her haunt. However, the barman, Winston, reveals that Daphne has actually been going only two weeks longer than Frasier. They opt to settle who gets to be a bar regular through a game of darts. Both are excellent players, so Daphne ensures that Frasier's anti-Brit sentiments are overheard by the regulars. When this culminates in a description of the Queen as 'a dowdy old sandbag with a flowerpot on her head', it's the final straw and Frasier wonders if he'll escape with his life . . .

Guest Cast: Claire (Gabrielle Fitzpatrick), Winston (Mark Ryan), Steven (Laurence Lau), Jimmy (Al Fann), Terrance (David Manis), Freddy (Adrian Neil), Young Frasier (Andrew Dorsett), Young Niles (Michael Welch).

Where Everybody Knows Their Name: Among Martin's card-playing buds, we're pleased to welcome back Frank (Ron Dean), Leo (Bill Gratton) and, best of all, Duke himself (John LaMotta). Paul Cusimano's waiter makes his first appearance in nearly two years – welcome back! There are references to Sherry Dempsey (she and Martin are hoping for a quiet night in) and Frasier reminisces about the Cheers bar in Boston.

Subtitles: A Long Time Ago In A Prep School Far, Far Away; So Authentic There Isn't An Ice Cube In The Joint.

Strange Bedfellows: Roz is enjoying being one of the boys in this episode, playing cards, going for crude jokes and opting for Angie Dickinson, 'if I had to choose'.

Full-on Moon: For an episode centring on our Daph, there's surprisingly little revealed about her except that she's been going to the Fox and Whistle for only a month, is friends with Claire and tells Steven she models underwear. We do see that she plays a mean game of darts, however.

Out Of Sight: It is Maris's birthday and her estranged husband has bought her a restored antique saddle, and Frasier wonders if his brother is proposing to wear it. The saddle is, according to Niles, 'bejewelled but not overdone – much like my Maris'. When he says it has been expertly restored and 'you can barely see the stitching', Frasier cannot resist saying, 'Again, like Maris.' However, when she uses the saddle, Maris's cellulite cream reacts badly with the restorative oils in the saddle causing her to stick to it. One hour and a whole bottle of nail-varnish remover later, she's free but her thighs are so chafed she has to sit astride a frozen turkey, which makes her teeth chatter.

The Buddy Show: Another poker game with Martin's buddies takes place at the apartment featuring Martin, Roz, Frank, Duke, Leo and Jimmy (but not the Jimmy from 1.16, 'Can't Tell A Crook By His Cover'). Roz isn't offended by the dirty jokes, even the one about Leo and Martin in a strip joint. We learn during the discussion about Roz's pregnancy that Frank is married to Annie and remembers, 'There is nothing more beautiful than a pregnant broad.'

Frasier Has Left The Building: Frasier and Martin's police buddies gather round the piano for a rousing chorus of 'Roll Out the Barrel', while Martin nicks their winnings.

On The Couch: A peculiar episode this, far reminiscent of a Season One show than a Season Five one. The jokes are good (especially the waspish banter between Frasier and Daphne) but it all seems a bit uncentred, a bit off key. While Frasier's yelling of 'I score again' during the darts match is greeted with 'That's something we don't hear out of your mouth very often' from Daphne, it all seems a little forced. It's nice to see Frasier knocking back beer rather than sherry with gay abandon (so, his *Cheers* days weren't quite as out of character as we thought), and the flashbacks to Frasier and Niles at prep school are inspired (great child actors and very clever setting up of the future – maybe we should see more of this), but it all adds to the disjointed feel of the story. Is it about Daphne and her free time? Is it about Frasier and Niles drifting apart? Is it about Frasier enjoying speaking in English idioms (or, rather, clichés)? Or is it about a bar packed with (presumably) a bunch of American actors again believing that the English sound like Dick Van Dyke (yes, even Scousers) with only poor Mark Ryan as Winston waving a genuinely British flag?

5.11

'Ain't Nobody's Business If I Do'

Written by Jay Kogen
Directed by David Lee
First UK Transmission: 20.03.98

Skyline: A shooting star passes overhead.

Synopsis: Daphne meets up with Niles and Frasier at Café Nervosa – she's found an engagement ring in Martin's room and Niles speculates that Martin is going to propose to Sherry. 'You know what this means,' he gasps. 'Yes,' says Frasier, 'we're going to hear what Mendelssohn's "Wedding March" sounds like on the banjo.' They realise that they still know very little about the woman they could soon be calling

Mother. Or Mamma. Or Ma. But Frasier says so long as Sherry makes Martin happy, then it's none of their business and is horrified at Niles's suggestion that they should do some dirt-digging.

Sherry is organising a party for Martin to meet some of her friends, and tells him that someone has been making rather indiscreet enquiries about her both with her neighbours and her boss at McGinty's. Martin immediately suspects Frasier and Niles have hired someone but they vehemently deny it. When a mollified Martin is out of earshot, Frasier berates Niles for trying to prevent Martin's happiness.

At Café Nervosa, while Roz gets a jaywalking ticket (it doesn't help her case when she erroneously congratulates the rather plumpish cop on her pregnancy), Niles is paying off the detective he hired. The detective passes them the information he has gathered – Sherry has a string of failed marriages behind her, but does Martin know? Niles feels it's their duty to tell Martin, but back at the apartment, Daphne blurts it out to their father. He's livid that they've investigated Sherry and don't trust him to have good judgment – and, yes, Sherry told him all about her past the very week they met. He goes off to meet her at McGinty's and then Daphne finds he's left the engagement ring behind. Hoping he can get there before Martin proposes and finds he hasn't actually got the ring, Frasier dashes off after his father . . .

Guest Cast: Policewoman (Linda Kerns), Detective (Tucker Smallwood).

Where Everybody Knows Their Name: Sherry Dempsey (Marsha Mason) is on fine form. She has a couple of friends from Atlantic City, Ray and Lola Sherwood, who used to do a knife-throwing act. She asks Martin not to look at Lola's eye because she gets self-conscious. Another friend is Edie, who's just met her fiancé because they've had a pen-pal relationship due to his being 'detained these last few years'. Sherry has been married six times before: Johnny Dempsey, Ned Foley, Mark Wallis, Vincent Mayhew, Milton Mandel and a man called Walt. She also got engaged to a Danny

Mitchell but called it off. While trying to work out ways of asking Martin if he's aware of all of these failures, Frasier sardonically suggests asking their father if he's planning a visit to 'the Sherry Ex-Husband Convention'.

While discussing marriage, Martin reveals that he believes Hester Crane is 'a hard act to follow'. Lilith and Nanette are both alluded to when Frasier discusses multiple marriages with Niles.

Subtitles: Mamma Mia!; Give Me A Ring Sometime.

Culture Vultures: When Daphne explains that she 'found a ring in your father's underwear drawer' Frasier is immediately appalled that his beloved furniture could be stained thus. Even Niles thinks Frasier is being stupid about this one. Frasier is also decidedly derogatory in tone about Sherry upon discovering she graduated 'from high school' and has almost paid off her Subaru.

Frasier Has Left The Building: Eddie is barking pointlessly at a fish sculpture which Sherry previously used as a pincushion into which she inserted food on cocktail sticks.

On The Couch: 'Who'd have guessed that something so innocent as spying on a man's girlfriend and rifling through his underwear drawer could turn so ugly?' A brilliant episode, with more good jokes per minute than most. Best of these is the buck-passing scene when Daphne blames the boys for digging into Sherry's past and Frasier blames her for digging in Martin's underwear! There are a couple of other terrific moments, such as Daphne's sarcasm when Frasier asks for her opinion after constantly telling her to shut up, and the story of Cousin Donald, who was married for two years before discovering his wife was previously a man.

But the highlight must be the final scene of bonding between Martin and Frasier at McGinty's over a beer and a Sonics game. Frasier finally, after five years, has learnt when to analyse and when to just shut up. Beautifully written stuff.

Of course, the episode has one major letdown – the departure of Sherry. After bringing such a breath of fresh air into the cast, who after five years are unsurprisingly looking a bit jaded in some shows, she also provided a marvellous comedy foil for the snobbery of the Crane boys that was far from exploited. Marsha Mason's performances were always endearing and it's a tragedy to see such potential wasted. We can only hope it was Ms Mason's decision to leave and not a short-sighted one on the part of the producers. That said, the leaving scene is marvellous and maybe one day she'll crop up again, even if it's just to say hello, or play something dreadfully on her banjo.

5.12
'The Zoo Story'

Written by Joe Keenan
Directed by Pamela Fryman
First UK Transmission: 27.03.98

Skyline: A helicopter rises up from the skyline and departs.

Synopsis: The new owner of KACL is putting everybody's contract under review and Bebe is in Café Nervosa, ready to sort things out for her clients. Frasier still won't have anything to do with her (see 4.17, 'Roz's Turn') and is horrified to find out Bebe is actually representing Roz and her unborn baby. Bebe intends to put Roz on Dr Clint Webber's medical show in a slot called 'Pregnant Pause' but this still doesn't impress Frasier. He is determined to find a new agent who is both good and honest, as opposed to someone 'whose ethics would have raised eyebrows in the court of Caligula'. Bebe is convinced that no one can be both good and an agent and reminds him that if he should fail in his quest, he always has her number. 'Still 666?' he asks her.

At the apartment Niles explains that Maris wants a new therapist because the current one counselling them is intolerant over her doing catalogue shopping during their sessions. Frasier tells him that he must say no to Maris, stick to his principles and never back down. Niles agrees that this is a good idea. To prove it, Frasier says he will not go back to Bebe under any circumstances and introduces everyone to Ben, his new agent, who doubles as a pigeon-loving, meals-on-wheels-delivering, toy-building, scout-mastering, churchgoing Samaritan from Salt Lake City.

Ben has a plan to increase Frasier's visibility – the Mercer Island Zoo has just bought a rare crane and he has suggested they name it Frasier, and then the real Frasier can introduce it to the press. They go along to the zoo for this, but discover Bebe has had the same idea, using Roz to pose with a pregnant chimp called Boobo. To top it all, the crane escapes and attacks Martin in front of the television cameras.

Frasier is a laughing stock as a result of this and, while they wait for Ben to come up with a new angle to deflect this failure, Niles explains that Maris is withdrawing sex unless Niles agrees to drop their counsellor. Frasier persists with telling his brother not to let his principles go. Ben then arrives with a toy couch and says he's arranged a photocall so that Frasier can give counselling to the crane.

The next day, Frasier arrives at Café Nervosa to talk to a decidedly sexually frustrated Niles. Frasier has himself been attacked by the bird now and Bebe seizes her chance to try one last attempt to woo him back. After Gil's salary is cut and Roz is given her own slot, the temptation is strong, but Frasier is resolute. Ben is the agent for him . . .

Guest Cast: Ben (Robert Stanton), Toffee Macintosh (Heather Lee), Mr Twembly (Palmer Scott).

Where Everybody Knows Their Name: A riotous return for Bebe Glazer (Harriet Sansom Harris) at her devilish best, stealing every scene in which she appears. There is an all-too-brief appearance by a distraught Gil Chesterton (Edward Hibbert), who chooses to have a drink with Aunt Penny, the Story Lady, rather than sit with Roz and Bebe. And there is an expanded role for the new waitress (Amy Landers), who at least now gets the coffee orders right.

Subtitles: Bye Bye Birdie; Maybe It Was A Disgruntled Former Zoo Worker.

Full-on Moon: A bizarre piece of Daphne dizziness as she can't tell the difference between cranes, pelicans and loons (although a Brit would actually call it a diver). Martin, on the other hand, knows a loon when he sees one!

Out Of Sight: Maris, we discover, rarely wears earrings because they make her head droop. And one hour of passion can satisfy Maris for a month because she stores it all up like a sexual camel, apparently. There's a mental image to conjure with!

The Buddy Show: After a mix-up at the video store, Niles took home the Charles Bronson movie, while Martin and Duke had to sit through Malle's *My Dinner With André*.

Frasier Has Left The Building: Frasier returns home to find Daphne analysing Eddie on Ben's tiny couch. He is not amused.

On The Couch: 'Your face is riddled with bird bites, your name's a punchline and your career is five minutes from over and he's only been your agent for three days!'

Any episode featuring Bebe Glazer is good, but rarely is she this good. Capitalising on the brilliant repartee set up last season when Frasier reckoned that, rather than her being a devil-worshipper, he worships her, we get some great lines in this. In ranting about how hard she's worked to get Frasier where he is today, Bebe claims, 'I have been to hell and back so often I've frequent-flyer miles,' while Frasier, on seeing her in the café for the first time, just mutters, 'Ah, Rosemary's Bebe.'

Although there are many excellent moments in this, the actual story about the crane, and indeed Ben himself, is a bit weak. There is no way, even in the bizarre world of Frasier, that Ben could be a successful agent, and the bird plot goes on a bit too long.

That aside, the idea of Frasier keeping to his principles and thus causing Niles terrible frustration because he won't give up until Frasier does is excellent. Niles's constant attempts to chat up other women is a delight, although his best piece is the simple but evil grin and chuckle he greets Frasier with after the incident at the zoo.

Bebe also revels in that, but in a more erudite way – she sends Frasier a bunch of Birds of Paradise. 'Her idea of floral irony,' laughs Niles.

A good, well-written character tale, this one, but how much more exciting it might have been had Ben been a really good agent and had some sort of showdown with Bebe.

5.13

'The Maris Counsellor'

Written by David Lloyd
Directed by Jeff Melman
First UK Transmission: 03.04.98

Skyline: Lights go on in various buildings.

Synopsis: It is sweeps week at KACL, and Roz is fixing the callers to ensure that only the juiciest, most outrageous ones get on the air. Martin meanwhile is trying to get a dinner invite from fellow Elliot Bay Towers resident Mrs Crowley – although Daphne thinks he's playing too hard to get. Frasier points out that the Crane men don't really have a good record where women are concerned – and then Mrs Crowley phones and invites Martin over.

At this point, Niles arrives – he and Frasier are co-hosting Niles's couples group therapy. He tells his brother about a doctor, Bernard Shenkman, whom he believes has got his and Maris's marriage off the rocks and well on the way to a reconciliation. Niles heads back to Maris's mansion to surprise her in bed. Trouble is, the surprise is on him –

he finds himself sharing the bed with Dr Shenkman, who explains that he and Maris have been having an affair for the last two weeks.

Distraught after confronting Maris and having the affair confirmed, Niles returns to the couples therapy group but cannot cope very well.

Later that evening, the Crane men ruminate on their lives. Niles's marriage is finished and Maris has filed for a divorce, Frasier is loveless and Martin's date turned out to be with Mrs Cowley's bizarre mother . . .

Guest Cast: Doctor Bernard Shenkman (Bob Dishy), Janice (Amy Van Nostrand).

Where Everybody Knows Their Name: In the various discussions at the end, there are passing references to Frasier's failed relationships – implying Lilith, Nannette and Diane. Martin also mentions his own lack of success with Sherry Dempsey.

Who's On The Line?: Mary (Bess Myerson), who is indecisive, comes on first. Then it's a battle between Roger (John Waters), who starts off as merely disgruntled with his career and ends up a transsexual congressman, and Bill (Rob Reiner), who used to wet the bed and now, apparently, does it when sleeping with his best friend's wife. Roger, by the way, appears to win.

Subtitles: In Case You're Wondering, It's A Brown Ermine; The Going Rate For Closure Is $1411.80.

Out Of Sight: It looks like we're getting ready to call 'time' on Maris now after fifteen years of marriage, so references to her seem likely to decrease. But Dr Shenkman appears to be pushing the right buttons, as Niles explains: 'It's as if he's discovered the magic elixir to repair the shattered fragments of her psyche. I don't know exactly what it is.' 'The words "Crazy Glue" leap to mind,' observes Frasier. Later, Niles reminds us that Maris meditates in her Zen garden (see 1.24, 'My Coffee With Niles') which always makes her 'randy as a stoat'. And it seems clear that Dr Shenkman has uncovered previously unseen sides of Mrs Crane – 'I've never known a woman so warm, so nurturing, so unselfish . . .' We, too, share Niles's incredulity at this – could it truly be a case of mistaken identity?

Frasier Has Left The Building: Martin answers the door to Mrs Crowley's dotty mother who gives him a cake dish which, when he takes the lid off, is empty.

On The Couch: Undoubtedly one of the most manic and probably the most downbeat episode of Frasier ever, this is a magnificent parade of everything that makes the show good. Topped off by a startling performance from the often under-used David Hyde Pierce, showing Niles going through elation, horror, devastation, hope and finally wry acceptance, the episode is unmissable. The humour is always top notch – the sequences in Maris's bed chamber as Niles and Bernard get ready for their unforgettable tryst and Roz's hysterical attempts to ensure decent callers to Frasier's show demonstrate that the writing is as sharp as always.

To top the whole thing off, the final scenes in the apartment, particularly on the balcony, are sublime.

5.14
'The Ski Lodge'

Written by Joe Keenan
Directed by David Lee
First UK Transmission: 10.04.98

Skyline: A streak of lightning crosses the sky.

Synopsis: Roz has won a skiing weekend, complete with a French Olympic ski champion as instructor, but Frasier bribes her with big-screen television to give it to him (well, in her condition . . .). He takes Niles, Martin, Daphne and Daphne's model friend Annie, who is celebrating her birthday. At the Lodge they meet Guy, their instructor/chef/handyman, and Daphne takes an immediate fancy to him. However, there are a few problems. Firstly, Niles wants Daphne. And she of course wants Guy. Annie meanwhile wants Niles. Frasier wants Annie, Guy wants Niles and thinks Daphne wants Annie, Martin wants a television set in his room and no one, but no one, seems to want poor Frasier.

But who, if anyone, will get the object of their desire when no one can actually be honest enough to say what they want?

Guest Cast: Guy (James Patrick Stuart), Annie (Cynthia LaMontagne).

Where Everybody Knows Their Name: We meet Connie (Lisa Robinson), KACL's resident raffles/bring-and-buy sales/charity obsessive who receives an earbashing from Roz immediately prior to giving her the prize from the church raffle. Roz has the decency not to be a hypocrite and care too much mere seconds after Connie's departure. Martin talks about how he proposed to Hester over a mug or two of his favourite, and very strong, rum tot.

Subtitles: Could Guy's Name Be Feydeau?

Frasier Has Left The Building: Annie goes to Frasier's bedroom after all but, when he doesn't answer, she leaves again. Then Frasier emerges from the kitchen.

On The Couch: The subtitle says it all – this is pure bedroom farce à la Georges Feydeau and as such is absolutely marvellous. Although you already know it's going to be complicated from the moment you realise Annie wants Niles not Frasier, when you suddenly understand what Guy wants, well, it's pure fun all the way. A tremendously witty show that, unusually, takes the cast out of the trappings of the usual sets and still manages to work well. There are passing similarities to the previous cabin farce (see 4.13, 'Four For The Seesaw') but that episode never achieved the success of this one. As we watch each person misinterpret everyone else's intentions, all muddled up further by Martin's hearing problem (a convenient plot device, yes, but rarely has one been used so well), you grip the seat wondering just how anyone is going to escape this one without egg on their face.

If there are any faults with this, they lie firstly with the ever-reduced role Roz gets to play and, more annoyingly for British viewers, with the apparent insistence on once again casting an actress to play one of Daphne's friends who cannot do a convincing English accent. This one sounds like Janet Street Porter on acid and thus has about as much chance of winning our sympathy as someone running their fingernails down a blackboard.

5.15
'Room Service'

Written by Ken Levine and David Isaacs
Directed by David Lee
First UK Transmission: 17.04.98

Skyline: The light atop the Space Needle glows.

Synopsis: Talk of leaking water during Frasier's show sends Roz scurrying to the loo, where she bumps into Lilith, who claims she has come for a convention. In fact she has come to see Frasier for moral support – she explains to him and Roz that her marriage to Brian (see 2.10, 'Adventures In Paradise II') is over as Brian has sought out someone 'a bit more feminine' and has found him – a contractor called Stan who was hired to rebuild the master bedroom.

Frasier meets up with Niles at Café Nervosa to tell him not only of Lilith's arrival, but also that he has invited her to accompany them to the Union Club that evening. Niles is having problems, however – every time anyone brings up the matter of his divorce settlement with Maris, he gets a bout of narcolepsy. If that were not problem enough, Frasier has to confess that he is finding Lilith very vulnerable and therefore exceptionally sexually attractive. He asks Niles to ensure that he does not get carried away. When Lilith arrives that evening in a low-cut dress, looking ravishing, Niles has a battle on his hands to stop his brother succumbing.

However, it appears to have worked when, the following morning, Lilith awakens in her hotel room after a night of lovemaking with a man who isn't Frasier. Trouble is, it's Niles.

When the waiter rouses them by bringing in the breakfast they ordered, they are worried in case Frasier finds out. When Frasier then turns up desperate for sex with Lilith, Niles is quickly banished into the bathroom. Trouble is, he keeps falling asleep . . .

Guest Cast: Waiter (John Ducey).

Where Everybody Knows Their Name: A riotous return for Lilith Sternin (Bebe Neuwirth) plus mentions for husband Brian and her and Frasier's son, Frederick.

Who's On The Line?: Betsy (Halle Berry) who is going on a cruise but dreams about floods.

Subtitles: The Ice Woman Cometh; Strange Interlude; Long Night's Journey Into Day.

Culture Vultures: Apart from the Crane brothers displaying horror at the idea of breakfast in the bathroom, they also adore Eggs Benedict. Indeed, Niles points out that it's what he always has after a night of passion. 'That's very rich,' admonishes Lilith, but Niles points out that he only has it 'once a year'.

Full-on Moon: Gasp with astonishment as we discover that Daphne does not receive a psychic headache to warn her (or Martin) of the impending arrival of Lilith on their doorstep.

Out Of Sight: When Niles falls asleep against the ice box in Frasier's refrigerator, he has a dream about dancing a tango with Maris.

Eddie Takes The Biscuit: Martin has taught Eddie to roll over although, having just seen a programme about a stunt dog that rescues babies from blazing buildings, Daphne is suitably unimpressed. He also makes a very fast exit when Lilith approaches him with a surprisingly unmenacing 'Hello, Eddie'.

Frasier Has Left The Building: Lilith is happily eating her breakfast, with copious amounts of tomato ketchup, in the seclusion of the bathroom.

On The Couch: Not the strongest Lilith episode by any means but, nevertheless, she still illuminates it. A glorious conclusion to Frasier's on-going fascination with his ex-wife, the episode's only down point is that amidst all the yelling and shouting in the last few moments – when Frasier finds out that his ex is sleeping with his brother – their perfectly well-reasoned arguments get a little lost, particularly annoying as they seem to all be very valid. Although the narcolepsy routine becomes a bit tiring (excuse the pun) very quickly, the episode has some great moments. Firstly, Frasier's reaction on seeing Lilith at KACL is almost identical to his response the time Diane Chambers returned (see 3.14, 'The Show Where Diane Comes Back'): similar scream, different studio window. Martin and Daphne's reaction to Lilith's imminent return is amusing, as is Eddie's, not to mention Niles's affirmation that he owes Martin five dollars on hearing that Brian has left Lilith for another man.

However, the classiest segments of the episode are those involving the hotel waiter (great performance by John Ducey) and the final few moments. 'Are we okay?' Niles asks his brother. 'No. But we will be,' Frasier reassures him gruffly. And we know that to be true because they are the Crane brothers, after all.

5.16

'Beware of Greeks'

Written by David Lloyd
Directed by Jeff Melman
First UK Transmission: 24.04.98

Skyline: The elevator goes up the Space Needle.

Synopsis: Frasier's show ends and he is greeted by his cousin, Nikos, who is getting married but is disappointed that Frasier isn't coming to the wedding. Frasier protests that he knew nothing about it – obviously this is another example of Nikos's mother, Zora, continuing a family feud between them. Years before, Frasier advised Nikos to follow his heart not his mother's and so Nikos became a street juggler rather than a doctor. As a result, Zora and her husband, Martin's brother, have not spoken to Martin's side of the family.

At the apartment, Martin is still angry with Frasier over the whole thing. 'Can you imagine,' he moans, 'what it is like to live in the same city as your brother and not see him for five years?' Frasier, with a glance at Niles who has been similarly berating him, icily shakes his head. 'No, but I'd like to give it a try.'

Deciding that enough is enough, Frasier goes to Constantine's, Zora's restaurant, and faces his aunt. Finally, after Frasier promising to plug the place on his show every day for a month, Zora welcomes him back into the family and invites them all to the pre-wedding dinner. There, while Daphne and Martin are recorded on cousin Ed's camcorder discussing Walt's stupidity and Zora's loose morals, and Niles flees from the amorous advances of his nymphomaniac cousin Yvonne, Frasier realises that the woman Nikos is marrying is nothing more than a spoilt rich-kid out to upset her parents. Nikos's real love is a fellow street entertainer called Crystal. But he has promised Zora that he won't interfere with Nikos's life any more and so wonders if he can get through the evening without trying to bring Nikos and Crystal back together . . .

Guest Cast: Zora (Patti LuPone), Nikos (Joseph Will), Walt (John Mahon), Yvonne (Lori Harmon), Ed (James Gleason), Mary Ann (Valerie Dillman), Crystal (Heide Karp).

Subtitles: Welcome To Hell's Kitchen; Lord Of The Dance.

Culture Vultures: As Niles is led away by Yvonne to go drink some bubbly, Zora proudly announces that there is, 'None of that sissy French wine. It's real Greek Champagne.' Smiling at the departing Niles, Frasier ironically begs him to 'save some for me'.

Strange Bedfellows: Roz is immediately attracted to Nikos, of course – until she learns he's a street entertainer rather than a well-paid doctor.

Full-on Moon: Amidst the Crane family arguing about how Frasier has caused the rift between them and the Greek side of the family, Daphne just notes that she, at least, likes zither music. The fact that the zither is more commonly associated with Bavaria than Greece seems to have by-passed both her and the Cranes . . .

The Buddy Show: Poor Martin is delighted to finally catch up with his brother Walt after five years of separation due to Frasier and Zora's dispute (this probably explains why he once mentioned not actually having a brother, see 1.22, 'Author, Author'). However, when they do meet, they have nothing to say to each other and end the episode saying goodbye once again, thanks to Frasier and Zora!

Frasier Has Left The Building: Ed's camera is on Niles and Yvonne – and then topples over just as Niles makes his escape, pursued by his devoted cousin.

On The Couch: Patti LuPone steals the show with a bizarrely overblown performance as the most horribly stereotypical dominating Greek mother, the frightening Zora. Indeed, this is another occasion when the writer has become a bit lazy and opts to deliver a series of staple sitcom caricatures (similar to Del Gato in 5.06, 'Voyage of the Damned') which *Frasier* usually strives to rise above. Nevertheless, although by no means the best of the season, the episode does give us a new branch of the Crane family tree and some great lines. When Zora is discussing the Sous Chef in her restaurant, she tells Frasier that the last time he was drunk on duty, 'He got his head caught in the duck press.' Frasier winces and wonders how he got there of all places. Zora shrugs. 'With my help.' Somehow, you just knew she was going to say that . . .

5.17

'The Perfect Guy'

Written by Rob Greenberg
Directed by Jeff Melman
First UK Transmission: 01.05.98

Skyline: Nothing happens.

Synopsis: The on-air staff at KACL are preparing for a new round of publicity photos because they've just welcomed aboard a new broadcaster, Dr Clint Webber, who, in most people's eyes, is drop-dead gorgeous. Frasier, however, begins to take a dislike to him as he realises that there doesn't seem to be anything Clint isn't the best at. He begins to try to outfox his new co-worker but is thwarted at every turn.

Niles, meanwhile, has taken Martin to Frenchies, a specialist French shop from which he buys his cheeses. Martin buys Eddie a very expensive can of dog food but offends the store owner, Robert, who bans him from the shop. When Eddie refuses to eat anything else, Martin has to eat humble pie and returns to the store with Daphne to apologise. Just as everything is amicably sorted, Daphne picks an argument with Robert and, once again, Martin finds himself banned and Eddie going food-less . . .

Frasier has decided to hold a party in Clint's honour at his apartment but, when Clint begins to woo even the delightful

Sharon away from him, he resolves to find just one flaw in the doctor and exploit it. Before long, an opportunity presents itself, and Frasier cannot help but encourage Clint to make a fool of himself . . .

Guest Cast: Robert (Francois Giroday), Clerk (Doug Budin).

Where Everybody Knows Their Name: We learn that Dr Clint Webber (Bill Campbell) has been brought in to replace Bert the Backyard Gardner. We also meet Sharon (Lindsay Price), a KACL employee attracted to Frasier, and it's a long overdue return for Bulldog, who is initially infuriated by the fact that Clint is undoubtedly going to steal all his 'chicks'. But stealing the show is Gil Chesterton (Edward Hibbert) who finally confounds everyone by 'inning' himself. As Frasier, Roz and Bulldog discuss Clint's movie-star looks, Gil says he hasn't noticed. Surprised by this, the others ask how that can be and Gil is horrified to realise they all think he's gay (although he had no problem with them thinking this when everyone at KACL heard about Frasier's erotic dream involving him – see 4.03, 'The Impossible Dream'). He reminds them that his wife is called Deb (they all thought Deb was his pet cat) and he proudly explains that, 'Mrs Gilbert Leslie Chesterton is a Sarah Lawrence graduate and owner of a very successful auto body repair shop.'

Who's On The Line?: Marie (Jill Clayburgh), who is unable to drag herself out of bed and feels very irritable. Frasier deduces she has problems that lead her to seek the security of her bed. Dr Webber suggests she may be hypoglycaemic.

Subtitles: Out And In; Bone Appétit.

Culture Vultures: As Frasier starts up his rivalry with Clint, they discuss universities. Frasier, as we know, graduated from Harvard, while Clint graduated from Oxford before studying in France, learning history and French cuisine. Clint plays squash expertly, his godfather is Jose Carreras, he speaks fluent Mandarin and knows the lyrics to Rogers and Hart songs. Oh, and he's a pretty good doctor, too.

Strange Bedfellows: Roz just adores Clint (which is just as well as Bebe arranged for her to fake giving birth on his show – see 5.12, 'The Zoo Story') and spends most of her time in his company treating him to her trademark throaty laugh.

Full-on Moon: Daphne is similarly smitten with Clint, and wonders if he's single.

Out Of Sight: When Martin can't make Eddie eat, Niles suggests his father sleep-feeds the dog via an eye-dropper and a protein shake. Well, it worked for Maris . . .

Frasier Has Left The Building: Martin is outside Frenchies, paying someone else to go in and buy Eddie's exotic dog food.

On The Couch: So we finally meet KACL's new boy, and what a marvellous piece of manhood he is. Good looks, charisma, intelligence and culture. Everything Frasier would normally appreciate – but here he is bitten by the little green-eyed monster and desperately wants Clint to fail. His final smile at the party as the episode ends is a joy, and yet it's a rather odd ending. The actual episode is compiled of a series of amusing one-upmanship moments (interspersed with the witty but unconnected feud between Martin, Daphne, Niles and Robert, the owner of Frenchies) but goes absolutely nowhere. We are left with a lot of questions – is everyone really going to go off Clint because Frasier has exposed his flaw? Is Sharon going to choose him over Frasier? Is Roz going to try to bed him? The episode lacks any real point and, clever as the dialogue is (and would we expect less of Rob Greenberg?), the sum total is not as good as its parts.

But without a doubt, the scene in which Gil confesses his heterosexuality is the cleverest and most smile-inducing moment for this character in ages. And whilst we don't for one moment actually believe the evidence given here over previous shows, it does give him a moment to shine as he quite thought-provokingly protests, 'Honestly, the conclusions people make just because a man dresses well and knows how to use a pastry dish . . .'

Appendix I

ACTORS

Tony Abatemarco	Jimmy (1.16)
Brooke Adams	Marilyn (3.05)
Lynne Adams	Nurse (2.08)
Josh Adell	Curtis (2.24)
Cleto Agusto	Delivery Man (1.01)
Lisa Akey	Christine (4.14)
Marv Albert	Jerry (4.02)
Wayne Alexander	Peter Soutendeck (4.14)
Jamie Alexis	Sally (5.09)
Hope Allen	Maxine (4.18)
Joan Allen	Lydia (3.17)
Brooks Almy	Mother in Elevator (5.09)
Don Amendolia	Guard (1.21)
Joel Anderson	Father (2.02)
Steve Arden	Daniel Gill (5.07)
Vaughn Armstrong	Tony (3.10)
Tom Astor	Waiter (4.24)
Scott Atkinson	Clive (4.01)
Todd Babcock	Rick (5.04)
Kevin Bacon	Vic (2.10)
Diedrich Bader	Brad (2.23)
Becky Ann Baker	Marge (3.09)
Lisa Banes	Pamela (4.07)
Ashley Bank	Renata (1.15)
Billy Barty	Chris (3.17)
Charlee Baugh	Schoolgirl (5.05)
Laque Beamer	Husband (4.24)
Diane Behrens	Patron # 1 (3.11)
Jay Bell	Maurice (2.23)
Mark Benninghofen	Clerk (3.17)
David Benoit	Doug (4.19)
Halle Berry	Betsy (5.15)
Jack Betts	Ian (4.18)

318

Troy Blendell	Curtis (3.17)
Mark Blum	John (5.05)
Eugenie Bonderant	Diane (1.06)
Klee Bragger	Ned (3.09)
John Brandon	Harry the Cop (1.04)
Danny Breen	Clark (3.14)
Eve Brent	Hostess (1.03)
David Breitbarth	Chuck (3.23)
Matthew Broderick	Mark (3.01)
Mel Brooks	Tom (1.12)
Dr Joyce Brothers	Herself (1.09)
Benjamin Brown	Stage Manager (3.16)
Blair Brown	Jill (3.02)
Christopher M. Brown	Lenny (4.05)
Rosey Brown	Prisoner (4.10)
Susan Brown	Amber Edwards (2.01)
Wren T. Brown	Keith Bishop (1.18)
Phil Buckman	Leo (1.19)
Doug Budin	Clerk (5.17)
Donna Bullock	Adair Peck (4.19, 4.20)
Brandi Burkett	Wella (4.14)
Rebecca Bush	Kimberly Egan (4.19)
Dan Butler	Bob 'Bulldog' Briscoe (1.02, 1.09, 1.10, 1.12, 1.15, 1.20, 2.01, 2.06, 2.07, 2.09, 2.12, 2.13, 2.19, 2.22, 2.23, 3.01, 3.02, 3.04, 3.06, 3.07, 3.09, 3.21, 3.22, 3.23, 4.02, 4.03, 4.05, 4.16, 4.17, 4.18, 4.21, 4.22, 5.01, 5.03, 5.04, 5.05, 5.17)
Geoff Callan	Hank (4.05)
Bill Campbell	Clint Webber (5.17)
Jen Campbell	Sharon (4.02)
Mark Capri	Man in Hall (5.09)
Doug Carfrae	'Professor Pete' (4.17)
Beecey Carlton	Maid (5.06)
Tony Carreiro	Joe Decarlo (3.05, 3.12)
Myra Carter	Mrs Warner (2.01)
Shawna Casey	Stage Manager (1.15)
Cyd Charisse	Polly (3.07)
Tom W. Chick	Waiter (5.05, 5.08)
Tim Choate	Dirk Binderkott (3.12)
June Claman	Aunt Bobbie (1.11)
Jill Clayburgh	Marie (5.17)

Rosemary Clooney	Gladys (1.12)
Robert Colbert	Tony (1.13)
Lisa Coles	Joanna (4.24, 5.01)
Betty Comden	Linda (2.08)
Judith Corber-Wexler	Darla (3.14)
Maddie Corman	Gail (1.11)
Bob Costas	Jake (4.02)
John Coughlin	Jeffrey Corbett (4.19)
Brian Cousins	Gunnar (2.21)
Rick Cramer	Ranger (2.20)
Tony Crane	Mike (2.22)
Cindy Crawford	Dorothy (5.03)
Pat Crowley	Marion Lawlor (1.08)
Billy Crystal	Jack (3.04)
Keiran Culkin	Jimmy (4.03)
Macaulay Culkin	Elliott (2.11)
Valerie Curtin	Mrs Warren (1.19)
John Cusack	Greg (4.08)
Paul Cusimano	Waiter (2.14, 3.17, 5.10)
John Cygan	Doug Harvey (3.17)
Catherine Danielle	Bonnie Weems (1.12)
Jeff Daniels	Doug (1.05)
Ted Danson	Sam Malone (2.16)
Lisa Darr	Laura Paris (4.13)
Nathan Davis	Otto (2.23)
Jo De Winter	Mrs Greenway (2.02)
Ron Dean	Frank (1.16, 2.13, 5.10)
Sandra Dee	Connie (2.06)
Maria del Mar	Leslie Wellman (4.19, 4.20)
George Deloy	Father Mike Mancuso (1.10, 2.06, 3.01)
Lisa Dergan	Cheerleader (4.05)
Laura Dern	June (3.06)
Kirsten Devere	Mother (2.09)
Valerie Dillman	Mary Ann (5.16)
Bob Dishy	Dr Shenkman (5.13)
Amanda Donohoe	Catherine (1.07)
Andrew Dorsett	Young Frasier (5.10)
John Drayman	Walnut (1.09)
John Ducey	Waiter (5.15)
David Duchovny	Tom (3.22)
Patty Duke	Alice (4.12)
Marion Duggan	Patient (1.11)

Stephanie Dunnam	Mrs Newman (1.11)
Dominic Dunne	Jeff (1.12)
Griffin Dunne	Russell (1.01)
	Bob (3.11)
Murphy Dunne	Pete (3.16)
Christopher Durang	Rudy (4.03)
Shelley Duvall	Caroline (2.24)
Richard Easton	Mel White (4.18)
Kris Edlund	Amanda (4.24)
Mitchell Edmonds	Mr Spencer (2.18)
Michael David Edwards	Almond (1.09)
Trevor Einhorn	Frederick Crane (4.07, 4.16)
Maxine Elliott	Mrs Grey (1.18)
Pierre Epstein	Etienne (2.09)
Dean Erickson	Eric the Waiter (1.04, 1.16, 1.17)
'Dr J' Erving	Mark (4.02)
Christine Estabrook	Lou (1.12)
Al Fann	Jimmy (5.10)
Stephanie Faracy	Mimi Cosgrove (5.06)
Kevin Farrell	Rodney Banks (4.06)
Mrs Fields	Beth (3.19)
John J. Finn	Tim (1.12)
Carrie Fisher	Phyllis (3.01)
Aileen Fitzpatrick	Committee Member (1.18)
Gabrielle Fitzpatrick	Claire (5.10)
Jodie Foster	Marlene (3.13)
Jonathan Fraser	Man at Party (5.03)
Patricia Fraser	Marjorie (1.13)
Lindsay Frost	Samantha (5.07, 5.08)
Boyd Gaines	Phil Patterson (2.07)
Allen Galli	Male Fan (5.06)
Edward F. Gallick	Ed (2.12)
Art Garfunkel	Chester (2.09)
Teri Garr	Nancy (3.01)
J. B. Gaynor	Billy (5.09)
Helen Geller	Sister Joselia (2.06)
Marita Geraghty	Amanda (3.23)
Gerry Gibson	Tom (4.22)
Julie Gill	Waitress (1.08)
Francois Giroday	Robert (5.17)
James Gleason	Ed (5.16)
John Glover	Ned Miller (1.10)

Pamela Gordon	Marvella (1.21)
Maddie Gorman	Gail (1.11)
Eydie Gormé	Lois (1.23)
Justin Gorrence	Gary (3.16)
Jim Graci	Game Announcer (4.05)
Camille Donatacci Grammer	Eve (5.03)
Bill Gratton	Leo (2.05, 2.13, 5.10)
Adolph Green	Walter (2.08)
James Greene	Salesman (1.19)
Joshua Greene	Ethan (4.24)
Googy Gress	Ned (3.14)
Eddie Van Halen	Hank (1.07)
Demane E. Hall	Conductor (5.09)
Richard Gilbert Hall	Elliot (4.07)
Linda Hamilton	Claire (1.01)
	Laura (4.24)
Richard Hamilton	Big Willy (3.21)
Luck Hari	Waitress (1.22, 1.24, 2.07, 3.09, 3.11, 3.13, 3.18, 3.20, 4.10, 4.22, 4.23)
Lori Harmon	Yvonne (5.16)
Ed Harris	Rob (3.04)
Michael G. Hawkins	Conductor (3.13)
Patricia Hearst	Janice (1.23)
Glenne Headley	Gretchen (2.21)
Andrew Heckler	Dr Morris Claman (4.13)
Elaine Hensley	Nancy Linari (4.14)
Tom Hewitt	Bartender (2.23)
Aaron Heyman	Clarence (2.04)
Edward Hibbert	Gil Chesterton (1.23, 2.01, 2.12, 2.23, 3.01, 3.06, 3.09, 3.21, 4.01, 4.03, 4.18, 5.03, 5.12, 5.17)
Tommy Hilfiger	Robert (1.23)
Shawn Huff	Woman at Shiva (1.11)
Tom Hulce	Keith (3.01)
Eric Idle	Chuck (3.17)
Leslie Ishii	Stewardess (5.01)
Zelijko Ivanek	Dr Arnold Shaw (4.12)
Dana Ivey	Ms Langer (4.11)
Judith Ivey	Lorraine (1.04)
Robert Lee Jacobs	Waiter (2.23)
Conrad James	Albert (5.09)
Hawthorne James	Bill (1.12)

James Earl Jones	Norman (4.15)
Kathryn Joosten	Vera (4.17)
Jane Kaczmarek	Maureen Cutler (3.20, 4.09)
Heide Karp	Crystal (5.16)
Cindy Katz	Elise (4.23)
Paul Kent	Dr Sternstein (2.08)
Roger Keller	Waiter (1.14)
	Coughing Man (4.21)
Baron Kelly	Bailiff (3.19)
Linda Kerns	Policewoman (5.11)
Patrick Kerr	Noel Shempsky (1.13, 1.18, 3.06, 3.08, 4.18)
Lincoln Kilpatrick	Artie Walshe (2.08)
Larry King	Himself (5.07)
Bruno Kirby	Marco (1.07)
Robert Klein	Gary (1.06)
Pamela Kosh	Dierdre Sauvage (3.07)
Randy Kovitz	Fan (2.13)
Robin Krieger	Mother (2.04)
Bernard Kuby	Priest (2.14)
Kay E. Kuter	Wino (4.02)
Deborah Lacey	Customer (2.23)
Tom Lagleder	Dr Stephen Kagen (4.12)
Christine Lahti	Laura (1.22)
Cynthia LaMontagne	Annie (5.14)
John LaMotta	Duke (2.05, 5.10)
Amy Landers	Waitress (5.08, 5.12)
Nathan Lane	Phil (2.14)
Sherry Lansing	Angela (3.24)
Stu Lantz	Sportscaster (4.05)
Annie Larussa	Susan Rosen (3.04)
Harris Laskaway	Moving Man (3.07)
Laurence Lau	Steven (5.10)
Piper Laurie	Marianne (1.13)
Steve Lawrence	Howard (1.23)
Loren Lazerine	Fan (4.05)
Timothy Leary	Hank (1.14)
Heather Lee	Toffee Macintosh (5.12)
Beverley Leech	Jennifer (5.07)
Jay Leno	Don (1.10)
Tea Leoni	Sheila (2.16)
Ray Liotta	Bob (3.09)

Renee Lippon	Kari (2.19)
John Lithgow	Madman Martinez (2.19)
Amy Lloyd	Receptionist (1.11)
Shelley Long	Diane Chambers (2.10, 3.14)
Irene Olga Lopez	Marta (2.21, 3.08, 4.23)
Kristen Lowman	Mrs Kalish (3.02)
Patti LuPone	Pam (1.03), Zora (5.16)
Eric Lutes	Tom Duran (2.03, 2.22)
Jane Lynch	Cynthia (4.07)
John Carroll Lynch	Dr Franklin Crean (3.14)
Scott MacDonald	Henry (3.12)
Jane McFie	Gate Attendant (3.10)
Jillie Mack	Charlotte (3.20)
Allison Mackie	Adelle Childs (4.06)
Albert Macklin	Masseur (5.09)
Heather Macrae	Cathy (3.23)
Amy Madigan	Maggie (2.04)
Ken Magee	Guard (4.05)
Garrett Maggart	Bruce (2.12)
John Mahon	Walt (5.16)
Mako	Sam Tanaka (1.22)
Henry Mancini	Al (1.13)
David Manis	Terrance (5.10)
Joe Mantegna	Derek Mann (1.04)
Christopher Marshall	Customer (5.08)
Melora Marshall	Female Fan (5.05)
Mile Marsico	Johnny (4.24)
Marsha Mason	Sherry Dempsey (4.09, 4.11, 4.19, 4.20, 4.21, 5.02, 5.11)
Mary Elizabeth Mastrantonio	Eileen (3.03)
Armistead Maupin	Gerard (3.11)
Yasemin Maytok	Cindy (5.07)
Paul Mazursky	Vinnie (3.08)
Malcolm McDowell	Dr Helmut Bruga (1.19)
Reba McEntire	Rachel (1.20)
Michael McFall	Messenger (4.22)
John C. McGinley	Danny Kriezel (2.11)
Katherine McGrath	Linda (1.16)
Christine McGraw	Lacey Lloyd (3.13)
Rita McKenzie	Mrs Littlejohn (2.19)
Zachary McLemore	Big Kid (5.09)
John McMartin	Fletcher Grey (1.18)

Joan McMurtrey	Heather (2.14)
Lisa Melilli	Dream Girl (4.03)
Sara Melson	Carrie (1.20)
Robert Miano	Rocco (1.16)
Brett Miller	T.J. Smith (1.15)
Alan Mingo	Waiter # 2 (5.08)
Ben Mittleman	Ralph (3.11)
Michael Mitz	Ben (3.22)
Nick Mize	Man in Street (5.08)
Mark Monuz	Dr Krovitz (5.03)
Alvy Moore	Patient (2.04)
James Morrison	Brian (2.10)
Marnie Mosiman	Donna (3.10)
Megan Mullally	Beth Armstrong (4.13)
Brittany Murphy	Olsen (1.19)
Rosemary Murphy	Carol Larkin (4.14)
Bess Myerson	Mary (5.13)
Naomi	Customer (3.17)
Adrian Neil	Freddy (5.10)
Bebe Neuwirth	Dr Lilith Sternin (1.14, 2.09, 2.10, 4.07, 5.15)
Lorenzo Newton	Reggie Maclemore (4.05)
Scotty Nguyen	Brown (1.19)
Kathleen Noone	Aunt Patrice (1.05)
Jim Norton	Wentworth (2.18)
Any Van Nostrand	Janice (5.13)
Mike Nussbaum	Owner (2.23)
Ivory Ocean	Bartender (1.16)
Donald O'Connor	Harlow Stafford (3.19)
Marilyn O'Connor	Albert's Wife (5.09)
John O'Hurley	Thomas Jay Fellow (2.01)
Kim Oja	Felicity Stafford (5.01)
Kev O'Neil	Electrician (3.05)
Jerry Orbach	Mitch (3.17)
Milo O'Shea	Dr Schacter (3.02)
Pauly P	Rebecca the Waitress (4.03, 4.19, 4.20)
Cyndi Pass	Vanessa (5.07)
Jane Pauly	Rochelle (3.17)
Austin Pendleton	Dr Dorfman (4.11)
Edward Penn	Jack Reynolds (2.18)
Jessica Pennington	Yvette (2.09)
Miguel Perez	Carlos Del Gato (5.06)

Rosie Perez	Francesca (2.12)
Karen Person	Customer (2.14)
Andrew Philpot	Waiter (5.01)
Byrne Piven	Dr Sigmund Freud (4.03)
Richard Poe	'Chopper' Dave (1.10, 1.12)
Denise Poirier	Maggie (3.20)
Sydney Pollack	Holden Thorpe (2.07)
Hal Porter	Al (2.13)
Linda Porter	Mary (2.04)
Shirley Prestia	Saleswoman (5.07)
Lindsay Price	Sharon (5.17)
Faith Prince	Brandy (3.15)
John Prosky	Preston (4.07)
Robert Prosky	Ted Houghton (4.04)
Bette Rae	Elizabeth (1.12, 3.20, 4.03)
John Rajeski	Waiter (3.24)
Trish Ramish	Tawney van Deusen (1.18)
Gina Ravarra	Waitress (1.01)
Abdul Salaam El Razzac	Paul (3.23)
Alyson Reed	Cindy Carruthers (2.19)
Christopher Reeve	Leonard (1.02)
Carl Reggiardo	Maître d' (4.24)
Carl Reiner	Roger (1.09)
Rob Reiner	Bill (5.13)
Joe Reynolds	Waiter (5.06)
Norman B. Rice	Himself (5.05)
Eric Roberts	Chet (4.14)
Lisa Robinson	Connie (5.14)
Marc Robinson	Joey (1.19)
Marco Rodriguez	Leo (1.16)
Dulcy Rogers	Woman with Chair (4.24)
Rachel Rosenthal	Martha Paxton (1.06)
Steven Rotblatt	Bar Patron (4.04)
John Rubinstein	Phillip Hayson (1.06)
Murray Rubinstein	Allan Freedman (1.11)
Mercedes Ruehl	Kate Costas (3.01, 3.04, 3.06, 3.07, 3.10)
Mark Ryan	Winston (5.10)
Rich Schatz	Busboy (2.09)
David Sederholm	Date (2.01)
Harriet Sansom Harris	Bebe Glazer (1.09, 1.18, 2.22, 3.21, 4.17, 5.12)
Mark Sawyer	Bob Peterson (1.18)

326

Palmer Scott	Mr Twembly (5.12)
Tony Shalhoub	Manu (3.23)
Lin Shaye	Anne (3.23)
Alan Shearman	Sous Chef (2.23)
Bobby Sherman	Himself (4.16)
W. Morgan Shepperd	Mr Drake (2.18)
Carly Simon	Marie (2.12)
Gary Sinise	Sid (2.18)
Peter Siragusa	Bruce (3.05)
Pat Skipper	Gary (3.23)
Tucker Smallwood	Detective (5.11)
Lois Smith	Moira (4.14)
James Spader	Steven (2.01)
Don Sparks	Mr Carr (3.02, 3.14)
Nancy Stafford	Claire Barnes (3.13)
Lesley Stahl	Herself (5.08)
Claire Stansfield	Kristina (1.15)
Robert Stanton	Ben (5.12)
Mike Starr	Billy Kriezel (2.11)
Mary Steenburgen	Marjorie (2.13)
Linda Stephens	Elaine (1.13)
Perry Stephens	Stan (3.14)
Saul Stern	John Rajeski (4.10)
Ben Stiller	Barry (1.12)
Eric Stoltz	Don (1.12)
Hank Stratton	Andrew Lloyd (3.13)
James Patrick Stuart	Guy (5.14)
Mark Sullivan	Restaurant Waiter (5.08)
Jack Sydow	Alfred Larkin (4.14)
Jodi Taffell	Nurse (3.04)
Luke Tarsitano	Frederick Crane (3.09)
Jack Tate	Director (2.07)
Christopher Templeton	Molly (4.11)
Cali Timmins	Mary Anne (3.14)
Lily Tomlin	Rita (2.02)
Doug Tompos	Flight Attendant (3.10)
Constance Towers	Clarise (2.01)
Randy Travis	Steve (3.15)
Tom Troupe	Minister (3.03)
Gary Trudeau	Louis (1.23)
Shannon Tweed	Dr Honey Snow (2.15)
Mary Tyler Moore	Marjorie (1.23)

Gregory Eugene Travis	Ronald (1.06)
Neil Vipond	Judge (3.19)
Christopher Walberg	Boy (2.07)
Nicholas Walker	Francoise (4.08)
Jack Wallace	Joe (2.05)
Laurie Walton	Waitress (1.03)
Sela Ward	Kelly Easterbrook (5.01)
Wendy Wasserstein	Linda (4.05)
Laura Waterbury	Fan (2.15)
John Waters	Roger (5.13)
Carlene Watkins	Susan Rajeski (4.10)
Cameron Watson	Data Collector (3.23)
Kevin Weisman	Painter (3.05)
Michael Welch	Young Niles (5.10)
Tegan West	Jack (3.09)
Patricia Wettig	Stephanie (4.14)
Michael Whaley	Pete (3.04, 4.02)
Paxton Whitehead	Colin Campbell (4.07)
Elvin Whitesides	Driver (3.10)
Alan Wilder	Leo Pascalé (4.22)
Joseph Will	Nikos (5.16)
Katarina Witt	Brenda (3.17)
Wayne Wilderson	Teddy (1.10)
James Willett	Cop (2.14)
Jennifer Williams	Woman in Hall (5.09)
JoBeth Williams	Danielle (1.08)
	Madeline Marshall (2.09, 2.10)
David Willis	Patron # 2 (3.11)
James Winker	Mr Giroux (3.19)
Elijah Wood	Ethan (1.13)
Alfre Woodard	Edna (2.06)
Charlayne Woodard	Arleen (2.04)
Lesley Woods	Mrs Kelly (3.02)
Henry Woronicz	Leader (3.23)
Steve Young	Blake (1.23)
Harris Yulin	Jerome Belasco (3.15)
Joey Zimmerman	Dracula (5.03)

Appendix II

MAIN CAST'S PREVIOUS ACTING CREDITS

Kelsey Grammer

Before finding work in television, Kelsey Grammer had built a reputation as a fine stage actor in the early 1980s. Working first at the Old Globe Theater in San Diego, he moved to New York where he worked on high-profile Broadway productions of *Othello* and *Macbeth*. Small roles in television series such as *One Life to Live*, *Kate and Allie* and *The Tracy Ullman Show* eventually led to his casting as Frasier in *Cheers*, and subsequently, of course, to *Frasier* itself. While starring in *Frasier*, Grammer has appeared in the fairly unsuccessful motion picture *Down Periscope*, acted in a couple of made-for-TV movies (*The Innocent* – for which he also acted as Executive Producer – and *London Suite*), and been Executive Producer of the series *Fired Up*. Of course, Grammer also regularly provides the voice for the bitter and twisted Bart-hating Sideshow Bob Terwilliger on *The Simpsons*.

David Hyde Pierce

Prior to *Frasier*, Hyde Pierce appeared in the short-lived series *The Powers That Be*, and had played a number of roles in television and film. His notable work includes appearances in *The Fisher King* and *Sleepless in Seattle* in the cinema and, on television, guest roles in *Spenser: For Hire* and *Dream On*. His film work has continued, with roles in *Nixon* and *Wolf*, and a recent stint as a voice artist on a new computer-animated feature, *A Bug's Life*. On television, he has appeared more recently in *The Outer Limits* and two episodes of *Caroline in the City* (playing Niles Crane in one). In a wonderful casting coup in 1997, he 'appeared' on *The Simpsons*, playing Sideshow Bob's brother, Cecil.

John Mahoney

Despite a rich and varied acting career, it wasn't until *Frasier* that John Mahoney really achieved widespread recognition. He was a regular cast member in a number of television series before *Frasier*, including lead roles in *H.E.L.P.* and *The Human Factor* in the early 1990s. His more recent film work includes roles in *In the Line of Fire*, *The Hudsucker Proxy*, *She's the One* (with *Friends*' Jennifer Aniston) and *Primal Fear*. In 1992, he guested on an episode of *Cheers* ('Do Not Forsake Me, O My Postman', playing Sy Flembeck).

Jane Leeves

A handful of guest roles on television throughout the 1980s (including *Seinfeld*, *Hooperman*, and *Murphy Brown*) eventually led Jane Leeves onto *Frasier*. She has springboarded a feature film career off the back of *Frasier*'s success, appearing in the remake of *Miracle on 34th Street* and voicing a character in the animated version of Roald Dahl's *James and the Giant Peach*. Just like David Hyde Pierce, Leeves appeared on *Caroline in the City*, playing her *Frasier* role. Leeves also filmed the pilot for the US version of the science fiction sitcom *Red Dwarf*, playing the ship's computer Holly.

Peri Gilpin

Peri Gilpin appeared in a number of guest roles on television throughout the time leading up to *Frasier*. Appearing in *Matlock*, *21 Jump Street*, *Wings* and *Designing Women*, she also notched up a guest role in *Cheers* (in the episode 'Woody Gets an Election', playing Holly Matheson). Television roles since *Frasier* began have included a couple of made-for-TV movies and appearances on *Early Edition* and *The Outer Limits*. She has also played her *Frasier* role on another series; Gilpin plays Roz in an episode of *The John Larroquette Show*.

Dan Butler

Dan Butler's work before *Frasier* includes a string of feature film credits: amongst them are roles in the two (unconnected) Hannibal Lecter movies, *Manhunter* and *The Silence of the Lambs*. On television, Butler had a recurring role on *Roseanne* (spanning 1991–1992), and has appeared as Kenneth Arabian in two episodes of *Caroline in the City*, as well as guesting on various shows such as *The X-Files*, *Quantum Leap* and *Picket Fences*.